SEXUALITY AND DEMOCRACY

*to my mother and sisters,
whose lives and experiences thank
fully made me wonder (as only women can)
about whether I should ever become
(what is supposedly)
a real man.*

SEXUALITY AND DEMOCRACY
Identities and Strategies in Lesbian and Gay Politics

Momin Rahman

Edinburgh University Press

© Momin Rahman, 2000

Edinburgh University Press Ltd
22 George Square, Edinburgh

Typeset in Palatino Light
by Pioneer Associates, Perthshire, and
printed and bound in Great Britain by
MPG Books Ltd, Bodmin

A CIP record for this book is available from the
British Library

ISBN 0 7486 0958 X (paperback)

The right of Momin Rahman
to be identified as author of this work
has been asserted in accordance with
the Copyright, Designs and Patents Act 1988.

CONTENTS

	Acknowledgements	vi
	Introduction: The unhappy marriage of sexuality and democracy	1
1	Sexuality as identity	17
2	Understanding sexual subjectivity	48
3	Sexual subjectivity in social context	81
4	Que(e?)rying political identity	116
5	Exploring political strategies	149
	Conclusion: Liberty or equality?	196
	Bibliography	202
	Index	214

ACKNOWLEDGEMENTS

There are many people who suffered my thoughts, ideas and anxieties whilst I completed this book, most unwittingly the students taking Sociology of Sexuality at the Universities of Strathclyde and Stirling and those Honours and graduate students whose dissertations have focused on sexuality. To them I offer thanks for their enthusiasm and dedication. Similarly, I would like to acknowledge those who have made space and time in their lives to talk about the issues covered in this book: at conferences, seminars and, most importantly, in those 'non-academic' settings when we have mulled over sex, love, life, liberty and the 'pursuit of happiness'. To these friends and colleagues I owe my greatest debt and my warmest thanks: Terrell Carver, David Evans, Catherine Grant, John Hughes, Gordon Hush, Tom Mackie, David Morgan, Charlotte Pearson, Jane Scoular, Sue Scott, Brian Thomson, Jim Valentine and Anne Witz. Above all I would like to thank Stevi Jackson for her professional support and guidance throughout my career and for providing me with a much valued and refreshingly forthright intellectual relationship. Finally I would like to thank the staff at Edinburgh University Press and, in particular, my editor Nicola Carr for her enthusiasm, patience, support and good humour.

Extract from 'On the Pulse of Morning' by Maya Angelou. Copyright © 1993 by Maya Angelou. Reprinted by permission of Random House, Inc. and Little, Brown.

INTRODUCTION:
THE UNHAPPY MARRIAGE OF SEXUALITY AND DEMOCRACY

In the summer of 1992 I was working in the office of a Congressman on Capitol Hill. As an intern I was a failure, unable to compete with the drive of the young North Americans who were my colleagues and unmotivated by the basic donkey work that is required of such unpaid volunteers.[1] However, during July of that year I was lucky enough to go to New York City to work on Bill Clinton's campaign for the Presidency and even luckier to be in the Convention Hall at Madison Square Gardens when Clinton made his acceptance speech. After performing my own small act of Queer subversion in order to 'pass' on to the floor of the Convention (I was wearing security badges with an identifiably female name on them), I was carried away by the excitement generated by the razzmatazz of the occasion. Political events such as these seem always to be a mixture of the gloriously transparent manipulation of emotions and the genuine – if vague – sense of potential which we invest in an emerging leader. So it was for me with 'the man from Hope'.[2] Clinton's candidacy meant many things to many different people but, like Tony Blair in Britain in 1997, there seemed to be a consistent plea in his speeches for a new, broader sense of the political nation (*New York Times* 17 July 1992). Clinton's explicit endorsement of feminist pro-choice campaigns around abortion and his inclusion of lesbians and gays within his vision of the era he sought to usher in were the specific issues which anchored my somewhat vague sense of investment in this new kind of politics (Rahman 1994). The meaning that I took from the Convention speech, and a theme which runs throughout this study, is that the advance of lesbian and gay 'equality' demands a different kind of democratic practice.

At the time I had not formulated any specific thesis on sexuality and democracy; rather I had an emotional and political stake in lesbian and gay equality and an academic interest in democratic theory. I did not know whether a new form of inclusive politics meant simply widening the scope of representative democracy or challenging its very premises: my analytic exploration of democratic theory had only just begun in relation to women and their lack of political representation (Ibid). I *did* know that I felt that any positive mention of gay and lesbian issues in political circles was a still somewhat remarkable but welcome occurrence. Thus, Maya Angelou's poem, delivered at the first inauguration of President Clinton, served only to increase my giddiness:

> Come, clad in peace,
> And I will sing the songs
> The Creator gave to me when I and the
> Tree and the Rock were one.
> Before cynicism was a bloody sear across your brow
> And when you yet knew you still knew nothing
> The River sang and sings on.
>
> There is a true yearning to respond to
> the singing River and the wise Rock.
> So say the Asian, the Hispanic, the Jew,
> The African, the Native American, the Sioux,
> The Catholic, the Muslim, the French, the Greek,
> The Irish, the Rabbi, the Priest, the Sheikh,
> The Gay, the Straight, the Preacher,
> The privileged, the homeless, the Teacher.
> They hear. They all hear
> The speaking of the Tree.
>
> They hear the first and last of every Tree
> Speak to humankind today.
> Come to me,
> Here, beside the River.
> Plant yourself beside the River.
>
> (Verses 7–9 from 'On the Pulse of Morning',
> Maya Angelou, 1995: 269)

Introduction

I remember receiving a copy of the poem and being glad that we – gays (lesbians and gays in the American sense)[3]– had arrived. Were things really going to be different now?

Well, of course not. Clinton blundered into his first political crisis precisely because of the clash between principles of equality and the negative social construction of gay and lesbian identities and sexual practices: the Joint Chiefs of Staff of the Armed Forces and the Senate Armed Forces committee refused to comply with his wish to remove the ban on lesbians and gays serving in the US military (*Congressional Quarterly*, 6 February 1993: 272). Moreover, this particular political incident illustrated that insecurity of tenure was the defining condition of gay and lesbian organisations within the mainstream processes of democratic representative politics (*Washington Post*, national weekly edition, 1–7 February 1993). I began to realise that we could not be just another interest group or ethnic minority in the sense which is implied in Maya Angelou's poem. Moreover, this feeling echoed my experiences with lesbian and gay political activism at university and beyond; we often deployed discourses of political equality and human rights but more often than not, these appeals failed to ignite any enthusiasm amongst either our own constituency or heterosexuals. Although democratisation and the expansion of political and social citizenship has been a constant public and political issue since the new social movements emerged in the 1960s and 1970s (Deitcher 1995; Evans 1993) it seemed apparent that social and political equality for homosexuals was a complex and problematic issue in democratic states for both homosexuals and the moral and political majority which identified as heterosexual.

It was really my engagement with feminist democratic theory that allowed me access to a framework which could begin to explain my uneasiness, both with the direction of gay and lesbian (although mostly 'gay') politics and with the problems of representing our experiences and demands within democratic polities and systems (Phillips 1993; Young 1989). I began to think about using the debates around democracy and social difference to investigate the political condition of lesbian and gay politics.

This book is an attempt to bring some resolution to the tangle of questions which filled my thoughts at the start of this research. I knew that there was something about democratic structures and processes which conditioned gay and lesbian politics but I could not explain this relationship with exclusive reference to political theory. Questions of morality, the social significance of sexuality and gender, and the implicit acceptance of the 'natural' all underpin discussions of gay and lesbian political issues: in the realm of sexuality and gender, the social determines the political. Although my initial and ultimate aim was to raise questions about lesbian and gay politics, I needed to bring in a sociological analysis in order to untangle the social conditions and processes which dictated such a contradictory and controversial reception for demands for lesbian and gay equality. This is therefore an interdisciplinary study with the political questions forming both reference points at the outset and conclusion of my intellectual journey and guidelines to the sociological investigation which forms the bulk of the chapters. In the sections that follow, I outline how the various chapters relate to the political and sociological questions that I seek to address. I have organised these questions into four main themes: essentialism as a political strategy; personal lives and sociological analysis; the contemporary debate between Queer theory and sociology; and the translation of theory into practical politics. Although these themes are neither comprehensive nor mutually exclusive they serve as signposts along this journey in terms of both the content and structure of my argument. Furthermore, this journey is, at best, an exploratory one which will, I hope, point towards further research and more effective political strategies, and also one which will end in more discussion and dialogue rather than clearcut conclusions.

ESSENTIALISM AS A POLITICAL STRATEGY

Gay liberation is a long way from being achieved in Western societies, despite the fact that the idea of lesbian and gay equality has been around for some twenty-five to thirty years.[4] Drawing on feminist political and social theory, this book is an exploration of the difficulties of pursuing lesbian and gay political agendas within democratic polities. Although it seems that advances in legal and political equality are being made, I remain sceptical and uneasy about such advances because there is no consistency in such political gains and because what we mean by 'equality' and 'liberation' is by no means clear.[5] Many of the current strategies in use to expand lesbian and gay freedoms employ liberal democratic discourses of equality and citizenship but, as feminists who have long been engaged with democratic theory and practice point out, formal legal and political equality does very little to remedy structural gender inequalities (Pateman 1983; Phillips 1993; Young 1989). Is the

Introduction

cause of lesbian and gay equality similarly unaffected by democratic remedies? Despite the connections between feminist and gay politics and theory, there has been no significant lesbian and gay intervention in this academic debate. The current wealth of material coming from Queer theorists is still predominantly concerned with cultural politics, and the relatively new explorations of citizenship from sociologists (Plummer 1995; Weeks 1996) again fail to provide a rigorous critique of democratic practices.[6] This book is an attempt to address this omission, through a consideration of the implications of sociological theories of sexuality for democratic theory and practice.

This interdisciplinary approach bridges a divide between the literature on lesbian and gay identities in sociology and cultural studies, and critiques of democracy within political theory. I focus on strategies of engagement with democratic structures and processes in chapter 5, but my critique derives from the sociological discussion which precedes the final chapter. This sociological discussion begins with the first question posed above: what does it mean to seek equality and/or liberation for lesbians and gays? To understand the ramifications of such a question, it is necessary to explain and explore the social significance and construction of lesbian and gay sexualities in order to first understand the basis of social inequality. That there are inequalities in most Western societies is not in doubt, but why and how these inequalities are socially produced, manifested and sustained is the remit of the first part of the sociological investigation which I am undertaking.

In Chapter 1 – 'Sexuality as identity' – I explore the social construction of sexuality in Western societies. I begin with essentialism (the common cultural understanding of sexuality as an innate and immutable identity) and consider the sociological critiques of such an understanding. Drawing on the work of Foucault (1980), Weeks (1989) and feminist theorists of sex, gender and sexuality (Delphy 1993; Fausto-Sterling 1992; Jackson and Scott 1996; Richardson 1996; Vines 1993) I discuss the emergence and consolidation of the essentialist model of sexuality. In particular I focus on the historical transformation in explanatory frameworks: from a focus on types of sexual activity to an emphasis on social and political identities. I suggest that this epistemological shift – explaining sexuality through identity rather than merely behaviour – has gone hand in hand with the need to consolidate status and gender divisions in the emergent capitalist societies under study. I therefore argue that current essentialist understandings of identity cannot be the basis for an effective political strategy for lesbian and gay equality for two major reasons. First, essentialist understandings of sexuality enshrine the binary divide between 'hetero' and 'homo' sexualities, thus implying a permanent minority status for gays and lesbians. Not only is minority protection not easily guaranteed in democratic theory or practice (Young 1989) but, as feminist theorists have demonstrated, formal legal equality does little to affect the social inequalities suffered by the relevant group (Jonasdottir 1988; Phillips 1993; Young 1989). Second, since the common sense essentialist model of sexuality is conflated with religious and humanist ideas about an essential psychic self and based on a model of biological sexual drives or instinct (Weeks 1989), gays and lesbians will always be seen as morally, spiritually or biologically maladjusted and this will be reflected both in the application of the law and in policy making (Rahman and Jackson 1997). The moral divisions central to the current essentialist understanding of sexuality hamper any comprehensive political advance within democratic political structures because they are dependent on a heterosexual majority and thus heteromorality.[7]

I am therefore suggesting that essentialism cannot be part of an effective political strategy for lesbians and gays and this is a theme I reiterate throughout this thesis. In my concluding discussion of democratic theory and practice, I develop a detailed critique of the unhappy consequences of marrying essentialist understandings of sexuality with democratic practices. However, I cannot engage in that discussion without developing an alternative sociological theorisation of sexual identity upon which a more effective politics can be based. It is this subject which preoccupies me in Chapters 2 and 3.

PERSONAL LIVES AND SOCIOLOGICAL ANALYSIS

It would be both foolish and insensitive to ignore or decry the attachment which individuals have to a stable and essentialist sense of their own sexualities. Since serious sociological investigation of sexuality began, essentialist versions of self have been the dominant form in which individuals speak of their sexual identities (Gagnon and Simon 1974; Plummer 1975, 1995; Whisman 1996). In Chapter 2 – 'Understanding sexual subjectivity' – I suggest that it is the lack of a sensitive sociological theorisation of self which has helped essentialism to retain its hold on both our psyches and our political strategies. Whilst sociohistorical and Foucauldian approaches have demonstrated the historical specificity of both categorisations of sexual identities and the social significance attached to various sexual acts (Foucault 1980; Weeks 1977, 1989), these accounts have been difficult to apply at the level of subjectivity and agency (Holland *et al.* 1998; Jackson 1996b). In one sense this difficulty is largely inevitable because we are engaged at two very different levels of analysis, sociohistorical/structural/macro versus intimate/individual/ micro. Indeed, the controversy and debate which surrounds sociological perspectives on sexuality is in large part a result of the lack of effective theoretical linkage between historical conditions/social structures and the experience of those living within these contexts.[8] Too often it is unclear what – exactly – is being described as socially constructed and when that lack of clarity encompasses very personal issues such as desire and love, the reaction against academic intrusion is often borne out of insecurity and confusion because sociologists are seen to be suggesting that personal biographies, beliefs and experiences can be deconstructed and analysed to fit in with a particular abstract set of ideas (Vance 1989).[9] Throughout this text, I argue we need a more astute understanding of the perceptions of the intimate self and its connection to the social self, if we are to make connections between the sociohistorical emergence of essentialism and a contemporary critique of it which resonates with everyday experience. In this sense, I am attempting to develop the sociological imagination (Mills 1970) further in the realm of sexuality and I agree with Morgan in his discussion of the same when he suggests that 'sociology, at its best, has the capacity to render mysterious without mystifying' (1998: 660); we need to imagine a different way of thinking about sexuality which makes sense to people in a culture where sexuality is so often seen and understood as personal, intimate, and even a mysterious part of our selves.

In Chapter 2 I therefore begin an initial exploration and assessment of the major sociological perspectives on the sexual self. I review both symbolic interactionist and psychoanalytic explanations of sexual subjectivity but, given the ahistorical approach and residually essentialist premises of psychoanalysis, I suggest that it is the interactionist perspective used in the work of Gagnon and Simon (1973, 1974) and Plummer (1975, 1995) which has more to offer in understanding sexual subjectivity. However, the interactionist emphasis on agency over structure leaves it difficult to theorise an effective sociological analysis of how we achieve and sustain our sexualities in such a structured and patterned manner – divided at the very least according to gender – and how our intimate lives are linked to the social deployment of power.

I therefore engage in a review of structural accounts of sexuality, thus reiterating the importance of developing a perspective which combines the interactionist conceptualisation of the self as process with a recognition that subjectivity is profoundly influenced by our location within social structures. The structural development of gay and lesbian subcultures in the late twentieth century has produced gay 'ghettos' in terms of residential and social areas which have served to consolidate the perception of homosexuals as an exclusive sexual identity[10] (Adam 1985; Altman 1980, 1993; Evans 1993) – and thus somehow intrinsically different. Moreover, the continuing deployment of medical and scientific techniques in order to 'explain' homosexuality (or find its biological cause) serves only to reinforce ideas that all sexualities are somehow 'naturally' determined (Fausto-Sterling 1992; Vines 1993). Since the days of gay liberation, many gay political activists and organisations have used these biologically essentialist ideas about sexuality in order to put forward their claims for equal treatment and protection under the law and as a protective shield against the attitudes of others – 'we are naturally this way just like heterosexuals are naturally straight'. Essentialist ideas continue to be mobilised in contemporary times: in the age-of-consent debates in Britain over the last few years (Rahman and Jackson 1997); in campaigns in the USA to win anti-discrimination legislation; and in proposals for the equalisation of a whole range of legal and social policies across many Western countries (Rahman 1998). I am suggesting therefore that sociologically speaking, the sociopolitical conditions in which most gays and lesbians exist lead inevitably to a reiteration and consolidation of essentialist ideas about sexuality. That is why it would be both academically foolish and politically insensitive to ignore the strength of purchase which essentialism enjoys.

In Chapter 3 – 'Sexual subjectivity in social context' – I suggest that a materially grounded interactionist perspective is an analytical framework which allows us to include both everyday social practices and also material relations as both constitutive of subjectivity and reflective of social structures and power hierarchies. I argue that individuals construct and deploy a stable and core sense of sexual identity whilst living through the social process. An alternative sociological perspective on the self must therefore acknowledge this perception of the stability of self and we must be able to explain the reasons why we feel that we 'need' a stable perception of self and a sense of a core self. I suggest that the very process of social action requires a strategic and intentional engagement on the part of social actors which inevitably produces short-hand rationalisations of the mobilisation and deployment of the different components of our subjectivities which are translated into ideas about a core and stable – or innate/essential – sexual subjectivity.

Not only am I therefore trying to produce a sociological critique which has resonance with personal, intimate lives, but I am also trying to use interactionist ideas within a structurally contextualised framework. In terms of the overall aims of my research, I suggest that such a grounded interactionist perspective potentially provides us with a theorisation of political identity which is sociologically based and thus transformative, and so can be deployed to challenge essentialist ideas and their oppressive consequences. However, the translation of sophisticated theory into political identities and strategies needs to be achieved with an awareness of both the experiences which that identity is used to illuminate, and the structural context of democratic practices and ideas which govern the representation of these experiences. It is these questions which occupy me in the last two chapters.

THE TURN TO QUEER THEORY

It is difficult to pursue the study of sexuality in any relevant academic discipline without engaging with what has come to be known as 'Queer' theory. In many ways, Queer theory has challenged fundamental epistemological paradigms in a variety of fields and, although it is not my intention to map out these debates in any detail, it is as well for us to be aware that there are lines of division drawn between Queer theorists and some feminists and Queer theorists and sociologists.[11] Although it would be wrong to characterise Queer theory as a unitary school of thought, it is fair to say that many of those who are either described or self-identify as 'Queer', draw on a common Foucauldian understanding of power and discourse and thus a shared preoccupation with the articulation of 'truths' through hegemonic discourses. Moreover, the political strategies of Queer are often focused on the destabilisation of oppressive discourses through the deconstruction of their 'truths' and an appropriation of their language (Halperin 1995; Seidman 1996; Stein and Plummer 1996). I discuss the relevance of Queer theory for sociology in more detail in Chapter 4 – 'Que(e)rying political identity?' – but, in brief, I argue that this diverse body of theory needs to be addressed by sociologists precisely because Queer theorists are attempting to provide both a non-essentialist theorisation of sexual identity and a programme of strategic intervention into the cultural and political realm (Gamson

1996; Wilson 1997). My concerns in the central part of this thesis therefore converge with the areas of thought to which Queer theorists have devoted so much of their work.

I use the word 'converge' specifically to denote that whilst I have much sympathy with the rigorously anti-essentialist theorisation of sexuality and gender found in the exemplars of Queer theory (Butler 1990a, 1993), I do not identify as a 'Queer' theorist because I remain sceptical of Queer theory's lack of a sociological perspective. In one sense, the central axis of this study is the question of whether an explanation of oppression be articulated which is compatible with democratic remedies but does not rely upon essentialist understandings of sexual identities. In Chapter 4, drawing on parallel feminist debates (Fraser 1997; Jackson and Scott 1996), I argue that too much of Queer theory is an exercise in the deconstruction of discourses and discursive identities which leaves common experiences of oppression both difficult to explain with reference to structured and materially grounded inequalities of sexuality/gender, and often undermines the legitimacy of political identity within representative democratic systems. I suggest that within the structured democratic framework, we must place some limits on our intellectual desire and abilities to deconstruct identity and instead develop a thorough sociological understanding of identity which allows us to think through new forms of political representation, aims and strategies. Moreover, I suggest that a more sophisticated grounded interactionist perspective takes us a long way towards removing the emphasis on essential sexuality and refocusing it on oppressive social relations, and micro-level and individual experiences constructed through these social relations.

I do not dismiss Queer theory out of hand but rather I argue that we need a more sociological critique of sexual inequalities if we are to advance our understanding of both sexual subjectivity and effective political strategies. There is of course a wider debate to be had about the epistemological and disciplinary questions which post-modernist theorising raises in its many manifestations, not least the fundamental one of the relevance of sociology in a 'post-modern' world (Turner 1993). However, I remain an advocate of sociological thought, and argue throughout this book that the translation of theory into accessible frameworks is a necessary and welcome aspect of the process of theorising, particularly if that theory has a transformative political purpose. Moreover, this is a problem faced not only by 'traditional' structure/agency-focused sociology, but I argue that this problem is central to the putative usurper that is Queer theory. With this in mind, I

Introduction

suggest a turning away from Queer theory back towards sociology in an attempt to achieve an effective translation of theory into strategy.

EFFECTIVE POLITICAL STRATEGIES

> GLF brought together politics which had been flowering in the social movements of the sixties and other political ideas which had lain dormant for many years. The immediate inspirations were the Civil Rights and Women's Liberation Movements, combined with the style of the counter-culture. To this was added a variety of ideas borrowed from socialist and libertarian tradition.
>
> The particular emphasis that GLF gave to this brew came from the experience of being homosexual in a hostile society. For lesbians and gay men as individuals it meant coming out and taking pride in being gay, making the personal political, and trying to live out our ideals. It meant, too, challenging the roles of the heterosexual nuclear family and the ideal of monogamy.
>
> This complex development of our politics meant that challenges were thrown out in all directions – to 'straight' society; to the state and various institutions; to the left; and not least to the ways of existence that the gay male community had carved out for itself.
> (Birch 1988: 51–2)

I have quoted at length from Keith Birch's memoir of his GLF (Gay Liberation Front) involvement because he illuminates both the revolutionary and reformist aims of the movement; campaigns for civil rights were 'inspirational' but GLF also demanded a fundamental transformation of the social organisation of gender and sexuality in its challenge to the traditional family. Perhaps the revolutionary ideas seem naïve in the late 1990s after the excessive homophobia generated through the hysteria around AIDS and the associated New Right political prescriptions for a return to 'traditional' family structures and values to remedy moral, social and economic decline (Durham 1991). Moreover, in both Britain and the United States (the two countries which spawned Gay Liberation and had New Right political executives in the 1980s) gays and lesbians are now attempting to gain the right to marry and have families, join the military, share in workplace and tax benefits and generally become fully-fledged citizens in these proud democracies (Rahman 1998). Despite the romantic attraction of a revolutionary stance, my question is not 'where did it all go wrong?' but rather, what social and political conditions have led us to focus on the more reformist legacy of gay liberation rather than the revolutionary one?

There are a number of ways of answering this question and each is a valid perspective to take on the development of gay and lesbian politics. You could argue that gay liberation followed a pattern of demise and deradicalisation which is a common pattern in the experience of new social movements (Gamson 1996; Kriesi *et al.* 1995) and furthermore suggest that the emergence and institutionalisation of gay political lobbies (Button *et al.* 1997) has compounded the corruption of 'revolutionary' aims. However, these two views are predominantly a form of political analysis and my concern is rather to intertwine the political and sociological investigations of gay and lesbian politics. Sociologists of sexuality have always been aware of the very political aims of the gay liberation movement; indeed, many of the first wave describe themselves as having been directly involved or inspired by GLF (Altman 1971/1993; Plummer 1995; Weeks 1996) and those such as Foucault recount the impact of the other radical counter-cultural protests of the time (Halperin 1995; Schehr 1997). However, most sociohistorical or sociological work has focused on the commercialisation of the gay (and to a lesser extent, lesbian) cultural scene and how those material processes have led to the consolidation of an 'ethnic' or essentialist sense of identity and thus a focus on minority identity politics (Altman 1971/1993; Evans 1993; Epstein 1992; Gamson 1996; Kriesi *et al.*). In Chapter 5 – 'Exploring political strategies' – I argue that democratic structures and discourses have also had a conditioning effect on the social construction of sexuality rather than simply on gay and lesbian politics and that this relationship has compounded the turn towards reformist politics and agendas.

My aim is to suggest that gay and lesbian political strategies have not been comprehensively successful largely because democratic practices condemn homosexuals to operate as a numerical minority which reinforces their status as a deviant minority and also because democratic discourses focus on individualised rights which allow an abstract, formal liberty as opposed to promoting social equality. My concern is that lesbian and gay politics is in danger of failing to address the social construction of sexuality and its relationship with democratic discourses and practices. Homosexual political positions often lack a coherent critique of the essentialist models of sexuality which legitimise the social oppression of women and non-heterosexuals (see Liberty 1994 for example) and thus an implicit essentialism converges with the democratic settlement

Introduction

of individual rights as the path to formal equality, rather than a focus on the social conditions which produce sexual inequality.

I argue that effective political strategies must begin with a conceptualisation of sexual identity which is not individually based, whether that essentialism is configured biologically or psychologically. Using the sociological theorisation of sexual subjectivity which I develop in Chapters 3 and 4, I suggest that we need to evoke a new understanding of sexuality which both resonates with people's experiences but also undermines any essentialist frameworks of explanation. Drawing parallels with feminist debates in this area (Phillips 1998; Wilson 1997), I discuss whether effective political engagement based on such a model can be focused on the promotion of 'differences' as many Queer theorists advocate, or whether we need to keep a focus on inequalities as the defining condition of lesbian and gay lives. In conclusion, I argue that the structures of democratic processes produce a need to deploy a representative political identity and also to articulate a continuing critique of inequalities between gendered and sexual divisions, rather than simply promoting the tolerance or acceptance of differences. I end on a pessimistic note, aware not only that this has been a theoretical discussion but also that there are limits on the translation of theory into effective politics. The structures of democracy and the material and social construction of sexuality produce an almost irresistible movement towards essentialist political discourses. I question whether the unhappy marriage of sexuality and democracy can ever be remedied when sexual identity is being seduced both by sexual and democratic essentialism, and I suggest that the future promises political liberty as opposed to social equality.

A GUIDE FOR STUDENTS USING THIS BOOK

I hope that both undergraduate and post-graduate students of sexuality will find this text useful as an introduction to sociological perspectives on sexuality. At present, there are many readers on sexuality which draw material from a wide range of academic disciplines but we do not yet have an introductory textbook in Britain or the USA specifically concerned with the sociology of sexuality.[12] Given that I have engaged in a sociological critique of various approaches to sexuality, this text can be used to provide a guide to various perspectives on sexuality and how useful these are for sociological study.

Chapter 1 serves as an introduction to what we call 'essentialist' ideas about sexuality and gender, explaining both essentialism and the historical development of such understandings in the West. I draw on the sociohistorical work of feminist, gay and lesbian scholars and I introduce the ideas of the influential French theorist Michel Foucault. Furthermore, relevant sociological themes and concepts are introduced in this chapter in my discussion of the relationship between sexuality, modernity, social control and structure and agency. These issues form the framework of criticism for the subsequent discussion of the three broad areas of thought which have come to dominate sociological views on sexuality; psychoanalysis, symbolic interactionism and Foucauldian perspectives.

In Chapter 2 I engage in a detailed critique of both psychoanalysis (Freud and Lacan) and symbolic interactionist perspectives, focusing on the work of Gagnon and Simon. I concentrate on the lack of both a sociohistorical and a social structural element to these perspectives and therefore go on to discuss the importance of such an analysis in Chapter 3. In many ways, this chapter focuses on a central dynamic in sociological analysis – the question of structure, ideology, subjectivity and agency – and I discuss the importance of assessing different perspectives on sexuality with this framework in mind.

In Chapter 4 I continue the emphasis on structure and agency in my introduction to and critique of Queer theory. Queer theory can be understood as the contemporary manifestation of Foucauldian thought and I engage in a detailed sociological critique of both Foucault's theoretical framework of discourse, power and knowledge and the subsequent use of these ideas within the work of Queer theorists. In my conclusion to this study, I suggest the need for a return to interpretations and explanations of sexuality which incorporate more traditional sociological concerns such as the influence of socioeconomic structures and the structural contexts for action. Although there are discussions of lesbian and gay politics throughout this study, and particularly in Chapter 5, I hope that students will find the sociological chapters sufficiently accessible on their own to provide a critical introduction to the sociology of sexuality.

NOTES

1. In the USA an internship is a period of work experience which is usually unpaid, especially in the public sector.
2. Bill Clinton was born in Hope, Arkansas and 'The Man from Hope' was the title of a biographical video shown immediately before the speech in which he accepted the nomination for the Presidential candidacy.

Introduction 15

3. I focus on homosexual politics in both Britain and the United States since they are the liberal democratic states in which the political movements of gay liberation first emerged. However, I will use the terms 'gay' and 'lesbian' (both as nouns and adjectives) to refer to homosexual men and women respectively rather than use the American term 'gay' to include both men and women.
4. Statements published by the Gay Liberation Front organisations in both Britain and the United States are the first examples of a positive self-image for gays and lesbians – encapsulated by the slogan 'gay is good' – and also the first instance of a demand to social and legal equality as a right rather than as a plea for tolerance (Evans 1993; Watney 1980).
5. In 1998, the House of Lords wrecked the Labour Government's attempts to reduce the age of consent for male homosexual activity to 16 (and threaten to do so again in 1999, *The Guardian*, 26 January 1999). South Africa is the only country in which there is a constitutional bar on discrimination against lesbians and gays but this sits side by side with an unequal age of consent (19 for homosexuals as opposed to 16 for heterosexuals, *The Guardian*, 27 January 1998).
6. However, many Queer theorists argue that cultural politics should and does include analyses of structured inequalities (See Butler 1998 and my discussion of differences and inequalities in Chapter 5). My point here is that Queer theorists rarely engage with specific political procedures, remaining on the whole in the realm of abstract theorising (see Wilson's critique, 1997).
7. President Clinton – that great defender of lesbians and gays in the military – turned his protective gaze towards heterosexuals when he agreed to sign up to the Defence of Marriage Act (which proposed a ban on gay marriages in the USA) in an attempt to (re) identify himself with 'centrist, mainstream' values (*The Times* 24 July 1996). The age of consent proposal in Parliament in 1998 had a successful outcome in the Commons (lowering the age for gay men to 16) but was defeated in the House of Lords. The debates in both Houses still contained references to the 'unnaturalness' of homosexual practices, especially in terms of Christian morality (*The Guardian* 23 June 1998). The Bill has again passed through the Commons in January 1999 but was defeated in the Lords. The Government has thrown its weight behind achieving this reform using whatever Parliamentary privileges are necessary.
8. Angelia R. Wilson has identified this problem as a lack of 'Queer translation' (1997). For a good critical discussion of the debates between essentialist and social constructionist (sociological) views, see the collection edited by Stein (1992).
9. Although sociological perspectives are often referred to as social constructionist views, there is no exact fit between these two terms – I will discuss this in detail in Chapters 1 and 2 but for the moment, I will retain the term 'sociological'.
10. These inner urban areas are usually male-dominated – gay men enjoy the same advantage over lesbians in rates of pay and broader range of

employment which straight men enjoy over all women.
11. The debate about Queer theory and sociology is mapped out by Steven Seidman in his introduction to his edited collection (1996).
12. Useful readers include *Sexuality* edited by Nye, R., 1999 (Oxford: Oxford University Press); *Feminism and Sexuality*, edited by Jackson, S. and Scott, S., 1996 (Edinburgh: Edinburgh University Press). Useful introductory research texts include Joseph Bristow's literary review *Sexuality*, 1997 (New York: Routledge); Diane Richardson's (ed.) collection *Theorising Heterosexuality*, 1996 (Milton Keynes: Open University Press) and Jeffrey Weeks' historical overview *Sex, Politics and Society*, 1989, second edition (Harlow: Longman). There are various chapters on sexuality in some basic level undergraduate textbooks but these are relatively unsophisticated – try the chapter in *Sociology: A Global Introduction*, edited by Macionis, J. and Plummer, K., 1998 (Hemel Hempstead: Prentice Hall Europe).

Chapter 1

SEXUALITY AS IDENTITY

INTRODUCTION: CHALLENGING THE SELF-EVIDENT

What does lesbian and gay liberation mean? To a generation of activists who took part in the original liberation movements for women and for lesbians and gays, it seems that the personal and the political were very much entwined (Birch 1988; Dixon 1988; Gomez 1995; Watney 1980). The demands that came out of the women's movement and gay liberation were a combination of programmatic social and legal policy reforms (Dixon 1988; Evans 1993; Watney 1980) and exhortations to individual transformations in consciousness and lifestyle which, taken together, were meant to bring about revolutionary social change in gender and sexual divisions. That these inequalities remain in most Western societies is not in doubt, and the analysis of these divisions is my remit in this chapter. Moreover, I undertake this task in order to begin an exploration of the identities and strategies involved in pursuing gay 'liberation'.

In this sense, this first chapter is about laying down the themes through which I present a challenge to the self-evident, both in sociological and political terms. My overall aim in this book is to suggest that contemporary gay and lesbian politics is not guaranteed any comprehensive success, despite the advances made in recent times, precisely because of the convergence between oppressive constructions of sexual identity and limited political conceptualisations of 'equality'. I am therefore joining those who remain sceptical about the apparently inevitable extension of citizenship and its attendant rights to lesbians and gays (Altman 1993; Evans 1993; Richardson 1998; Sinfield 1994). My focus on questions of political strategy and the meaning of equality is sharper in the final chapter and conclusion but before I reach that point, I must engage with the question of sexual identity. This leads me to question naturalist understandings of sexuality in our culture, both in their own terms and, crucially, as a basis for political identity. Drawing on the work of Foucault (1980), Weeks (1989) and feminist theorists of sex, gender and sexuality (Butler 1991; Delphy 1993; Fausto-Sterling 1992; Jackson 1996b; Richardson 1996; Vines 1993) I explore the emergence of the model of sexuality which dominates contemporary times – the essentialist or nativist understanding of sexuality. Sociohistorical work on sexuality has demonstrated that the historical transformation in explanatory frameworks – which has led to our current nativist understanding – has developed in conjunction with the need to consolidate status and gender divisions in the emergent capitalist societies under study.[1] I therefore argue that effective political strategies for lesbian and gay equality must address gender inequalities rather than simply political reform for lesbians and gays.

Moreover, gay and lesbian politics must also include a critique of essentialism since it is essentialist understandings of sexuality *as* identity which construct the moral divisions which are used to deny lesbians and gays social and political equality. The perception that gays and lesbians are essentially different reflects the common understanding of sexuality as innate, God-given or biological. Within this framework, lesbians and gays are rigidly divided from heterosexuals on the basis of sexual activity, and they are then regarded as an aberrant minority. Given the dominance of essentialist constructions of sexuality, it is not surprising that these frameworks form the basis of political activity in both anti-homosexual and gay rights movements. Epstein (1992) notes that gay interventions into politics in the USA often involve the deployment of an 'ethnic' identity; a strategy which continues in the USA and is used in Britain as well around a variety of campaigns (Gamson 1996; Rahman 1998). One of the effects and aims of such a strategy is to emphasise parallels with race-based political aims and strategies. However, racial politics in Western democratic systems is primarily minority politics, based on the protection of a group who are in the numerical minority and who suffer from cultural discrimination and material and social inequalities. Whilst it may appear that this form of political identity is appropriate for homosexuals, my worry is that the acceptance of an ethnic or essentialist identity will limit the forms of political and social change possible.

Since essentialist constructions of identity are common to both racial and homosexual oppression, we should consider whether they play any

Sexuality as identity

role in sustaining oppression. There is a widespread cultural and political discourse which contains the assumption that the self-evident 'natural' differences between races will inevitably result in antagonism and discrimination.[2] In turn, the focus of public policy and political activity becomes these 'natural' attributes. What is less often addressed is why those attributes become the basis for social oppression (Guillaumin 1995). The incorporation of essentialism into political discourse and practice renders invisible the social hierarchies and structures within which those individuals are located and through which their identities are constructed.

Without becoming involved in the detailed history of racial inequalities in the West, it is fair to say that minority politics has not delivered substantial social and political equality for all racial minority groups (Guinier 1994; Solomos 1991). This in itself should make gays and lesbians think twice about the usefulness of an 'ethnic' political identity. If 'ethnic' is taken to mean 'minority', there will inevitably be tensions in the pursuit of equality within democratic polities when such equality requires undermining the privileges of the (heteromoral) majority. My concern is that the incorporation of essentialism into homosexual politics will result in the same disservice to the cause of equality as has been apparent in the politics of race. I contend that we must suspend our common way of knowing about sexuality and instead ask how it has come about that sexuality is such an important signifier of identity within our culture. My focus in this chapter is therefore not exclusively on homosexuality or on heterosexuality, but rather on the system that allocates identity by sexual activity. In the literature it is referred to as the naturalist or essentialist understanding of sexuality (Jackson 1990; Weeks 1989). Connell and Dowsett call it a 'nativist' model in order to stress that 'whether laid down by God, achieved by evolution, or settled by the hormones, the nativist assumption is that sexuality is fundamentally *pre-social*' (Connell and Dowsett 1992: 50). Although there have been a variety of sociological perspectives which have challenged different aspects of the essentialist understanding of sexuality,[3] the most influential sociohistorical investigation has been the combined works of the French theorist Michel Foucault (1980, 1989, 1990). Since a Foucauldian perspective underpins much of the subsequent discussion of sexuality in the academy – on both the emergence of categories of sexuality and the role of social control, social reproduction and power – I will begin with a brief summary of Foucault's main argument.

FOUCAULT: SEXUALITY AND POWER

Foucault begins by setting up the 'repressive hypothesis' and then proceeds elegantly to dismantle it (1980). He argues that there is a fundamental contradiction between the accepted wisdom that sexuality was repressed in Victorian times and the historical evidence of an explosion of discourse around sexuality in this period. In his analysis, he argues that the Victorian era saw a significant increase in the discussion of human sexuality and, for the first time, the emergence of terms which described sexual behaviours as types of people within psychiatry, jurisprudence and in the developing field of sexology. Moreover, he connects this obsession with sex to a longer tradition, suggesting that the Victorian attempt to categorise sexual identities according to particular desires is a continuation of the emphasis on the control of thoughts and desires which had become increasingly important in the church since the Reformation. The Christian church served as both instigator and referent for moral laws, especially those concerned with human sexuality (Boswell 1992; Weeks 1989). It had, in practice, shifted its focus from the immoral or sinful acts committed by individuals towards their immoral or sinful thoughts, regarding these as the motivation for committing sin. There was an incitement by the church 'to transform your desire, your every desire, into discourse' (Foucault 1980: 12). Foucault thus illustrates that the social control of sex and sexual identity has a long history which saw a particularly fruitful period during the Victorian era. He argues that the focus on sex evinces a concern with social control; first by the church as a method of asserting authority, and subsequently by the emerging professional elites in medicine, psychiatry and criminal justice during the mid-nineteenth century.

Foucault suggests a collective interest in sex, stating that there were 'power mechanisms that functioned in such a way that a discourse on sex... became essential' (1980: 23) and it is the association of power with sexuality that becomes his central theme. Although he mentions that the management of populations is an increasingly urgent concern for Western industrialising states at this time, Foucault is much more concerned with the emergence of the essentialist framework as an effect of power, and specifically power manifested as knowledge. He uses the term discourse to describe a framework of explanation which creates its own 'regimes of truth' or forms of legitimate knowledge. A discourse creates its own objects through the production of regimes of truth and knowledge which produce certain topics or concepts – such as sexuality –

Sexuality as identity

as legitimate understandings of the world. This essentialist discourse of sexuality transforms our understanding of human sexuality from simple lust into sexuality as an indicator of our core being, a sexuality which interweaves thoughts, desires, motivations, acts, and physiological and mental well-being within its meaning.

However, Foucault takes issue with the common understanding of the operation and effects of power as repressive – what he calls the juridico–discursive model. He argues that a key manifestation of power is the 'propagation of knowledge' (1980: 12) and, although this does act as a repressive and disciplinary power in that it creates 'regimes of truth' (discourses) around a particular area or object, part of its effect is creative or constitutive. Since power can be manifested as knowledge, and the essentialist construction of sexuality is a particular set of 'truths' and knowledge claims, the emergence of an essentialist understanding of sexuality is a direct effect of the generative operation of power. Power exists as a potentiality in all social relationships and is therefore diffuse, ubiquitous and a fundamental component of any social location. Since social categories of sexuality have been generated through the emergence of discourses, or knowledge claims, Foucault contends that power has multiplied itself through the creation of essential sexual identities.

More relevant to my subsequent discussion of Queer theory and political strategies is the idea of resistance, which is central to Foucault's concept of power, since all power is seen to allow for potential resistance. For example, Gay Liberation's slogan and outlook was an example of resistance through a counter discourse, whereby the 'deviant' social identity – 'gay' – is appropriated in order to produce an alternative set of truth claims – 'gay is good'. A more recent example is the political use of the term 'queer' which had, up until the late 1980s, been a term of abuse for gays and lesbians. Resistance is manifested using the same discourse which has generated social identities so that, in the case of homosexuality: 'The very discourse which sought to produce a regulative order managed to empower those it sought to subjugate. In other words, sexological categories could cut either way, depending on who was deploying them' (Bristow 1997: 178). For example, naturalistic or essentialist explanations of homosexuality mobilise resistance around a reverse discourse which proposes different moral conclusions from the heteronormative discourse, but which does not fundamentally disturb the dominant discourse of essential sexuality.[4] 'Discourse transmits and produces power; it reinforces it, but also undermines and exposes it, rendering it fragile and makes it possible to thwart it' (Foucault 1980: 101).

For those defined as 'perverse' within the hierarchy of the essentialist construction of sexuality, the Foucauldian connections between sexuality and power are attractive precisely because they suggest a radical anti-essentialism and a potentially transformative idea of power. We are all located within the intricate web of power but we are not simply trapped. We can move along various threads, using the momentum of the power which has generated our particular social identity. We may turn the tables using, so to speak, the power invested in us. This idea of resistance and the theoretical rationale behind it forms a key tenet of Queer theory and politics which I will deal in more detail in Chapters 2 and 3 when I discuss the criteria necessary for a viable theory of sexual and political subjectivity. For my purposes here, we can simply take Foucault's ideas about the emergence of an essentialist understanding of sexuality as the main influence behind a vast body of sociohistorical work.

FROM LUST TO LIFESTYLE: THE EMERGENCE OF SEXUALITY AS IDENTITY

What, exactly, is sexuality? As Stephen Heath (1982) points out, human sexual behaviour and desires have always existed but the particular concept which has recently dominated the way we think about human sexuality is a historically specific social construction. It is this later sense of sexuality which is under discussion in this chapter; the essentialist framework of sexuality which emerged in the mid-nineteenth century and is still current today. John Boswell describes how ancient civilisations and early Christian Europe (400 BC – AD 400) understood human sexuality simply as physical lust; a quality which was regarded as natural to humans (1980, 1992). He characterises three forms of regulation: that based on the ethics of responsibilities, that based on the notion of lust as threatening to good order and that based on a specific religious code. He suggests that many ancient societies were untroubled by sexual behaviour as long as it did not interfere with responsibilities to family or state. An identifiably Christian influence on sexual behaviour began to emerge around AD 400 with a new sexual code that emphasised the control of lust as necessary for a good religious character.

Boswell identifies two relevant strands of thought: the first regarded all desire as potentially dangerous and made no serious distinction between homosexual or heterosexual activity. The second view was that procreation was the only justification for sexual activity. The latter perspective came to dominate Catholic Europe by the Middle Ages and was incorporated into religious laws. However, in both strands, lust is still the focus of regulation and still conceptualised as an innate potential in all individuals; 'it was part of the old Adam, an aspect of fallen humanity to be wrestled with and defeated' (Connell and Dowsett 1992: 50). Anyone could be prey to lust driving them to sinful sexual behaviour but, as Boswell puts it, 'everyone in Catholic Europe was a sinner' and it was a temporary state ended by repentance (1992: 159).

There is a vast literature on the history of sexual regulation and it is not my intention to review it here. However, these historical perspectives (Connell and Dowsett 1992; Foucault 1980; Heath 1982; Weeks 1989) make it clear that 'sexuality' did not exist as the basis for identity in the past, but, more often than not, it simply referred to sexual urges or sexual organs. Stephen Heath points out that the Oxford English Dictionary definition of 'sexuality' changed from denoting sexual feelings or reproductive organs in 1800 to encapsulating a sense of being by 1889 (Heath 1982). Connell and Dowsett (1982) contend that a shift away from religious nativism to 'scientific nativism' was brought about after Darwin's *The Descent of Man* was published in 1874. Darwin argued that human beings were descended from anthropoid apes through a process of evolution. This argument drew on his theory of evolution, put forward in *The Origin of Species* (1859). Humans were thus located within the 'natural' order and so subject to the same laws of nature and, more importantly, subject to the same methods of scientific enquiry, classification and categorisation which had developed in the natural sciences. The religious incitement to procreative sex was thus reinforced by a scientific explanation which reduced human sexual behaviour to the 'natural' imperative to propagate the species.

As Connell and Dowsett (1992) have put it, scientific nativism began to displace religious nativism. They call the developing interest in sexuality a 'scienta sexualis' (after Foucault) and describe it as a fusion of biology, anthropology and forensics. In all of these attempts to classify and produce knowledge about sexual behaviour there is little conception of this behaviour as learned and socially influenced. The emphasis is on explaining 'natural' and 'unnatural' phenomena. However, if all such sexual drives continued to be seen as essential, natural attributes, there would have been no basis for the construction of a moral distinction between different desires. What seems to have happened is that the Christian focus on procreation began the process of constructing moral divisions according to sexual behaviour and desire (Boswell 1992). Natural and medical science then compounded these divisions through the process of classifying different behaviours within the moral/religious framework, thus defining in advance what was 'normal' and 'abnormal'. The sciences of sexology and medicine were not objective disciplines; their practitioners were often in search of explanations for 'abnormal' behaviour, the labelling of which was dictated by the religious codes of the day intertwined with a new medical justification for procreative sex (M. Jackson 1989; Vines 1993). The homosexual becomes, in Foucault's terms, a 'species' – unnatural, sterile, unmanly and named as such well before the procreative couple become labelled as 'heterosexual'.

The actual process of categorising sexual behaviour begins to alter the understanding of sexuality (Foucault 1980; Weeks 1989). Lusts and desires are classified and thus divided, allotted to either one category or another. Since these lusts are located within individuals, there develops an identification of the individual with their sexual behaviour. The emphasis in understanding sexuality thus shifts from the actual behaviour towards the category of person who engages in the behaviour. This shift marks the emergence of a conceptualisation of sexuality as an innate, psychologically essential, identity.

Jeffrey Weeks argues that this new development of an essentialist understanding of sexuality is based on 'the belief that certain social concepts are given, and correspond to eternal biological and historical truths' (Weeks 1977: 2). Sexual desire is conceptualised as 'an overpowering force in the individual' which is 'built into the biology of the human animal' (Weeks 1989: 2) and is extrapolated into a sexual identity which encompasses not only lust, but also a sense of being which acts as a fundamental reference point for both social and self identity. Since desire has long been understood as an innate and natural drive, sexuality, read off from desire, has come to be seen as a similarly essential property of the individual. His detailed description illustrates the ways in which the transformation of religious nativism into scientific nativism was incorporated into secular legislation and medical categorisation during the nineteenth century. Not only did the focus of regulation shift from a sin to a crime but, moreover, on to a criminal type: an identity rather than an act (Weeks 1989: 80–83, 99–101).

In many ways, the emergence of sexuality can thus be seen as part of the increasing rationalisation and categorisation which classical sociological theorists and historians have identified as central to the processes of change wrought by the advent of modernity (Hobsbawm 1995; Turner 1993; Weber 1976). However, as Foucault points out (1980) it would be foolish to suppose that the emergence of sexuality was merely a reflex of the structural changes occurring in the socioeconomic system during the Victorian era. There was also a development in medical and psychological understandings of human behaviour which, along with the classificatory frameworks of modern science, became incorporated into the new understanding of sexuality.

Centuries of thought have characterised humans as split between the mind and the body, with the body regarded as a complex physical mechanism. Anatomy was thought to dictate behaviour and impulses to behaviour were thus understood as the need to achieve a 'natural' balance within the body. This dualist view was conceptualised most thoroughly by the philosopher Descartes in the seventeenth century (1986). Physical urges were understood as bodily needs that had to be fulfilled. The concept of lust or desire was similarly understood as a bodily need and thus explained by anatomical reasoning. Control over lust, or any other 'base' impulse, could be achieved by exerting the mind. Although philosophers wrestled with the nature of the mind, the common cultural understanding of its workings was dominated by Christian concepts which located motivation within a framework of temptation and virtue. Lust, therefore, was an innate physiological attribute which could be regulated by the mind only insofar as the mind could overcome base, mechanistic impulses.

This is, of course, religious nativism. Foucault argues, however, that the emergent psychological–medical discourse around sexuality converged with and compounded the development of long-standing religious ideas around an 'inner' self (Foucault 1980, 1990; Rose 1989). His main focus is on the impact that the Christian practice of confession has in transforming understandings of deviant human behaviour from intermittent acts which simply, mechanically occur, to acts which must have an inner, psychological explanation since the subject is required to provide a mental reconstruction and verbal rationalisation through the ritual of the confessional. Moreover, this focus on the complexities of thought and motivation which underpin behaviour is compounded by the development of medical and psychological discourses during the late nineteenth and early twentieth centuries (Foucault 1980; Rose 1989; Weeks 1989). As scientists developed a less mechanistic view of the body, they extended their approach to the other side of the dualist divide, gradually displacing the dominant religious and spiritual explanations of the mind. However, religious nativism was not simply overturned but rather transformed and extended into a form of 'scientific' psychological nativism.

Arnold Davidson (1992) argues that an epistemological rupture occurred in science during the latter half of the nineteenth century which resulted in a new psychological reasoning replacing the previous focus on anatomical explanations of human behaviour. Psychological premises became incorporated as explanations of deviant or 'unnatural' sexual behaviour. Weeks (1989) describes this as the 'medical model' of sexuality and argues that its pathologisation of non-heterosexuals was crucial in confirming the focus on sexuality as an identity rather than a behaviour. This new psychological understanding translated sins driven by physical urges into disorders of the mind, which in turn affected the healthy functioning and balance of the body. This perspective perpetuates the essentialist drive model of sexual desire, but now connects this to the workings of the mind. Since the mind was understood as part of the essential spiritual self, sexual behaviour becomes integral to the idea of the self.

Psychological rationalisations became widespread in the developing field of sex studies: psychology became the basis of explaining 'deviant' sexual behaviours as pathological. This theme is evident in the work of the most prominent sexologists, such as Havelock Ellis' *Studies in the Psychology of Sex* (1942), and it was reinforced by the developing credibility of Freud's psychoanalytic approach to psychology, which became widespread during the early twentieth century, especially in the United States. In her review of sex manuals of this period, Margaret Jackson (1989) illustrates the incorporation of naturalist and psychological premises into the science of sexuality, resulting in advice which concentrates on heterosexuality as the 'healthy' norm, both for the body and for the mind. As both Jackson and critics of psychoanalysis point out (Butler 1990b; Evans 1993; Heath 1982), psychological explanations of the late nineteenth and early twentieth century relied on the idea of there being a radical biological and physiological difference between men and women. This framework has been shown to be a historically specific development in the West (Lacqueur 1990) which, during the nineteenth century, gradually displaced the previously held ideas about there only being variations on one sex, although even in this model the female version was regarded as inferior to the male. The development of the two-sex model has allowed a more rigid biological basis for the claims of sexologists that there were strict psychological differences between men and women based on a 'natural' biological complementary division. This, in turn, suggests the 'unnaturalness' of anything other than genitally focused, male-dominated heterosexuality and the inevitability of psychological disorders accompanying any deviations from this norm.

From the early part of the twentieth century the transformation in psychology has served to reinforce the medical model of sexuality. Indeed, the influence of medical/psychological science has confirmed essentialist beliefs rather than demystified them (Heath 1982; Weeks 1977). The premise that sex is somehow vital to a well-balanced and fulfilled individual was the rationale behind the Victorian emphasis on regulated and moderate sexual activity for men (Jackson and Scott 1997; Weeks 1977). During the twentieth century the change in sexual mores has led to an incitement to have sex as often as possible, for both men and women, but the premise of sex being essential to bodily and mental wellbeing remains constant (Heath 1982; M. Jackson 1989; Plummer 1995; Weeks 1989).

Sexuality has emerged as a highly significant gauge of our innate mental and physical wellbeing. It is in this specific sense that it can be regarded as an essentialist concept. The understanding of sexuality has been transformed from simple physical essentialism – a concept which defines lusts, desires and practices – to social and psychological essentialism – one which indicates 'a sense of being' (Heath 1982). With the increasing sexualisation of culture in late capitalism (Heath 1982; Weeks 1980), and the increasing tendency for social identity to be consciously constructed through diversified consumption, sexuality has become ever more central to what Giddens calls the reflexive project of the self (Giddens 1991a, 1992). It is in this sense that sexuality has become the very essence of late-modern identities (Plummer 1995); sexuality is regarded an expression of lifestyle, behaviour and character over and above simply an indicator of sexual desire (Altman 1980; Evans 1993). However, it could be argued that this particular essentialist construction of sexuality is no longer oppressive to either women or lesbians and gays and that, in fact, the political system in Western democracies provides us with a platform on which to assemble 'essential' identities as authentic political voices with legitimate demands for 'equality'. It is this particular argument which appears consistently in gay and lesbian politics and it is this argument with which I engage in this study.

I have hitherto demonstrated that the current understanding of sexuality as identity is a result of historically specific processes of change in both structural social factors and the development of particular disciplines of knowledge within medicine, psychology and biology. In this sense, sexuality is the product of modernity and, as we enter a late-modern, high-modern (Giddens 1990) or post-modern age, perhaps we can rest assured that the inevitable progress of democratisation, which began as a reaction to the advent of modernity (Hobsbawm 1995), has now finally reached the realm of sexual identities. As I suggested earlier in this section, however, our current understanding of sexuality cannot be explained simply as an effect of modernity and the developments in scientific thought brought about by industrialisation. Our current concept of sexuality also signifies a strand of thought about social control and morality which predates the 'scientific' Victorian era. Sexualities have become social as well as personal identities. Moreover, the categorisation of personal desires is achieved only through psychological and medical frameworks which have been constructed on a blueprint of moral divisions. There are those who have a 'healthy' sexual appetite and there are 'perverts': this binary divide permeates our whole culture. Heterosexuality is seen as natural since it is reproductive and there is an inherent moral component to this privileged status; natural is 'good' in religious and medical discourses and also good for the soul. Heterosexuals are seen as natural; they are not sick; they are not immoral and so their identity as heterosexuals need not be foregrounded or put under scrutiny. Although many gay groups have used similarly essentialist ideas to promote demands for equality or tolerance, we must consider how far the historical emergence of both essentialist moral divisions and social practices is linked to rationalisations and techniques of social control.

SEXUALITY, MODERNITY AND SOCIAL CONTROL

In the ancient Greek city-states, citizens (who were by definition men) often had younger male lovers (Boswell 1992; Foucault 1980, 1990). Men were not expected to be penetrated by those below their social standing since this was regarded as the submissive role. As long as the man was the 'active' partner, it remained unimportant whom he chose to have sex with, be they slave boys or girls, women, or other male citizens. Moreover, the central issue was to keep the social hierarchy intact, so that behaviour such as being penetrated by a lower status male or sleeping with another citizen's wife or daughter were equally unacceptable.

Social anthropology has contributed other studies which similarly illustrate that sexual acts are not always and everywhere equated with a sexual identity (Herdt 1982; Mathieu 1996; Miegs 1990). For example, Gil Shepherd's study of homosexuality in Mombasa shows how married

Sexuality as identity

men may legitimately engage in sex with boys without it disrupting their family life (Shepherd 1989). In his study of Chicano men, Almaguer argues that homosexual behaviour may be acceptable if negotiated within the traditional patriarchal system that keeps masculinity as dominant (1991). As in the example from antiquity, what seems important is that the pursuit of pleasure does not disrupt or undermine social hierarchies, particularly those constructed on gender divisions. These brief examples suggest that sexual desire, although understood as an innate and 'natural' force, has also been perceived as problematic for social order (Boswell 1992). Sexual codes have existed throughout history but they have tended to focus on the control of gendered behaviour rather than on the control of 'forms of desire' (Stein 1992). What I want to consider is the relationship between social control and the emergence of the essentialist framework of sexuality during the period of industrialisation which sociologists have characterised as the advent of modernity.

Jeffrey Weeks locates the emergence of the essentialist conceptualisation of sexuality in the context of the fundamental social changes that occurred during the transformations of British society into the world's pre-eminent capitalist state. Although he agrees with Foucault that the social significance of an essential sexuality is an effect of power, Weeks focuses much more explicitly on the class divisions which underpin the operation of power. He argues that the mass, property-less workforce created through industrialisation and urbanisation had to be sustained and reproduced (1989). Therefore it was inevitable that sexual behaviour became harnessed to the needs of social stability in this time of fundamental social upheaval. The aim of social control thus became the 'definition of acceptable sexual behaviour within the context of changing class and power relations' (Weeks 1989: 23).

Drawing on the work of feminist scholars such as Davidoff and Hall (1987) and specifically Hall's concept of the 'domestic ideology' (Hall 1982; 1992), Weeks (1989) describes how this ideology was crucial in redefining the family unit and masculine and feminine roles. Industrialisation created the bourgeoisie as the dominant class. In turn, bourgeois ideological dominance followed which legitimised both the political settlement of a limited liberal capitalist state (which consolidated the idea of public and private spheres with the state limited to action in the former), and the social settlement of class and gender divisions. The main focus in Weeks' analysis is on marriage and the family as the institutionalised path to securing property and inheritance and, in particular, the bourgeois family as the model of moral and religious superiority for the lower classes. It is not that the family had never served these functions before but rather that the roles of men and women within this institution were transformed during this period.

This is a complex and vast area in which the feminist research has attempted to draw out the relative importance of patriarchy and capitalism and trace the development of each (Barrett 1980; Davidoff and Hall 1987; Jackson 1992b; Walby 1990). One important theme in this body of work is the shift in the understanding of masculinity and femininity that comes to dominate society by the mid-nineteenth century (Davidoff and Hall 1987; Heath 1982; Jackson 1992b; Weeks 1989). Jackson (1992b) argues that working-class campaigns were organised to exclude women from skilled labour and that these coincided with the development of a reform campaign, instigated by bourgeois males, aimed at keeping women at home. These exclusions were thus differentiated across class divisions and varied across specific contexts (Barrett 1980; Jackson 1992b) but the overall effect was that women were separated from the workplace (both factories and middle-class businesses). Given their developing material and ideological dominance of capitalist society (Hall 1992; Weeks 1989), and their religious articulation of the work ethic and family life, the bourgeoisie in particular sought to instal wives in the home as the revered carers of children and caretakers of the domestic refuge from the competitive, amoral, dirty, industrial world.

The historian Thomas Lacqueur suggests that the conditions of modernity produced a cultural imperative for a radical differentiation between men and women which displaced the previous conceptualisation of both sexes as variations on one blueprint (1990). This in turn provided a 'natural' basis for the hierarchical division of psychological and physical aptitudes between men and women. The physical essentialism of previous eras is replaced with a gendered, sociobiological and psychological essentialist construction of sexuality which suggests that subordinate roles for women within sexual relations, marriage, family, and society, are 'natural' and inevitable. Physical – 'natural' – divisions serve social relationships and institutions and thus essentialism becomes one of the techniques of social control. For example, the previously dominant idea of women as lustful is displaced by the idea of women's sexual nature as passive and dormant; domesticity changes women from sinful Eve to pure Mary (Cott 1978) in part because the perception of their bodies has moved from them being suffused with sexuality as part of the natural human condition, to one of their radical difference from men's bodies, aroused only by the touch of a man (preferably the husband) but essentially asexual (Lacqueur 1990; M. Jackson 1989). Meanwhile the masculine ideal stresses control over the 'natural' sexual drive, both in order to maintain balanced health and illustrate a moral character above the baser impulses of the less civilised classes and nations (Seidler 1989; Weeks 1977, 1989). Thus the role of sexuality within the domestic ideology served to enshrine a specific understanding of masculinity and femininity which in turn served the new bourgeois and continuing patriarchal social settlement.

Not only were gender divisions made more rigid but the religious emphasis on procreative sex was continued through the domestic ideology, particularly because the bourgeoisie mobilised their own religious morality in order to undermine the dissolute, but socially dominant, aristocracy (Hall 1992). Marriage and the family therefore assumed a regenerated legitimacy, whereby the family was seen as 'the unit of social stability' (Weeks 1989) and marriage was reinforced as the only morally legitimate sexual relationship (Jackson 1990). Essentialist and moral constructions of masculinity and femininity are thus mobilised within the family ideal to reinforce heterosexual relations as moral and natural. Since it is moral and natural, heterosexuality becomes the implicit, assumed, expected sexual identity. Indeed, it is not even named as such until it is defined in relation to its opposite: homosexuality.

The counterweight to the privilege of heterosexuality is the stigmatisation of non-heterosexual identities. The scientific and medical processes described in the previous section focus on regulating non-procreative sex, and are central to the construction of the concept of an essential sexuality, rather than sexuality as simply desire or behaviour (Weeks 1977, 1989). The concept of essential sexuality produces social practices and practices of the self which function as technologies of social control. Foucault argues that the generation of essentialist sexual identities occurred within a moral discourse which divided the 'natural' from the 'perverse' (1980). Of course, others had made this connection between sexual identities and social control before Foucault. Using labelling theory, Mary McIntosh (1968) suggested that the social construction of homosexuality as deviant serves to enforce and sustain heterosexuality in the majority.

The connection between this particular essentialist conceptualisation of sexuality and its role in social control has been widely documented and is implicit in many discussions of sexuality. What we need to consider is the question of whether sexuality be reclaimed simply as desire and behaviour; can it be divorced from social control? Within an essentialist framework, I would suggest not. The mobilisation of essentialist constructions by lesbians and/or gays is fraught with dangers. Of course, to a large extent, I have been engaged in describing the historical development of a particular form of essentialism which is dominant today, and it is possible to argue that not all essentialist constructions need be oppressive.[5] I have sympathy with this view only because an effective politics needs to resonate with the experiences and self-understandings of those it serves,[6] and most lesbians and gays tend to subscribe to essentialist explanations of their homosexuality (Cant and Hemmings 1988; Deitcher 1995; Whisman 1996). However, I will argue below that not only is this dominant form of essentialism oppressive to lesbians and gays, but also that essentialist ideas of sexuality *per se* are an extremely problematic way in which to explain and understand sexual identity and behaviour.

THE TROUBLE WITH SEXUALITY

The essentialist construction of sexuality is troublesome in two senses. First, given that it is a transcultural and transhistorical approach to human behaviour and social organisation, it does not stand up to historical analysis as a convincing explanation of human sexuality. In this respect, the reliance on biological drive models of lust and the psychological conceptualisation of the sexual self are particularly problematic. Second, the essentialist construction of sexuality and the practices and effects which derive from it, entail 'trouble' (Butler 1990a) for those on the wrong side of the moral divide. This is relevant to the aims and forms of any liberation politics.

In our current essentialist understandings of sexuality, biological arrangements have as Gagnon and Simon put it, been 'translated into sociocultural imperatives' (1974: 7). Gender is used as the equating function between anatomical sex and sexuality. Whilst we are able to perform a variety of actions with our sexual organs, within essentialism the only truly legitimate action – 'real' sex – is the vaginal penetration of women by men, because this is how to procreate. It is a crudely biological model of sexuality which only allows certain shapes into certain holes, like one of those children's activity centres. However, in this particular Fisher–Price world, experimentation only proves us wrong. Gay men can play, as long as they pretend to be one of the boys and put their peg into exactly the right hole; lesbians need not bother as, quite literally, they have no 'thing' to play with. Women can't play with other women; they just have to wait for the boys to show them what to do. Anatomical arrangements, underwritten by the reproductive process and rigidly divided by sex/gender, are used to invent a naturalist blueprint which renders alternative sexual practices individually unthinkable and/or socially unacceptable.

Biological rationalisations of human social activity are widespread. In the realm of sexual behaviour, these explanations are regarded as self-evident and underpin most discussions of sexuality. However, the common acceptance of biological explanations is more a reflection of the status accorded to medical and psychological science rather than an indication of incontrovertible fact (Vines 1993). Although science enjoys an image of neutrality – it is seen as a search for the truth, devoid of moral judgements or social influences – we have already seen how the medical and psychological sciences developed within historically specific conditions which governed the moral, methodological and epistemological framework of investigation: the development of sexology as a discipline which combines biological and psychological ideas has been the development of new forms of social control of women and non-heterosexuals. Feminist and gay scholars have criticised the androcentric and heterosexist assumptions underpinning the study of sexual behaviour (Fausto-Sterling 1992; Heath 1982; M. Jackson 1994; Vines 1993; Weeks 1989). The shift towards seeing sexuality as a condition was instigated by those within the medical and psychological professions and their views and research reinforced and promoted culturally specific versions of appropriate, gendered, sexual behaviour. Rather than 'discovering' how our sexualities 'work', it is more accurate to say that science actually helped to create the idea of essential sexuality.

Since the last century, scientists have sought to discover the biological bases for differences between men and women and the biological root of sexual perversion but the focus on hormonal and physiological differences failed to produce any significant causal or correlatory link between biology and behaviour (Vines 1993). Critics of such an approach to sexuality suggest that this is not surprising given sexual identity and behaviour are fundamentally social phenomena, which vary according to context and opportunity and according to the changing definition of what is and is not acceptable or appropriate behaviour. The medical approach to sexuality has shifted away from trying to cure various aberrant behaviours towards an incitement to 'healthy' sexual functioning as a necessary part of all-round physical and mental health. Many activities previously regarded as perverse are now regarded as 'healthy' expressions of sexuality. Masturbation, previously thought to cause madness, is now positively encouraged as a necessary fulfilment of 'needs' and non-procreative intercourse is similarly constructed, with a massive industry devoted to selling us advice on how to do it right (Jackson and Scott 1996).

These shifts in medical rationalisations may seem to indicate a morally neutral approach to sexuality; it appears that we have progressed from a Fisher–Price toy to the more sophisticated Meccano set – fitting anatomical parts together is still important but the emphasis is now on the skill with which we handle [sic] a wider variety of parts and tools. The rules about the sex we can construct with our parts and tools are more relaxed which means that we can play around more, as long as there is a peg in a hole somewhere along the way.

This 'health'-based understanding of sexuality seems to offer diversity for all. It is not difficult to see how lesbians and gays may well feel able to play with this toy; after all, shapes and holes don't seem to matter so much. The influence of medical views of sexuality have provided the cultural backdrop to the potential recasting of previously 'perverse' sexualities as merely diverse expressions of the same, natural, healthy, biological drive for sexual pleasure and release. This is certainly a theme in gay culture and particularly through the added impetus of safer sex advice. The emphasis on healthy biological needs is still, however, constructed within the dominant moral and essentialist culture in which the emphasis continues to be on 'real' sex as penetrative heterosexual sex. The essentialist construction of sexuality is not solely about biology, and the other facets of an essential sexuality – moral and mental well-being – have not been displaced.

A 'health' or 'needs' discourse may allow 'perverse' people to join in the game, but the ultimate aims of the game are the same. After all, anything apart from penetration, while it may be fun and good for you, is still only *fore*-play. Heterosexuals are still the only truly biologically legitimate type. The most striking and depressing example of this understanding of sexuality was the reaction to the AIDS epidemic in Britain and the USA. Money and resources were not forthcoming when the disease was considered as simply a 'gay' problem, and even when the problem was acknowledged, the health dimension of the disease was overshadowed by the moral judgements applied to both gay sexual behaviour and lifestyle (see collections edited by Aggleton, Davies and Hart 1989, 1990; Weeks 1996). Furthermore, much of the safer sex advice directed at heterosexuals focused simply on condom protection during intercourse, rather than suggesting alternatives to penile penetration (Holland *et al*.

Sexuality as identity 35

1998; Ramazanoglu and Holland 1993). Of course, with gay men, the blunt advice of non-gay governmental and medical agencies had been to stop having penetrative sex. Only straight men, it seems, have real biological 'needs'.

Despite the social construction of biology as a resource for the heterosexual and patriarchal status quo, naturalist explanations have been given further weight by the current crop of scientific research into 'gay' brains and 'gay' genes. These are welcomed by the straight world, as confirmation of their naturalness and our aberration from their norm, and by those who would wish to see 'cures' or treatment for the condition of homosexuality. These apparent explanations are also welcomed by many gays and lesbians. It seems that we cannot let go of the elusive potential for mobilising nature on our behalf.

The two best known studies are Le Vay's study on the hypothalamus region of the brain, and a genetic study of 40 pairs of gay brothers. To be fair to each group of scientists, neither has claimed that they have discovered a 'cause' for homosexuality. The methodological and causal problems with the research have been thoroughly criticised by those better qualified to do so (see for example, Fausto-Sterling 1992; *New Scientist* 24 July 1993; Vines 1993), and instead I would like to emphasise the common cultural conditions and assumptions which underpin these studies.

Simon LeVay's study of brains from 19 gay men, 16 straight men and six straight women found that a part of the hypothalamus was smaller in gay men than in straight men – in fact, gay men showed similarities to women's brains (LeVay 1993). LeVay's study has serious methodological problems which derive from the uncritical acceptance of essentialist precepts of both gender and sexuality. For example, the straight brains were from men and women presumed to be heterosexual. This assumption of heterosexuality is based on the lack of identification as homosexual, by either the man or woman concerned (on their medical records), or by the medical authorities. Since the homosexual identity has not been asserted, either by the subject or by the labelling authorities, there follows an assumption that homosexual behaviour cannot have been part of the subject's lifestyle or experience. In a classically essentialist mode of thinking, LeVay accepts the identification of socially constructed categories of identity with behaviour, without knowing anything about the actual behaviour exhibited by these subjects.

There seems to be an equally unsound basis for identifying homosexuals. The 'gay' brains were from men who had died of AIDS-related illnesses and whose patterns of sexual behaviour were unknown. Even LeVay himself stated that it was not possible to tell if the brain differences found were caused by HIV, AIDS or sexual behaviour, or had actually caused the assumed behaviour. Furthermore, the variety and frequency of the sexual behaviour of these men is not known, nor is there any information about their general lifestyles. This lack of information could be taken to suggest that the actual behaviour of these men is less important than the fact that they have identified as gay. Of course, LeVay is assuming that that self or medically labelled identities can be equated with a particular type of behaviour but he presents no evidence to support this.

The central flaw in this and similar research is that it accepts the social framework of gender divisions and sexual identities without question, particularly that aspect which assumes that sexuality is divided rigidly by gender, eternally and exclusively focused on one gendered object or the other. Thus LeVay can make a claim that gay men have feminine brains and we can all understand what he is trying to get at or explain. But do we stop to think whether brains can be 'masculine' or 'feminine' or indeed whether sex is a relevant distinction at the level of the brain? That we do not is, perhaps, unsurprising, since it is the essentialist construction which is culturally dominant, but it is more evidence that 'the scientific community, in turn, picks up these cultural ideas and plays them back to us, now vested with scientific authority, as facts of nature' (Vines 1993: 117). Furthermore, we have to consider that general culture is also reproduced at the level of the self, and ask therefore why is it that these morally constructed arguments about sexuality and gender have such a hold on the personal beliefs of many gays and lesbians. I would argue that the attraction of a 'natural' explanation of homosexuality is easy to understand. Surely it would be easier, both politically and personally, to frame homosexuality as a natural difference, like being left-handed or red-headed? This must seem increasingly attractive given that we live in an era where discrimination based on supposedly 'natural' differences – such as sex, race or physical ability – has by and large been legislated against in many Western liberal and social democracies. Moreover, gays and lesbians in these cultures are no longer being subjected to institutionalisation on medical/psychological grounds, no longer being treated with electroconvulsive shock therapy (ECT) in order to 'cure' their diseased desires. This is not to argue that all is well and good for lesbians and gays, but it must appear to many that there has been a significant movement towards emancipation over the last 30 years, and that part of this linear progress has been the cessation of hostilities from the medical profession. However, this understanding of gay and lesbian liberation as one component in the inevitable progress towards social equality in democratic states misses the point about homosexuality. It will never be like being left-handed as long as that difference remains socially insignificant. Homosexuality, on the other hand, is a social identity which has emerged specifically to categorise, identify and, above all, stigmatise certain people as deviants. Biology serves morality.

The pursuit of a natural cause may well be followed by the pursuit of a natural cure, as has already been mooted by those opposed to gay lifestyles and behaviour. It is the cultural context which determines the agenda of science: this is made abundantly clear when one realises that nobody is looking for a cause for heterosexuality. In LeVay's study, heterosexuality is taken as the unexamined, 'natural' norm, against which deviations can be measured. There is an assumption that we know what makes people heterosexual: it is 'natural'. This may leave the option open of suggesting that homosexuality is 'naturally' occurring too, but it does not guarantee that the moral good attached to nature will outweigh the deviant label attached to homosexuality. Racial minorities, who are constructed as 'naturally' different, do not find their 'natural' identity much use in overcoming cultural oppression (Guillaumin 1995).

From a sociological perspective, it would indeed be astonishing if scientists could find a cause for lust (of any kind), since human sexual behaviour is so much more than a stimulus–response procedure. The biological 'needs' used to justify male sexual dominance and aggression and heterosexual 'naturalness' are, in fact, the interpretation of biological arrangements within an essentialist framework which serves the patriarchal and heterosexual status quo. Biological explanations are, in this sense, excuses for a particular hierarchy and practise of sexual desire. When one considers what is actually involved in the process of lust, you realise that it cannot be understood outside the social context in which it is produced and practised. The premise of reducing thoughts, desires and situational contexts to a chromosome or neural impulse is absurdly simplistic. Neither homosexuals nor heterosexuals desire all of the potential partners whom they meet, and many engage in both heterosexual and same-sex experiences over the course of a lifecycle (Caplan 1989; Weeks 1996; Wellings *et al.* 1994). Moreover, the desire for a particular object choice is not constant; people fall in and out of lust and emotions play a significant part in our sexual lives (Jackson 1993). This kind of variety suggests that the biological drive, if indeed it exists, is of relatively minor significance.

Even if science progresses to the point of being able to identify causal or contextual reasons for sexual preferences, the empirical variety of these preferences suggests that cultural factors will remain the overwhelming influence on human sexuality. More important is that the context of such a continuing enquiry will not change: it will continue to be the essentialist agenda which constructs scientific 'truth'. As such, we should stop searching for easy answers or false prophets in the realm of science, and instead engage in a critique of the social and cultural constructions of essentialist sexuality which underpin biological explanations.

THE TROUBLED SELF

The acceptance of 'natural' sexual divisions is central to biological explanations of sexuality. Not only have historical analyses demonstrated that the idea of two distinct sexes is a relatively recent one (Lacqueur 1990) but theorists of gender have also recently turned their attention to the categories of biological sex, arguing that in fact it cannot mean anything without the prior existence of a meaningful framework of gender divisions (Butler 1993; Delphy 1993). Not only are understandings of sexuality and gender historically variable and subject to social factors, but so indeed are understandings of apparently 'natural' and eternal classifications such as physiological sex. Normative heterosexuality is justified as 'natural' by an appeal to the logic of the complementary genital arrangement needed to procreate: 'healthy' sexual desire and practice is still underwritten by the goal of vaginal penetrative sex. However, although desire is understood as a natural instinct or drive it is not simply an exclusively physiological phenomenon. In the current essentialist model of sexuality it would seem that sexual urges, whilst being biologically 'natural', are also psychologically or spiritually influenced. This understanding suggests possible tensions at the heart of the sexual self.

The faculty of human reason has been traditionally regarded as more developed in men than women (and absent in animals): men have been seen as more capable of overcoming baser instincts through the application of reason to their behaviour. Self-control defines men's rationality (Seidler 1989). However, the essentialist understanding of sexuality defines sexual drives as both natural and masculine (M. Jackson 1989; S. Jackson 1990; Seidler 1989). This immediately suggests that sexual lust

Sexuality as identity

poses a threat to the rational and moral composition of the self. Does this mean that the male sexual self is constantly at war with itself? At the very least, the essentialist understanding of male subjectivity is fraught with tension and instability (Jackson and Scott 1997) and this imbalance is distinct from the trouble suggested by the previous religious conceptualisation of physical essentialism – lust as sin. The problems of physical essentialism could be remedied after the act through repentance (Boswell 1980, 1992): sin can always be absolved. This is not true of psychological essentialism which suggests instead that deviant behaviour indicates a problem in mental (that is, psychological) faculties which cannot, of course, be treated through absolution but must be uncovered, analysed and worked through. Psychoanalysis, as one subdiscipline of psychology, is the exemplar in these terms; sexual problems must be 'resolved' through an analysis of the unconscious mind. Are we to understand that the male psyche is in fact, fundamentally riddled with tensions between the physical and psychological? If social organisation reflected this feature of men, one might have expected women to be more prominent in public activity and moral leadership, given the Victorian understanding of women as untroubled by lust.[7] That this has not happened indicates that essentialist understandings of sexual subjectivity are perhaps not as definitive of a 'natural' hierarchy as we are led to believe. Indeed, it suggests that essentialism has been pressed into the service of pre-existing gender divisions.

This contention is supported by the fact that different essentialist constructions have been mobilised at different times in order to legitimise masculine dominance. Although 'the masculine man was in control of his sexuality, the feminine women was controlled by hers, at the mercy of reproductive capacities which defined her as the deviant sexual category' (Jackson 1990: 43). This Victorian construction of a passive feminine sexuality which incorporated an unstable undercurrent of lust, echoes the tension central to male subjectivity but, unlike men, women were regarded as unable to exercise any control over their 'natural' sides.

The 'manly' Victorian man, while sexually dominant, was supposed to be in control of his lust; his subjectivity was not to be overridden by its baser instincts (Weeks 1977). In the latter half of this century, men are still supposed to exert control, but now only over their sexual performance rather than over their desires. The culture now encourages men to have sex often, but to be good at it. This suggests that far from being eternal, 'essential' sexuality is in fact historically variable. Moreover, the consistent identification of essentialist masculine sexuality with some form of control, and with sexual aggression and dominance, indicates that sexuality is being deployed as yet another technology for asserting and reflecting the social status of men.

The corollary to this deployment is the constant theme of dependence in the construction of women's sexuality. Women are seen either as dependent on a man to stimulate sexual responses and emotions, or they are governed by overpowering biological impulses located in their reproductive organs. Women are allowed neither the calming influence of a rational will (since rationality is the preserve of men), nor an autonomous erotic life. The constant theme of dependence suggests that the female sexual self is a construction which functions as the complementary 'other' to male sexuality. There seems no logical reason to suppose that the tensions in women's sexual subjectivity are any more problematic than those central to men's subjectivity, and yet it is evident that the essentialist construction of women's sexuality serves the social dominance of men. Women's sexuality is always regarded and understood as problematic in comparison to men's sexuality, whether this is cast in moral or physiological terms.

The essentialist construction of the sexual self as indicative of subjectivity must be brought into question since this understanding is founded on supposedly 'natural' sexual/gender differences which are, in fact, socially constructed and sustained. These differences are the basis for the confused and contradictory understandings of the subjectivity for both men and women. However, the idea of the 'natural' within the realm of sex, gender and sexuality is simply not credible. It is the concept of gender which defines the way in which physiological distinctions and sexual acts are both understood and made socially significant. Desire is taken to be indicative of our general subjectivity and yet subjectivity is defined according to gender; physiological sex is used as the ultimate referent of both desire and gender, and yet the framework of 'sex' can only be understood within the context of gender. It is this tortuous construction which defines our current conceptualisation of sexuality. Within this essentialist framework, explanations of homosexuality exist only in terms of the inversion of subjectivity and a perversion of the 'natural' direction of the biological drive: thus gays and lesbians are not real men or real women. Furthermore, we cannot claim a simple natural status since any judgements of our essential sexualities will not simply be about sexual desires and practices; they will be made in the context of social norms of gender divisions, normative heterosexuality and

Sexuality as identity

patriarchal morality. From whatever angle it is approached, the concept and practice of essentialist sexuality creates trouble for lesbians, women and gay men.

CHALLENGING 'ESSENTIAL' SEXUALITY

Since gays and lesbians have been constructed as deviant sexual identities, organising around these sexualities may imply an acceptance of their validity as essential sexualities. This is a classic example of the 'dilemma of difference' discussed by Iris Young when she considered the potential reinscription of oppressive essentialist ideas through the very process of organising around essentialist identities for political and representative purposes (Young 1989). While it could be argued that equality should be advocated regardless of moral judgements, the essentialist understanding of sexuality is premised on a heterosexual masculine hierarchy and its attendant moral framework, both of which inform political and social oppression. Both political and social equality requires, therefore, a fundamental critique of the essentialist construction of sexuality and the corresponding institutionalisation of heterosexuality.

Sociological perspectives have been developed as a challenge to the essentialist understanding of sexuality. That said, there is great variance in the extent to which they have succeeded in providing alternative understandings of sexuality. A large part of sociological theorising about sexuality is devoted to illuminating the social processes which have been involved in producing our current framework. This is a predominantly sociohistorical approach, taken by feminists who began to question the 'truth' of sex as it was then understood, and by Foucault (1980, 1990) and those influenced by his work (Jackson 1996b; Weeks 1989, 1996). A major concern of both feminists and gay theorists was to show that gender and sexuality were not eternal truths about men and women but constructions of particular cultures and times. Research on the historical construction of sexuality was reinforced by the emergence of anthropological studies which demonstrated that the equation between sexual behaviour and sexual identity, which is so central to psychologically essentialist understandings of sexuality, not only varied across cultures and across timespans, but was also a relatively recent development in Western culture (Caplan 1989; Vance 1989). It is through these developments, which both followed and paralleled feminist research on gender, that the idea that sexuality is socially constructed took root.

Sociological explanations have come to be known as social constructionist approaches, with a widely held perception that these approaches are both anti-essentialist and epistemologically relativist (Stein 1992). This, however, is a somewhat crude characterisation of a vast body of literature and theory. Because social constructionist perspectives have often gained credence through their anti-essentialism, social constructionism is often defined by the fact that it is anti-essentialist rather than by an understanding of its positive contribution the theorisation of sexuality.

Related to this negative definition of social constructionist thought is the charge that it is a relativist perspective. There is a common perception that social constructionist perspectives deny the existence or importance of human sexuality. A social constructionist does not deny that human sexual activities – including homosexual acts – have existed throughout history, or indeed, that human sexuality is important to social or self-identity. A constructionist position would be simply that sexual acts have varying social meaning and significance in different cultures and historical periods and do not always translate into an innate psychobiological identity (Heath 1982; Vance 1989). In this sense, a constructionist perspective suggests that identities, sexualities, moral frameworks and their social significance are all culturally and historically variable. Cultural relativism is a central premise in constructionist approaches to the extent that these perspectives are anti-foundational – they do not start with a positivist epistemological position which seeks out a certain truth.

A constructionist position, however, whilst historically and culturally relativist, does not imply an unstructured variety and fluidity of sexual identity through time and within or across cultures. While in many approaches the connections between structures and sexuality are under-theorised, it is the pervasive effect of the essentialist understanding of sexuality which forms the context of a subject's negotiation and formation of sexual identity and, more often than not, structures such as gender divisions, racial and class stratification, are central to such a description of essentialism. Feminists in particular have been extremely sensitive to the dangers of denying structural divisions of power and resources, particularly with regard to Foucault (Ramazanoglu 1993) and Queer theory (Grant 1996). How then does one begin to negotiate a way through the enormous diversity of sociological/social constructionist theory? What are the central issues that need to be considered in thinking through an alternative to essentialist sexuality? Once it is accepted that sexual acts have varying social significance, the question of what, precisely, is socially constructed becomes important (Stein 1992; Vance 1989).

Negotiating our way through sexual lives is precisely about our social relationships with gendered others, the institutions of society (such as marriage) and our understanding of our 'selves'. It is in this last area that social constructionist thought is under-developed, although it seems to me that a key part of constructing a fully social explanation of sexuality is a theorisation of the formation of the sexual self. I suggest, therefore, that a first step in challenging the current construction of sexuality must be to provide a more thorough sociological understanding of our 'selves' in order that political claims and identities do not rely on the problematic understanding of sexuality as 'natural' or an 'essence' of self. In this sense, the structure/agency/subjectivity dimension is as central to understanding human sexuality as it is to any sociological theory. My focus in the next chapter will therefore be on the explanations of sexual subjectivity given by social constructionist theories. Broadly speaking, there are three major approaches: Lacanian psychoanalysis, symbolic interactionism and the Foucauldian approach. I will assess the relative merits and problems of each approach, thereby drawing out common issues and themes which should suggest how social structures and processes construct subjectivity and shape our sexual identities. In this sense, before I return to questions of political identity and the meaning of equality, I am searching for a sociological explanation of how we become sexual, both in terms of desire and identity.

CONCLUSION: SEXUALITY, MORALITY AND POLITICS

I set out to analyse the social construction and significance of sexuality and I have arrived at a thoroughly anti-essentialist point of view. Sociohistorical and theoretical work has demonstrated that the rigid natural equation between sex, gender and sexuality is, in fact, the result of a combination of shifts in our cultural epistemological frameworks and the needs of social control in the era of modernity. The current essentialist understanding of both anatomical sex and social and sexual subjectivity is therefore a social construction which primarily serves the divisions of gender in society. Moreover, I have argued that the idea of the 'natural' cannot therefore be understood as outwith cultural moral frameworks and thus essentialist versions of sexuality cannot serve as an effective basis for a lesbian and gay politics of liberation. My discussion throughout this chapter therefore leads me to argue that we need a more astute understanding of perceptions of the intimate self and its connection to the social self, if we are to make connections between the sociohistorical emergence of essentialism and a contemporary critique of the same which resonates with everyday experience.

Can lesbian and gay politics reflect these sociological insights or does it serve to reinforce an essentialist understanding of sexuality? My worry that the latter is the case has been the impetus behind this research. Lesbian and gay politics is often projected or perceived, both by activists and sympathisers alike, as the latest wave in a long tradition of emancipation movements (Plummer 1995). Although I have no fundamental disagreement with the aim of emancipation, it seems to me that we can learn more than we have done from the frustrating experiences of other movements with which gay and lesbian politics often tries to identify. The dependence of categories of sexuality on gender divisions should ally our cause much more consistently to feminist politics; a simplistic sexual libertarianism which is exclusively focused on homosexual identities and is based on the premise of liberating our 'natural' sexual desires seems to me to misrepresent the underlying matrix of moral and social oppression which has been given force through essentialist ideas about the self, gender and sexuality.

Of course this is a brief and simplistic characterisation of the vast diversity of lesbian, gender and gay politics. Moreover, my aim is not to undermine or deconstruct sexual identity, *per se*, as the basis of a strategic political identity. There are too many inequalities and oppressions for those who identify as gay, lesbian, bisexual or heterosexual feminist to invalidate any political mobilisation around these common and patterned experiences.

There is also an abundant awareness of the fact that our sexualities are, as Jeffrey Weeks puts it, 'necessary fictions' which encompass the paradoxes of an essential identity with the importance of that identity as a signifier of social location and its historically specific, contingent, existence (Weeks 1996). Moreover, there is an emergent politics which is against the essence, against foundational meta-narratives of morality and cultural organisation, and which does celebrate difference (Phillips 1993; Plummer 1995; Weeks 1996). However, this is a politics which is allied to and identifies with democratisation and its tenets of citizenship and rights and there is still, in my view, a real danger that the focus on the individual evinced within democratic theory and practice will reaffirm and compound the problematic individualist understanding of sexuality.

In democratic politics, organising around a 'natural' difference has often provided a basis for claiming minority protection and the equalisation of formal rights, but these forms of protection have usually been ascribed individually, through rights legislation. The social relationships or structures which construct a group of people as different have rarely been addressed. It is unsurprising that claiming a natural difference is a strategy which preoccupies gay and lesbian politics at present: the influence of biological explanations for homosexuality and the commercialisation of gay and lesbian subcultures have contributed to the image of an essential, natural, and exclusive homosexual identity (Weeks 1980). An example of this strategy is provided by the civil rights organisation Liberty, which has recently published a comprehensive report on the lack of rights enjoyed by gays, lesbians and transsexuals in the UK (Liberty 1994, in consultation with the gay and lesbian political groups Stonewall and OutRage!). In this report they argue that the protection afforded to other social groups should be extended to gays and lesbians because 'sexual orientation is an immutable part of every person, like their race or and gender' (1994: 11). Not only do Liberty seem to have accepted sex and gender as 'natural' (while at the same time seeking to defend those who are transsexuals and therefore not immutably of one sex or the other), but they also state that a 'debate continues about whether sexual orientation is a biologically innate characteristic or a conscious political choice' (Liberty 1994: 11). Although they argue that either view strengthens the case for the protection of gays and lesbians, their footnotes suggest that scientific research appears to link orientation to genes or brain structure. The report also compares homosexuals to other 'minority' groups, implicitly accepting the essentialist divisions which locate non-heterosexuals as permanent minorities. Whether intentionally or not, this argument endorses current essentialist understandings of sexuality and uses these ideas as a basis for formally equal, individual rights (Rahman and Jackson 1997).

The essentialist model of sexuality seems to me to dictate a limited agenda for liberation; one which echoes the classic liberal argument for freedom from state intervention, in which the legality of certain actions is taken as the primary indication of freedom. Moreover, the legality of an action is regarded as distinct from the morality of the action. This is the seductive point for lesbians and gays: we can argue that we do not need moral approval to live our lives, but simply the legal guarantees which heterosexuals enjoy. However, since the essentialist understanding of sexuality is precisely about creating moral and immoral sexual identities,

I would argue that there is no guarantee that the importance of legal liberties will take precedence over essentialist morality. In the realm both of sexuality and of sex and gender, the traditional liberal formula is reversed and morality determines legality (Rahman and Jackson 1997). As David Evans (1993) points out, the Wolfenden Report, which led to the decriminalisation of homosexuality in England and Wales in 1968, argued that it was an immoral and offensive behaviour, despite its contention that it was the innate biological or psychological condition of a significant minority.

A libertarian sexual rights agenda may well increase legal freedoms and ensure some level of formal civil equality, but it is difficult to see how this would contribute to effective social equality, given that such an agenda does not fundamentally challenge the moral underpinning of social oppression. The state might allow us, as two abstract individuals, to get married but once we walk out of the registry office we are on the street, and then holding hands marks us out, not as individuals whose rights are assured in law, but as part of the group of queers, against whom it is socially legitimate to discriminate. Whether framed in spiritual or biological terms, the argument that homosexuality is a permanent and eternal identity merely validates heterosexuality as the same and legitimises the continuing privileging of heteromorality. In turn, this merely reinforces the current social conditions and practices which favour institutionalised heterosexuality. Being 'naturally' different but formally equal does not guarantee that our difference will be seen as acceptable or equivalent to the dominant form of sexuality.

The moral judgements used to justify naturalist explanations of deviance remain unaffected by a politics which claims an 'ethnic' basis. As an alternative, sociological perspectives undermine the 'natural law' status of heteromorality. Sociohistorical accounts illustrate the processes underlying the emergence of moral and immoral sexual identities: they help us to understand the shifts in the meaning and regulation and social understandings of sexuality. We need to be able to construct a politics of sexuality which is focused on the social processes of becoming sexual, in order to illustrate that there are no natural moralities, only invented ones (Weeks 1996). However, I suggest that we also need to develop alternative explanations of the sexual self as socially constructed. With a social understanding of the formation of subjectivity, we can reclaim sexuality as a less definitive concept, perhaps ultimately removing the need to use it as a necessary fiction, or at the very least being able to

Sexuality as identity

show that differences in sexuality are, after all, irrelevant as exclusive indicators of our moral and psychological selves.

NOTES

1. My focus is on the USA and UK as the original centres of gay liberation.
2. The most frequent manifestation of this discourse is the argument that strict immigration policies are necessary for the maintenance of good race relations. This argument has been a constant theme underpinning immigration policies in the UK since the influx of Eastern European Jews in the early part of this century (resulting in the 1905 Aliens Act) right through to the present day preoccupations with controlling immigration from the Indian subcontinent. For discussions of immigration policies in the UK and European Union, see Dummet and Nicol 1990, Bunyan (ed.) 1993.
3. I discuss the various approaches in more detail in the next chapter, but for my purposes here we need focus only on the Foucauldian perspective on sexuality.
4. As Bristow reminds us, sexologists first coined the term 'homosexual' in the late nineteenth century to describe a 'natural', if inverted, form of manmanly love and thus applied this term without moral judgement (1997: 180).
5. For a thorough review of the permutations of essentialist and social constructionist positions and the related political implications, see Stein 1992.
6. A more detailed discussion of this point in relation to developing a viable sociological perspective appears in Chapter 3.
7. Indeed, women did lead campaigns for moral purity in the nineteenth century, but this occurred during a time when they were denied the vote in both Britain and the USA as well as access to higher education and many of the professions, and were still legally dependent on husbands (Weeks 1989: 160). Women were not, by any contemporary standards, equal in public activity or legal and social status to men.

Chapter 2

UNDERSTANDING SEXUAL SUBJECTIVITY

INTRODUCTION: THE SEXUAL AND POLITICAL SUBJECT

As Steven Epstein (1992) argues, the self-understanding of lesbians and gays shapes their politics. The reformist argument for incorporation into the polity on the grounds of equal citizenship is partly a reflection of their increasingly essentialist or 'ethnic' self-understanding (Epstein 1992). Furthermore, as Simon Watney suggests, the liberationist analysis of sexuality as a political institution did not extend to an understanding of the self as socially constructed (Watney 1980). There may have been a politicisation of self-identity, through the process of coming out and through the identification of homosexuals as revolutionary subjects, but there was no thorough consideration of the self and its desires as socially constructed. This left the self-understanding of many lesbians and gays mirroring the dominant cultural understanding of sexuality as an essential quality.

In most democratic states, the influence of liberal thought has sustained a conceptualisation of the organic individual subject as the inviolable focus of political and civil rights (Parekh 1994; Phillips 1993; Young 1989). Liberal individualist rights and legislation focus on the protection of the individual rather than on the social causes of oppression or inequality, thus reducing social divisions to their manifestation within individual life experiences and so rendering invisible the social significance of group identity as the basis for social stigma and oppression. I suggest that this form of political essentialism unfortunately serves to reinforce the idea of an essential sexuality and thus the related notion that the arena of intimate life is determined by nature and so outwith the influence of politics (Rahman and Jackson 1997; Rahman 1998). What I want to suggest is that a sociological understanding of the sexual self is a necessity for a politics conducted within the democratic framework. It is only with such an understanding that we can illustrate how the sexual subject comes to inhabit social categories of sexuality. Forging this connection makes it easier to reassert the realm of sexuality as a legitimate site of political activity since we can illustrate that the sexual subject is but one dimension of the social, and therefore political, self. My aim in this chapter is therefore to focus on the theorisations of sexual subjectivity put forward by sociological theorists and to discuss the implications of these perspectives for political strategies and identities. The latter part of my task serves merely to introduce the themes which will occupy my discussion throughout the rest of this book, but my prior engagement with sociological perspectives is fundamental to developing a comprehensive understanding of the context of lesbian and gay politics within democratic societies.

Anti-naturalist perspectives on sexuality are of relatively recent origin. Stein (1992) cites Foucault's study of sexuality (1976/1980), and McIntosh's labelling theory approach to homosexuality (1968) as the twin origins of academic challenges to essentialism. To this I would add Gagnon and Simon's contemporaneous interactionist study (1974) as perhaps the first properly sociological account of sexuality. Since sociohistorical and anti-naturalist analyses have emerged from a variety of literary, cultural, psychological, anthropological and sociological disciplines, it is the term social constructionism which has generally been used to describe such perspectives. Social constructionist ideas about sexuality are extremely diverse in terms of theoretical frameworks, epistemological approaches and empirical focus but, at the very least, different thinkers agree that 'identical sexual acts may have varying social significance and social meaning depending on how they are defined and understood in different cultures and historical periods' (Vance 1989: 18). More specifically, sociological approaches provide an understanding of sexuality as both socially significant and socially constructed – sexual identities and sexual conduct are formed through social processes of negotiation, regulation and interaction. Although there is a fierce debate about the extent to which the latter point is true, for our purposes here we can focus on the fact that all sociological perspectives challenge the idea that an individual's sexuality is a presocial indication of their eternal biological moral or psychospiritual nature.

Social constructionist approaches therefore reveal sexuality as a legitimate arena for social and political struggle. The development of these theories occurred in the context of post-Stonewall gay liberation politics and, whilst the demands of the Gay Liberation Front (GLF) in both Britain and the USA were not rigorously constructionist, they did echo the sociohistorical accounts of sexualities as socially produced categories (Epstein 1992). GLF principles were based on an analysis of sexuality as constructed through patriarchal social institutions, social practices and the consequent ideological colonisation of subjectivity (Altman 1971/1993; Evans 1993: 16; Watney 1980). In common with other liberation movements which proliferated at the time (the women's movement, Black Power, left-wing student protests, anti-war protests) political activity was revolutionary in character and intent.

With hindsight it is easy of course to dismiss the goals of the various revolutionary liberation movements of the time as hopelessly unrealistic. However, as both Evans (1993) and Altman (1971/1993) point out, the specific demands of GLF, both in Britain and the USA, were often reformist ones, designed to secure certain formal rights and conditions of citizenship within the status quo. After the demise of the various GLF movements, more reformist political groups flourished for a while, such as the Gay Activists Alliance in the USA and the Campaign for Homosexual Equality in Britain. The subsequent emergence of public policy orientated lobbying groups such as Stonewall in the UK (Evans 1993), has confirmed the reformist and incorporationist bent of much gay and lesbian politics. Although there have been discussions of why and how revolutionary sexual politics became incorporated into reformist democratic processes, the focus has been on either the institutional conservatism of the political process, or on the structural and material conditions which have led to an increasingly 'ethnic' or essentialist sense of sexual and political identity (Evans 1993; Epstein 1992, 1996; Gamson 1996). In order to achieve my overall aims, I want to suggest in conclusion to this chapter that sociological theorisations of sexual subjectivity are necessary not only to provide an alternative academic understanding of the social construction of sexual subjectivity, but also as a basis for political identity. Precisely because ethnic versions of sexual identity dovetail with essentialist understandings of political identity, I begin by arguing that essentialist understandings of sexuality have not simply converged with democratic practices based on individualism, but in fact that we must understand the historical construction of the sexual and political subject as an intertwined and interdependent set of social processes.

THE 'MODERN' IDENTITY OF GAY POLITICS

The development of the distinctively gay self and social identities has been discussed in the previous chapter in the more general context of the emergence of our current understanding of sexuality as a biologically and psychologically innate quality of humans. However, it is important to recognise that the honing of modern gay and lesbian identities proceeded apace after the short-lived period of Gay Liberation and the political reforms which accompanied the heyday of revolutionary activity. Most important among the structural reasons for this rapid change in identity was the commercialisation of the (now decriminalised) gay male subculture. New lifestyles became possible within the commercial scene which burgeoned during the 1970s in major conurbations in the USA, UK and Australia (Altman 1980). These scenes were, and remain, male dominated – ordered around the relatively privileged lives of affluent, predominantly white, men. With many of these gay men enjoying the economic advantages over women that heterosexual men do, they were able to build communities based on exclusively gay clubs, bars and a range of services provided for gays by gays – not to mention creating a high profile target for the 'niche marketing' of mainstream advertising companies. Gay male sexual identity paralleled (and often led) the general commodification of sexuality which has come to exemplify the late twentieth century capitalist phenomenon of the construction of social identity through consumption (Altman 1980; Evans 1993; Heath 1982).

For the first time in Western culture, gay liberation provided a positive social identity around which homosexuals could organise and with which they could identify. The very term 'gay' was a departure from clinical or stigmatised terms such as homosexual and queer: the slogan 'gay is good' was an affirmation of both personal and social identity. Through commercialisation and the associated colonisation of urban areas, sexuality became the definitive referent for the self, both in terms of gay pride and in the distinction it denoted in terms of social groupings – being gay meant being away from straights and away from heterosexual culture. Even in towns and cities with small gay scenes, where there may literally be only one pub, club or sometimes one gay/lesbian 'night' in straight places, these arenas still function as precisely those spaces in which it is safe to be gay. It has been within these urban communities and commercial locations that the distinct, separate and exclusive nature of homosexual identity has been reinforced (Epstein 1992; Mort 1980; Weeks 1980), thus giving credence to the current essentialist understanding of sexuality which characterises homosexuals as a distinct, separate and exclusive deviant minority. Homosexual politics began to shift away from its radical emphasis on the social processes and institutions which construct our sexualities, to a position which is based on the politics of identity which, more often than not, does not question the social formation or contingent nature of the identity 'gay' or 'lesbian'.

An emphasis on the politics of sexual identity further removed gay politics from its association with the politics of gender. Gay Liberation challenged patriarchal constructions of sexuality (Edwards 1994; Watney 1980) and shared with feminism the assumption that sexuality and gender were socially constructed, but in both the USA and the UK the alliance between the gay movement and feminism was short lived. Many lesbians, disillusioned with the male-dominated agenda of gay politics, turned their attention to the women's movement (Edwards 1994; Evans 1993; Jeffreys 1990; Stanley 1982). Those left tended to focus their politics on homosexuality *per se*, rather than an analysis of sexual categories as dependent on gender divisions.

Outside the gay and lesbian communities themselves, the state was also important in contributing to the current condition and identity of lesbian and gay politics. With financial crises in the mid-1970s, there emerged a political project associated with the New Right, both in the USA and across Western Europe; although only in the US and UK were such governments elected (Durham 1991). The aims were to rein in state spending on the provision of social welfare and education, whilst at the same time emphasising the importance of a traditional patriarchal family unit in the provision of social needs (Abbott and Wallace 1992; Durham 1991). Most of these monies are spent and administered at the level of local government (whether this is at council level in the UK or state level and below in the USA) and the few inroads into public policy and resources that had previously been made by lesbians, gays and feminists were often at the level of local government, both in the USA and in the UK. Funding for projects and the emphasis on diversity in policy and education have all been under attack since the early 1980s, with lesbians and gays in particular being used as the deviant presence around which to mobilise attacks on local government in Britain (Durham 1994) and federal government in the USA (Stychin 1995).

Furthermore, with the hostile response in the USA, and the 'incoherent' response of the British state to the AIDS crisis (Freeman 1992), gay identity and gay communities came under further attack. Cutbacks and homophobia only served to emphasise how vital these communities

Understanding sexual subjectivity

were, both for political organisation and for the provision of education, care and support for those living with HIV or AIDS (Weeks 1996). Moreover, the issue of safer sex served to emphasise the fluidity of sexual behaviour across the supposedly binary categories of sexualities (Richardson 1990; Schramm-Evans 1990; Weeks 1989). It became apparent that targeting specific groups of people – gays, women, men – was ineffective because there were disparities between people's self-identification and their sexual behaviour. Thus such categories as 'men who have sex with men' were born. In a profoundly painful way, because of the difficulties of illuminating the variety of sexual behaviours and communicating appropriate safer sex information 'AIDS reminds us of the complexities of contemporary identities' (Weeks 1996: 20). The continued dominance of essentialist understandings of sexuality have hampered the provision of information and resources. AIDS is a set of illnesses, a syndrome, and yet it has not been treated like any other viral disease: rather it has been used as a symbol of concern about changing sexual values, practices and moral codes (Weeks ibid.).

Illuminating the complexities of sexual identities and self-understandings has been central to the effective responses to AIDS developed within gay organisations and, to some extent, has influenced state agencies. The devastating impact of AIDS and the associated frustrations with the policy process have produced direct action tactics from groups such as ACT UP (AIDS Coalition To Unleash Power), which echo Gay Liberation 'actions' and, to some extent, have resurrected alliances between gays, lesbians and feminists (Jackson and Scott 1996; Whisman 1996).

In many ways, the factors discussed above confirm the continued marginalisation of gays and lesbians: within urban ghettos, within niche markets, within high-risk categories, and as moral deviants. Underpinning the directions to these marginal locations is the continued understanding of sexuality as essential to our selves rather than an understanding of the self as itself social. As in the case of AIDS, we need to challenge the categories that construct us as marginal, but this is profoundly difficult when those categories are grounded in material relations, social institutions, within our subjectivities and, moreover, within the very framework of democratic political processes.

The politics of identity has often been associated with the decline in class politics which has been a feature of late-modern, post-industrial capitalist democracies (Giddens 1990). Those putting forward this argument suggest that new dimensions of social identification have emerged in a world conditioned more by mass consumption and mass media than by class relations centred on production and, as a consequence of these social changes, new political demands are being made which challenge the traditional social order (Laclau and Mouffe 1985). Sexual politics have thus often been characterised and analysed as part of the wave of new social movements (Kriesi *et al.* 1995; Gamson 1996) which were organised around social identities other than class.

Sexuality – as a socially significant identity – cannot however be understood simply as a late-modern or indeed post-modern identity politics. Neither is sexuality simply an effect of the epistemological and social changes brought about by modernity; elements in the social construction of sexuality predate the advent of industrialisation and have combined with certain consequences of class and gender divisions during modernity to produce our current understanding of sexuality. One of the threads which had been drawn into the construction of sexuality during the Victorian era was the idea of the inner self (Foucault 1980; Rose 1989). Moreover, this understanding of the self served as the basis for conceptualisations of both sexual and political subjectivity (Seidler 1989). Psychosexual health came to signify not only moral well-being but also the triumph of rational reflective thought and the ability to exercise this thought as control over the baser instincts of the mind and soul. The ideal of a rational, autonomous and unencumbered self was incorporated into the emerging democratic settlement in liberal capitalist states which of course meant that women were excluded from political power as, initially, were the intellectually inferior working classes of both genders (Hobsbawm 1995; Phillips 1993; Seidler 1989). The development of political citizenship has, therefore, been part and parcel of the process of the development of ideas and practices based on an essential identity, and specifically, an essentialist conceptualisation of sexuality (Richardson 1998). Women have also been either formally excluded or informally excluded by the social and material costs of participation in the political realm (Chapman 1992; Rahman 1994).

Gay and lesbian politics is modern only in the everyday sense of the word. It is a contemporary form of activity precisely because gays and lesbians have been legally regulated and/or socially marginalised until legal reform and structural changes in gender divisions and material conditions provided the context for the development of contemporary identities and politics. However, the politics of identity, in the sense that an essential identity underpins concepts of sexual and political subjectivity, is neither a contemporary – 'modern' – development nor simply an effect of modernity. Deploying contemporary versions of essential sexual identities within the political realm is thus not simply a contextually convenient strategy for furthering interests within democratic systems, it is a necessary method for engaging with democratic traditions of citizenship and rights, which have developed within the essentialist paradigm over a period which predates the advent of democracy but has become central to democratic practice and theory. Essentialist identities and democratic strategies are therefore linked, I would suggest, in a complex relationship. I will return to this issue in some detail in the final chapter but I hope that it is clear that I see the development of sociological perspectives on sexual subjectivity as a challenge to essentialist conceptualisations of both the sexual and political self.

CRITERIA FOR VIABLE POLITICAL AND SEXUAL SUBJECTIVITY

I want to trace the development of theories of sexual subjectivity in order to suggest what we may have gained and lost in the theoretical development of our understanding of sexual self as social. My approach is not only an attempt to be comprehensive; by dealing with older sociological theories I hope to illustrate that the premises of the currently popular body of work known as Queer theory should not be such a revelation for sociologists of sexuality, despite the fact that they appear novel to lesbian and gay theorists in other academic disciplines. I will begin with the three broadly sociological approaches to sexuality: the Foucauldian perspective, the interactionist approach (initiated by Gagnon and Simon 1974), and Freudian and Lacanian psychoanalysis. Each has spawned theoretical derivatives, from post-structuralism derived from Foucault's work to the concern with narratives emerging from interactionists such as Plummer (1995). For my purposes, I will concentrate on whether the various perspectives are useful in helping us to understand the connections to be made between sexual and political subjectivity. There are a number of criteria that I will use to judge this.

First, a viable theory of sexual subjectivity needs to resonate with everyday understandings of self. Essentialism is reproduced precisely because it provides a framework of explanation for the self which then becomes incorporated into our constructions of subjectivity; we explain ourselves and our actions from essentialist perspectives because this is how we have learned to interpret the sexual world. This is not to say that any alternative theory must therefore be essentialist, but rather, that a viable theory of sexual subjectivity must illuminate how it is that our sexualities are socially constructed within the framework of our lives in a way that people can make sense of and accommodate into their framework of self. Second, a theory of sexual subjectivity must necessarily be anti-naturalist (and in this sense anti-essentialist) if it is to open up the possibilities of transformation through political activity. Third, we need a consideration of sexual subjectivity which explains the current construction of sexualities, but does not suggest that this is all that is possible. In this sense, viable sexual subjectivity and political activity depends on an explanation of sexuality which does not take for granted the institutionalisation of heterosexuality and gender divisions or the associated moral framework.

In using these criteria, I may seem to emphasise the importance of transformative social theory. Of course my political intent derives from my position as a gay man, but my political desires are tempered by theoretical developments. In the attempt to theorise sexual subjectivity I am not looking for a meta-narrative of the construction of subjectivity. Instead, I am on the bandwagon of difference: seeking to illuminate that the differences in sexuality are the result of social processes and practices and not indicative of some essential moral or natural worth. In this sense, I do not expect to uncover a single set of explanations for the formation of sexual subjectivity. What I do hope to illustrate is the variety of social influences, and thus points of access for transformation, which are apparent in the formation of sexuality.

These criteria are underpinned by what Jeffrey Weeks has called the 'paradoxes of identity' (Weeks 1996). He describes these paradoxes thus: how we see ourselves as fixed, essential, identities whilst at the same time engaged in a process of practising acts and relationships which deny this possibility; how our intimate lives also indicate our various social locations; how sexual identities are historically produced categories and yet contingent on our identification, and how we use our identities as 'necessary fictions' in our social negotiation of the world (ibid.: 98). In all of these paradoxes, the question of how subjectivity relates to social categories is the key dimension and I have already argued that this is the key to a sociological perspective on the sexual self that can displace essentialism. Therefore, I will use this framework to assess the criteria for a viable understanding of sexual and political subjectivity and I begin with Freud's perspective which has dominated characterisations of sexuality for most of the twentieth century.

FREUD, SEXUALITY AND SUBJECTIVITY

There has been much cross-theoretical development in approaches to sexuality but, in the realm of sexual subjectivity, it is the Freudian view which has been particularly influential during this century. Despite this dominance, my argument in this section is that the underlying precepts of psychoanalysis can only be understood as derivatives of the essentialist paradigm which developed in the same historical period. As Heath puts it:

> The genuine originality of Freud's [work] should not hide the fact that his work is in many respects part of a whole context of investigation of the sexual and movement towards the conception of sexuality. (Heath 1982: 53)

Freud's rejection of the traditional physiological model (stimulus–response creating observable behaviour) is part of the rupture in modes of reasoning around sexuality which occurred in science during the latter half of the nineteenth century. Freud suggested that sexuality was a central component in the workings of the mind and so was crucial to the formation of our subjectivities. This view was radical in that it forced a focus on the importance of sexuality but, as Heath (1982) points out, Freud's characterisation of sexuality as central to subjectivity further consolidated – and in psychological terms furthered – the medico-scientific view of an essential sexuality. Freud was the first theorist to provide a coherent account of the importance and relationship of sexual identity to our subjectivities and society. However, Heath reminds us that Freud's work followed on the heels of Krafft-Ebbing's *Psychopathia Sexualis* (1886) and Havelock Ellis' *Studies in the Psychology of Sex* (1896) and reflected the explosion in interest around sexuality and the concern with perversions, homosexuality and children's sexuality which are all found in the sexological works of the time (Bristow 1997; Kennedy 1997; Rosario 1997).

Freud published *Three Essays on the Theory of Sexuality* in 1905, in which he developed his argument that childhood sexual experience fundamentally shapes adult sexual and mental identity. He first outlined this theory in his work on hysteria – a condition which he claimed was the result of sexual abuse in childhood – although he had abandoned this so-called seduction theory by 1898 (Gay 1995). However, in this earlier work Freud had developed his theory that an unconscious part of the mind develops in co-existence with the conscious mind, and this unconscious serves as the repository for all those desires and experiences which must be repressed in order for the person to become appropriately socialised and gendered (Bristow 1997: 64). Moreover, Freud argues that the development of sexual identity (gender and sexual desires in his terms) occurs at the level of the unconscious. In his first essay on 'The sexual aberrations' (1905) Freud appears resolutely anti-essentialist. Basing his theorising on sexological studies (including Krafft-Ebbing and Havelock Ellis), he argues that there is no proof that inverts (meaning homosexuals) are degenerate or innately inverted. Indeed, his argument is that cultural values must be considered when using a term like degeneracy and that perversions of the sexual aim (the act towards which the sexual instinct tends) and inversion of the sexual object (the object of attraction) are particular manifestations of a sexuality that is common to all people. Freud makes this claim by suggesting that the cause of aberrations are to be found in 'Infantile sexuality' (1905), which is the subject of his second essay.

Freud argues that infants are innately polymorphously perverse – they will seek pleasurable stimulation of their senses through any means available. Since the infantile sexual aim 'consists of obtaining satisfaction by means of an appropriate stimulation of the erotogenic zone which has been selected in one way or another', children seek pleasure from their own bodies in all manner of ways, from thumb or sensual sucking to anal and genital stimulation. Freud asserts that the first peak of infantile sexuality occurs around the ages of 3–5 years, where perversity is often visible, since the repressive cultural and biological mechanisms may not have been fully constructed or developed. It is also during this period that the instinct for knowledge develops and the knowledge of genital distinction dawns on children.

The genital trauma and the associated Oedipus complex are the most problematic of Freud's ideas, both in terms of their resonance with self-understandings of sexuality, and in the emphasis they appear to give to institutionalised heterosexuality and the dominant position of men in society. Freud suggests that a male child assumes that everyone has a penis since he has one. Upon recognising that girls do not, the male child must struggle with this apparent inconsistency. For girls, the same process produces penis-envy in them, since all they have is a clitoris and so they too must now struggle with their 'lack'. Why the absence of a penis is regarded as lack is not explained but rather, it is assumed that the male organ is somehow inherently desirable.

Where this becomes even more problematic is in the significance this distinction has for the formation of male and female subjectivities. Freud develops this theory in his later essays 'The dissolution of the Oedipus complex' (1925a) and 'Some psychical consequences of the anatomical distinction between the sexes' (1925b). Freud argues that all children identify their mother as their primary love-object since it is she who cares for them and stimulates their polymorphous erotogenic zones through physical contact. For boys, this creates the Oedipus complex (desiring the mother and wishing to take the place of the father) which leads to the castration complex in which the boy realises he cannot continue to desire the mother since she is 'owned' by the father and that his father may castrate him to remove the threat of his desire. Furthermore, he cannot position himself in supplication to his father since that would imply his subordination which means being like a woman – that is, without a penis and so inferior like his mother and sister. The male child thus turns away from the Oedipus complex because of his castration anxiety: he internalises the authority of the father and accepts his superiority over women. In 'The transformations of puberty' (1905), Freud's third essay on sexuality, he discusses how the boy must choose a new sexual object and how his choice is based on the rediscovery of his desire for his mother. However, since he has resolved his Oedipus complex by identifying with the father, and because of taboos on incest, he is able to choose other women as his sexual object.

This whole process is different for girls and, in many important senses, much more problematic. The genital distinction leaves girls feeling inferior. Again, we might ask why would girls automatically envy a penis? Freud suggests that the masculine complex within women's unconscious means that they will either still hope to acquire a penis or disavow its lack and pretend that they have one (1925). Both inferiority and disavowal as responses to this 'lack' are recognised by Freud as recipes for future neurosis or inversion. He suggests that the common response is for the girl to accept her inferiority. The penis-envy which accompanies the genital distinction also loosens the girl's attachment to the mother as love object since she is identified as lacking a penis and thus subordinate to the father. The girl transfers her affections to her father and so the genital distinction creates the mirror of the male Oedipal drama whereby she desires her father and seeks to replace her mother. In their transformation during puberty, this is not resolved but is reinforced, although again the incest taboo in society will push girls towards choosing a male object other than their father. Women, therefore, mature into heterosexuality as psychological and sexual subordinates.

One implication of Freud's theories is that genital trauma, castration anxiety and the subsequent resolution of the Oedipus complex are universal; both transhistorical and transcultural. Since this is a universal theory of sexual subjectivity, it cannot account for the variations across time and cultures in both gender divisions and the identifications of self that depend on these divisions. Moreover, Freud's emphasis on the unconscious as the location of sexual/gendered subjectivity does not permit any access to these aspects of identity except through psychoanalysis. This form of psychotherapy in clinical practice has proved a difficult experience for many women, lesbians or gay men precisely because there is an implicit suggestion within Freud's theories that the fully developed form of sexual subjectivity is a gender-divided heterosexuality. Despite the fact that Freud did not regard homosexuality as an illness, mental or physical, and that he *did* regard the moulding of sexuality into genital heterosexuality as damaging and repressive to psychic life, he still manages to suggest that homosexuality is an immature form of sexuality because the homosexual has somehow not resolved the Oedipal complex, and homosexual desire is thus inevitably a perversion of the natural sexual aim. Lesbians are again regarded as immature, in that they do not accept their lack of a penis and so pretend to be men.

In 'The transformations of puberty' (1905), Freud asserts that 'the strongest force working against a permanent inversion of the sexual object is the attraction which the opposing sexual characters exercise upon one another'. He thus posits a natural basis to sexual desire and so endorses genital heterosexuality despite his misgivings about its effects in the repression of our innate perversity. Moreover, this position sanctions the subordination of women within heterosexuality, since his version of the Oedipal drama for women depicts female subjectivity as inherently unstable.

It is interesting to note again the characterisation of lesbians and gays as immature or inverted. This inversion is based on the blueprint of anatomical sex equating with gender and thus sexuality – a biologically essentialist construction of sexuality. The model of natural gender divisions is used to contain the social concepts of masculinity and femininity and so anatomy becomes the reference for sexuality. As I have discussed in the previous chapter, anatomy or sex is not an eternal truth but must rather be understood as part of a historically specific development of frameworks

Understanding sexual subjectivity

of thought around the body and gender (Delphy 1993; Lacqueur 1990). However, in Freud's view, the formation of sexual subjectivity is grounded in anatomy, excluding the possibility that social processes and structures will be allotted any explanatory or conditioning role, either in terms of sexual categories or the development of subjectivity.

It seems that Freud ultimately relies on the widespread assumption that there is some transcultural and innate biological mandate to reproduce. In doing so, he not only removes sexuality from a social or political arena, but he also seems to contradict himself. Freud relies on the concept of a sexual drive in children which is polymorphously perverse and seen as a 'set of pleasure seeking drives' rather than a biological mandate for genital heterosexuality (Fletcher 1989: 96) yet assumes natural attraction to the opposite sex. This inconsistency only seems to reinforce the sense that Freud could not transcend the cultural prejudices and preoccupations of his time (Heath 1982).

The Freudian perspective does not meet any of the criteria for providing a social understanding of subjectivity. The pathologisation of lesbians and gays within clinical psychoanalytic practice has produced a hostility to Freudian theories which means that few homosexuals tend to understand their sexual identities in this way.[1] Furthermore, despite the apparently positive view of perversions and inversions (which place morality firmly in the realm of culture), both the penis and heterosexuality are invested with a natural and eternal significance, which undermines any claims that deviations from the 'correct' use of a penis or the 'correct' sexual aim are not somehow inherently unnatural or immoral. Perhaps the most problematic dimension is the conflation of gender and sexuality. Freud seems to rely on the dominant Victorian bourgeois constructions of his own culture in order to determine what is appropriately masculine or feminine. That this involves a passive female sexuality does not seem to have troubled him, since he conceptualises the gendered behaviour of men and women as natural effects of their anatomy. There is, therefore, no possibility that intervention in social processes and relationships will bring about change in the condition of either heterosexual men and women, or homosexual men and women. Indeed, that there could be anything but men and women in this heterosexual construction seems impossible within the Freudian framework. Even homosexuals merely serve as the mirror confirmation of the correctness of gender divisions based on anatomy.

The attraction of Freud lingers on, however, partly because the perspective does try to explain, however unconvincingly, the centrality of sexuality to our subjectivities. In the Lacanian interpretation of psychoanalysis, the emphasis on language suggests a greater explanatory weight given to cultural factors over seemingly 'natural' ones. In turn, this has led many feminists and some lesbians and gays to embrace psychoanalysis as an understanding of subjectivity which emphasises the importance of social relationships and hierarchies in the construction of sexuality.

LACAN AND LANGUAGE

From a Lacanian perspective, it is still argued that 'anatomical difference comes to figure sexual difference' (Rose 1982: 42), but the way in which the relationship between anatomy and sexuality is conceptualised suggests the possibility of a sociological account of desire and subjectivity. Lacan attempted a recovery of Freud's subversiveness by emphasising the need to read him symbolically (1975). The crucial difference lies in Lacan's interpretation of the unconscious as a system of signs. This approach derives from the discipline of semiology – the science of signs – which was influenced by the work of Ferdinand de Saussure (1959) in structural linguistics.[2]

Saussure argued that language is a self-contained and structured system of signs which is organised around the signifier and signified. Thus the spoken or written 'cat' symbolises the sound 'kat', written word, or image of a cat (both signifiers) with the related concept of a four-legged feline (the signified). Signs do not express any essential quality of the object which they signify; they are arbitrary and only achieve meaning through their relationship with other signs in the system and this works because it is a system of differences. Thus 'cat' does not mean 'dog' because they signify different concepts within this particular system – they gain meaning in relation to each other. Language is therefore central to the development of conceptual and social awareness in a subject.

Since language constructs and defines all meaning, Lacan argues that the unconscious is created and structured through language (Lacan 1975; Rose 1982). In describing the unconscious as a structured system of signs, 'Lacan's is a linguistic theory of the Unconscious and the subject's development' (Cameron 1985: 19). Psychoanalysis is the only way to understand the unconscious but this analysis is mediated through language (that is, the discussion between analyst and patient). Thus a semiological approach is set up as the 'correct' approach to

Understanding sexual subjectivity

analysing the unconscious. Lacan draws on Freud's conceptualisation of the unconscious as the site of the genital distinction trauma and associated Oedipus complex but suggests that it is the entry into language – becoming speaking subjects – that sets in motion the trauma in the unconscious which in turn determines our selves as gendered, sexed subjects. This trauma occurs as we develop our conceptual understanding of the world and realise that the law of the phallus rules the world. We don't need to see a penis, rather it is that 'the concept of the phallus stands for that subjection [of patriarchy] and for the way in which women are precisely implicated in its process' (Rose 1982: 28).

One can see how the focus on language provides the means by which social and cultural practices and meaning are incorporated into subjectivity. Rather than relying on anatomy as a natural container for gender and sexuality, Lacan asserts that the meaning of gender and sexuality are mediated and constructed through our entry into language – the world of concepts and social meaning. This approach may seem to overcome the biological essentialism which runs through Freud's work and is no doubt the reason why some feminists, lesbian and gay theorists use Lacanian psychoanalysis whenever they are discussing the formation and development of subjectivity (Mitchell 1974; Rose 1982).[3]

There is a residual universalism in Lacanian psychoanalysis which is not so easily disposed of; this perspective still relies on the universality and consistency of sexual division. It takes these divisions as pregiven and so there cannot be anything but male or female desiring subjects which correspond with male or female object choices. This is demonstrated by the fact that Lacanian psychoanalysis cannot provide an explanation of homosexuality which does not echo the Freudian view that these are somehow immature sexualities. Gays and lesbians are still defined through reference to the binary divides of gender – the cross-sex grid (Sinfield 1994) – and the implication is, therefore, that we get the codes of masculinity and femininity wrong.

In a subversive sense, getting gender wrong may indeed be the supreme achievement of lesbians and gays, but this judgement only makes sense within a framework which accepts the essentialist conflation of anatomy, gender and sexuality – within a framework which privileges normative heterosexuality. As Judith Butler puts it, 'the rules constituting and regulating sexual difference within Lacanian terms evince an immutability which seriously challenges their usefulness for any theory of social and cultural change' (Butler 1990b: 329). Butler recognises that there need to be alternatives beyond our current conceptualisation of masculine/feminine, hetero/homo if we are to overcome the oppressive construction of gender and sexuality. Although Lacanian psychoanalysis seeks to explain the social sources of sexual subjectivity, it does this through a process which may be learned but is in no sense adaptable. This ultimately makes it a theory which collapses into an implicit endorsement of normative gender divisions and thus can have no transformative effect, despite its anti-essentialist credentials.

Furthermore, Lacanian psychoanalysis does not explain the paradoxes of identity very well (Weeks 1996). The central question of how our subjectivities relate to social categories is barely addressed; the focus is much more on individual subjectivity rather than the social categories of identity. In part this is a reflection of the emphasis on the unconscious. Since the process of subjectivity formation is located in this part of our minds, we can never understand the process except through psychoanalysis. In many ways, this individualises the process of becoming sexed and gendered because the influence of social relations and hierarchies are reduced to their representation in language and subsequent mediation through the individual unconscious. As Monique Wittig has argued, this focus on the linguistic construction of identity ignores the material exploitation fundamental to the maintenance of gender divisions (Wittig 1992) which has been demonstrated as a central structural context for the transformations in the understandings of gender and sexuality which occurred during the early part of modernity.

I suggest that it would be impossible to formulate a construction of psychological essentialism which is as internally consistent and difficult to refute as psychoanalysis. Psychoanalytic explanations are products of the very paradigm which they seek to challenge; they make sense of our social world and our selves precisely because they reflect that world rather than explain it. Nonetheless, the focus on the production of meaning through our entry into language seems to me to represent an excellent beginning in a properly sociological approach to sexual subjectivity. However, it is only a beginning, and I agree with Wittig (1992) when she argues that we need a broader vision encompassing both material social relations and the materiality of social practices. Moreover, although the development of conceptual skills and understanding is fundamental to our psychological formation, Lacanian perspectives tend more to explanations of the transmission and internalisation of meaning rather than its production and significance. Thus psychoanalytic perspectives have no sociological explanation for the attribution of deviant meaning or status to some sexualities, implying a reliance on the framework of moral divisions which is constructed through the essentialist paradigm – or at least, being so open to this interpretation that they serve no useful purpose in the attempt to construct an alternative understanding of sexuality and sexual morality.

DEVIANCE AND ESSENTIALISM IN THE INTERACTIONIST APPROACH

One major source of social constructionist ideas on sexuality derives from the symbolic interactionist approach to deviance, which is associated with labelling theory. There is an emphasis in labelling theory on the social creation of deviant identities. For example, David Matza argues that the process of becoming deviant cannot be considered without taking into account the authority which labels the deviants. He calls the procedure of being labelled, registered, and so defined as deviant, the process of signification (Matza 1969). Signification creates subjects who come to represent the act which is regarded as deviant. In his example, he suggests that the characterisation of those labelled as 'thieves' serves to imply that it is only these types of people who will commit the act of theft. In the realm of sexuality, this process resulted in the understanding of sexual acts as indicative of a type of person – the congenital sodomite, for example, rather than the particular act of sodomy (Weeks 1989).

It is not difficult to see why this perspective would seem appropriate for studying sexuality; McIntosh's application of labelling theory to homosexuality leads her to conclude: 'The way in which people become labelled as homosexual can now be seen as an important social process connected with mechanisms of social control' (1968: 184). Labelling theory challenges the deviant status accorded to homosexuals, emphasising instead that a set of homosexual practices and feelings have become equated with a deviant identity through a social process of signification (McIntosh 1968). This explanation of the social significance of homosexuality predates Foucault's argument that the creation of discourses on sexuality led to the 'perverse' implantation of deviant identities which served to define the normality and thus privilege of marital heterosexuality (Foucault 1980). In both a Foucauldian and interactionist approach, deviance is explained as a technique of social control; one implication of which is that, unlike psychoanalysis, deviant status may therefore be challenged politically by contesting social meaning – the social significance of homosexuality.

In their study of sexuality, Gagnon and Simon suggest the centrality of social meaning to our interpretation of physical acts, bodies and what they call social scripts – the contextualised mechanisms through which we negotiate sexual situations. In terms of the way subjectivity is conceptualised in both their work and the earlier use of labelling theory, the major influence has been social action theory, developed by G. H. Mead (1967). A central premise of Mead's theory is that the self is formed through social interaction. He differentiates the self into two components – the 'me' and the 'I'. The 'me' functions as the reflexive understanding of identity that is arrived at using social interactions as comparisons and reference points. The 'I' is the particular moment of the 'me' engaging in social interaction. This is an anti-essentialist perspective on the self in that there is no presocial form of subjectivity; it is not there at birth or contained in some spiritual essence; rather it is an ongoing process of negotiation with others (referred to as significant or generalised others), social practices and norms.

The symbolic interactionist approach in Gagnon and Simon's work relies on this conceptualisation of self-identity: the idea that social conduct is mediated by the self and that the self is in a constant process of interaction and transformation is at the heart of *Sexual Conduct* (1974). The focus is on the processes through which social meaning creates subjectivity and guides conduct. In this sense, they develop the understanding of subjectivity inherited from social action theory. Social conduct results from the interpretation and negotiation of the meanings of social objects whereby objects are any people, events, situations or physical entities which are given a meaning. Common or shared meaning, between different subjects, creates an object and sustains its existence as that object. Joint action is any social action wherein each actor is adjusting to and interpreting other actors' behaviour in order to take action. It is joint (or social) action that is the basis of social life. Moreover, social meaning is thus internalised into the self through the very process of interacting with the social world – a much broader view of social influence on subjectivity than is admitted in Lacanian psychoanalysis.

THE INTERACTIVE SELF, SOCIAL MEANING AND SEXUALITY

> We have allowed the organs, orifices, and the gender of the actors to personify or embody or exhaust nearly all the meanings that exist

Understanding sexual subjectivity 67

in the sexual situation. Rarely do we turn from a consideration of the organs themselves to the sources of the meanings that are attached to them, the ways in which the physical activities of sex are learned, and the ways in which these activities are integrated into larger social scripts and social arrangements, where meaning and sexual behaviour come together to create sexual conduct. (Gagnon and Simon 1974: 5)

Gagnon and Simon suggest that sexuality is a phenomenon best understood through an exploration of its social meaning, and that sexual subjectivity is formed through the process of interaction of the self with sexual scripts. They propose that sexuality is not an essential quality of humans but that it is a social and self-identity which is learned and developed through the negotiation of social meaning – where that meaning is invested in certain organs and acts – and social scripts. In this perspective, subjectivity may be understood as a process rather than an essence, and yet as an identity that is fixed at certain points in time in the reflexive understanding of self that is mobilised as the subject 'I'. This flexible idea of the self suggests that interactionism will provide a more coherent account of the paradoxes of identity mentioned by Weeks (1996) than psychoanalytic perspectives.

In rationalising their approach to sexuality as an object of sociological study, Gagnon and Simon (1974) point out that society places a great emphasis on sex as central to our sense of identity. Their initial discussion of the social weight given to sexuality develops into a critique of psychoanalysis; *Sexual Conduct* provides a number of valuable insights that develop some of those made by psychoanalysis. Gagnon and Simon agree that childhood is a time of pleasure seeking, both for gratification and desire, but they argue that this cannot be regarded as having a sexual meaning, since it is only in adolescence that sexual scripts are made available to children. Thus it is only at that point that they may begin to develop a sense of sexual self and relate their gendered and general conduct to this aspect of their self-identity.

Retrospective accounts of sexual awareness project the developed sexual self (of the adult) on to the presexual self and seek to integrate the latter with the former to display some coherence to the development of self. In this sense, Gagnon and Simon fracture the closed circular reasoning of psychoanalysis, which does not take into account either the reconstruction of narratives of the self, or the defining influence of a foundational structure (the Oedipus complex, for example) on which that retrospective narrative is built. Psychoanalysis filters both conduct and identity through its own meanings and then declares that these meanings have been confirmed as truths. As an alternative view, Gagnon and Simon argue that sex and sexuality become a special area of social life not because of the eternal psychological 'family romance' of the Oedipus complex, but precisely because sexual knowledge and identity is constructed as special by society. Sexual knowledge and activity is regulated and discouraged until adolescence and yet is rehearsed through gender identity before this period, as something similarly essential to individual being. Key to the development of sexuality is the acquisition of a gendered identity: 'The decision whether to raise a child as male or female is probably based on the most significant labelling experience that the child will receive' (Gagnon and Simon 1974: 29). Although sexuality is constructed as a supremely intimate and individual identity, they argue that in fact it is often determined by other social identities, particularly gender. This emphasis is a key difference from psychoanalysis: in interactionism gender and sexuality are not conflated. Gender is regarded as central to identity formation but it is also understood as presexual. The formation of sexual subjectivity is explained in this perspective with reference to social processes and situations rather than as the effect of an exclusively internal and inaccessible psychological trauma. It is in this way that the essentialist understanding of self that most subjects incorporate into subjectivity, the gendered construction of subjectivity and the function of sexuality as a social category as well as intimate identity can all be accounted for as a social process in the interactionist perspective.

The institutionalisation of heterosexuality; the existence of gender divisions; and the culturally dominant explanation of sexual identity as innate are all described as contents of the scripts through which we learn appropriate sexual behaviour and incorporate the knowledge and experience into our sense of self. Moreover, these sexual scripts are divided by gender, with different scripts available to men and women (ibid.). There are however, major gaps in interactionist thought which undermine its potential use as a theory of social transformation. The emphasis on meaning in symbolic interactionism does not extend to a thorough consideration of how meaning is produced and sustained in a structural sense. For the most part, this is down to the vague theorisation of the concept of scripts which, after all, are the major source of meaning for subjects. It is this weakness which prevents any attempt to account for the historical specificity of particular sexual identities – such as the modern essential homosexual – and which leaves unconsidered the viability of social transformation through the provision of alternative scripts and meanings.

SCRIPTED SEXUALITY

The central problem of interactionism is that social arrangements are not explicitly acknowledged as social structures which provide the sources of social meaning. In their chapter 'Social change and sexual conduct', Gagnon and Simon (1974) discuss four factors which they see as influencing sexual change: increasing affluence and emphasis on consumption, new social movements such as the women's movement, the erosion of rigid gender divisions and the sexualisation of cultural and commercial life. These factors suggest structural and cultural social changes, whether it be women's position in the labour and education markets, or the emphasis on consumption rather than production as a referent for class location. Indeed, as discussed at the beginning of the chapter, many of these factors form the structural conditions which have underpinned the development of the modern gay identity. If these transformations are influencing social arrangements and the meanings attached to them, then it must be accepted that it is social structures which produce and transform social meaning at a general level, outwith the contexts of specific instances of interaction. However, the reluctance to develop this point in interactionism may well be because this line of argument seems to echo traditional structuralist positions which do not accommodate agency or social meaning within an explanation of social action.

Interactionism, on the other hand, is clearly a social theory which places its explanatory emphasis on agents and how they create the social world (Blumer 1966). Interactionism privileges the agent to an unparalleled degree with an almost hyperactive subject as the focus of analysis (Evans 1993). This is a consequence of its relativist epistemological approach to social life which places it at odds with positivist or realist structuralist theories such as found in functionalism or Marxism or, more pertinently, psychoanalysis. The emphasis on social life as a process of interpretation and negotiation means that 'symbolic interactionism is notable for its lack of internal theory and its emphasis on the particular rather than the abstract and general' (Cuff et al. 1992: 145). Perhaps the most radical implication of this perspective is its argument that social action is dependent on the particular meanings that a situation has for actors. Social action cannot therefore be understood or explained without an understanding of the meaning it has for those engaged in it (Blumer 1966).

This, of course, returns us to the problems with social scripts as the vehicle for meaning. Defining a script is a difficult task since 'The term script might be properly invoked to describe virtually all human behaviour in the sense that there is very little that in a full measure [can] be called spontaneous' and we should view 'the script as the organisation of mutually shared conventions that allows two or more actors to participate in a complex act involving mutual dependence' (Gagnon and Simon 1974: 19–20).[4] It is clear that a script must function as the means of translating meaning into conduct. The script is thus a framework for action: 'the organisation of mutually shared conventions'.

As I have argued above, the mutually shared convention and meaning arrived at through interaction must be underpinned by social structures. Without such an understanding of scripts, it becomes impossible to explain the permanence of both social meaning and scripts. Consider heterosexuality, for example. If, as Gagnon and Simon argue, this is a socially produced script then we need some explanation of how it is sustained and reproduced and how this affects the subjectivity of those interacting in terms of the script. Of course, there are sources of sexual scripting that interactionists mention: sites such as the family, significant others, the strength of gender divisions, schools, the church, the law (Gagnon and Simon 1974; Plummer 1975). These are clearly social arenas where heterosexuality is institutionalised and so exists, within these contexts, as a structural influence on sexual scripts. Furthermore, there must be some weight given to the coercive nature of scripts if we are to understand why most people identify as heterosexual. In his criticism of social constructionism, Steven Epstein (1992) notes that all the anthropological, social and cultural research published does not reflect the variation in human sexualities which interactionists imply. The potential for extreme emphasis on hyperactive subjects in a state of continual transformation is clearly untenable in the face of empirical reflection. Social meaning must have some relationship to social structures if we are to explain the relatively few variations in human sexual identity in our current Western cultures.

I argue therefore, that scripts, as conventions of behaviour and meaning, are defined with reference to stable social meanings which are sustained and reproduced within institutions, social practices and ideological formations, as well as being incorporated into the subjectivities of those

Understanding sexual subjectivity

engaged with the script. Subjectivity is still a process developed through experiential learning but it is patterned experience that counts – what Blumer has described as the reinforcement of 'recurrent affirmative definition' (1966: 13). In this sense, the social script functions as the contextual embodiment of structural relationships and social identities through the mobilisation of particular conventions of behaviour and meanings.

To admit the importance of structures may imply a collapse into determinism that would negate the fundamental principles of interactionism. However, if we retain the concept of the script as interactive, then it becomes possible to retain the notion that the individual or collective actor has the opportunity to adapt the conventions and negotiate their meaning since the actor is the momentary deployment (the 'I') of an ongoing process of social experience and identity (the 'me') which has its reflexive understanding of its own particular history, experience, expectations and potential for action. This position recognises the myriad differences in individual negotiation of identity and self while placing these in the context of general 'social scripts and social arrangements'. Individual subjectivity is mobilised into a particular social category at the moment of interaction – we identify, or are identified, as sexual only in particular circumstances, and the meaning that this has for us varies, not only between men and women, but for each individual. Gagnon and Simon develop such a position in their later work, which describes different levels of scripts and the conditioning effect these have on interaction (1986). They attempt to account for the structural existence and effects of their concept of scripts, as indeed many other interactionists have attempted to deal with the theoretical issues of structure and agency (see for example, Becker 1971; Denzin 1969; McCall and Simmons 1966). However, despite this development of their work, their emphasis remains very much on the agent as the conscious negotiator of social meanings, even if these are conceptualised as denser and more complex than they were initially.

A more promising perspective is developed by Dorothy Smith in her work on feminist standpoint theorising which draws on symbolic interactionism and ethnomethodology (Smith 1988). She resists being identified in either way, in part because she acknowledges the importance of social structural relations in creating the context – specific conditions within which we interact. As Smith puts it: 'Though bureaucracy, discourse and the exchange of money for commodities create forms of social relations which transcend the local and particular, they are constituted, created and practised always *within* the local and particular.' (1988: 108). My characterisation of social structures as instrumental in creating social meaning and defining social practices is an explicit statement of the potential connection between structures, meaning and the self which is similarly explored in Smith's work.

That this explicit development of interactionism is necessary is demonstrated by the gaps in interactionist thought when applied to homosexuality. Whilst the majority identify as heterosexual, there is also the social category of homosexuality with which a minority identify. However, when they turn to homosexuality, Gagnon and Simon (1974) seem less sure of themselves. In the context of their times it is clear that they are attempting to de-emphasise the need to 'explain' homosexuality as illness or deviance, arguing that any such explanation must address heterosexuality as well. Their discussion of male homosexuality and lesbianism details the importance of social scripts for these identities and subjectivities in much the same vein as their discussion of heterosexuality. This supports their arguments about the self as process, and the diversity of sexual subjectivity, but they fail to tease out the gaps in institutionalised heterosexuality which have led to the development of homosexual identities. Whilst they demonstrate that gays and lesbians suffer from a lack of available scripts they do not investigate thoroughly why it is that they come to want different scripts. Where does the meaning come from – both to desire the same sex and to identify as homosexual and how do lesbians and gays actually manage to escape from the institutionalised heterosexual script? Again, this seems to be a reflection of the emphasis on agency rather than social structure. Moreover, this suggests a less than thorough consideration of sexual desires as socially constructed, and how the construction of desire connects both to subjectivity and social structures.

LEARNING DESIRE

The interactionist characterisation of the self as a process opens up the potential for transformation in social identities and potentially explains the myriad differences in subjectivity which are apparent in human beings. However, the explanation of desire is less well detailed, particularly when it comes to homosexuality. This is a problem because desire becomes incorporated into our subjectivities: we come to identify as gay or lesbian not just as a social identity but as a marker of sexual conduct. We therefore need a sociological account of desire because we must be

Understanding sexual subjectivity

able to challenge 'naturalist' explanations of it whilst remaining sensitive to it as a very personal component of self-identity. In understanding desire as socially produced and constructed, we may go a long way to removing the stigma attached to 'deviant' desires within the essentialist framework.

Gagnon and Simon's original work on homosexuality is tentative to say the least. The title of their chapter on lesbians – 'A conformity greater than deviance' – reflects their argument that lesbians must still negotiate identity primarily as women.[5] However, the reasons for this sexual 'deviance' are not investigated thoroughly, for either gay men or lesbians, although the importance of gender identity is hinted at. In both cases, they cite respondents' feelings of being 'different' from other boys and girls as the beginnings of an alternative sexual identity. A more thorough consideration of male homosexuality can be found in Ken Plummer's study *Sexual Stigma* (1975). From an interactionist perspective, Plummer contends that the condition of homosexuality is created by the societal and individual reaction to it and the self-negotiation of these processes. He identifies three stages of the homosexual career: sensitisation, signification and coming out.

The first stage is where real or imagined same sex experience creates the potential for a homosexual career, particularly in conjunction with a registering of difference from prevailing gender socialisation. In a society and culture where gender difference is equated with sexual difference, feeling different from the other boys or girls may lead to a consideration of the self as homosexual (as the inverse of the 'normal' heterosexual). In signification – the second stage – the self must be reconstructed with this new conception of identity which is primarily determined by society's norms and therefore understood as deviant (Matza 1969). The final stage is the resolution of signification which results in 'coming out'. This is an acceptance of one's identity as homosexual. This does not necessarily mean gay pride, since the negotiation of the gay self must still continue in relation to a predominantly heterosexual world. However, the homosexual subculture (the 'scene') could provide a pool of similarly out significant others but even then it seems unlikely that all significant others (families for example) will be supportive of the new identity.

Both Plummer's (1995) later work and other studies have contained an emphasis on desire as socially constructed. From a feminist perspective, there has been a variety of work detailing the production and maintenance of heterosexual desire through social and ideological practice (see Holland *et al.* 1998; Irigary 1985; Jackson 1996b; Mackinnon 1989, Rich 1986; Richardson 1996; Wittig 1992). In all of this theory and research into the creation and meaning of desire, there is a recognition that having and practising sexual desire are part of the process by which we construct our self-identity and our subjectivities. Socially produced and conditioned desire is therefore a central component in the social construction of our subjectivities. We learn sexual desires just as we learn desires for commodities, status, wealth. Desire cannot therefore be an indication of some natural moral essence, but rather it is a manifestation of the social creation and ordering of sexuality. Desires must be understood as central to subjectivity and yet created by, linked to and sustained through wider social mechanisms.

CONCLUSION: ACHIEVING SUBJECTIVITY

It is orthodoxy now in most sociological approaches to consider subjectivity as a process (Benhabib 1992; Giddens 1991a, 1991b; Gilligan 1982; Laclau 1991; Laclau and Mouffe 1985, 1987; Plummer 1995; Weeks 1996), thereby dictating a non-essentialist understanding of the self and social identity. These insights have been heavily influenced by the interactionist concern with the importance of meaning to human social activity and the impact this activity has on identity through time and space, as well as the contribution made by post-structuralist theorists to understandings of subjectivity. Whether in the realm of consumption, sexuality or class analysis, there is a consensus that subjectivity is a state which is achieved through interaction with social relations and divisions, rather than being a pregiven, presocial state or one that is functionally and predictably determined by structural forces. In the exploration of sexuality, symbolic interactionism has provided a more sociological framework of analysis than has psychoanalysis, although the latter perspective has certainly been more popular when the origin and meaning of desires are under consideration. What I have tried to show in this chapter is that we can retain the premise of the interactive self and relate it, without too much inconsistency, to social structures as the source of social meanings. If we think of the specific situation as the contextual embeddedness of structural relations (Smith 1988), then we begin to have a way of thinking about how subjectivity is constructed by social forces and how desires are similarly constructed and used as a core referent for self and social identity.

Although I have only very briefly sketched how this relationship between sexual subjectivity and social structures can be conceptualised, I feel that I can safely claim to have met two of the three criteria which I laid down as necessary for a viable theory of sexual subjectivity. The interactionist approach is both anti-essentialist and can be used to provide a framework of explanation for sexuality which illuminates the social forces, contexts and relationships involved in constructing sexuality as central to subjectivity. However, as a potentially transformative way of thinking, interactionism suffers from an over-emphasis on the fluidity of subjectivity and social relations which bears no relationship to the world of rigidly demarcated sexual identities and social categories (Epstein 1992). This is not to say that individuals do not develop their sexualities differently within categories of sexual identity, but rather to emphasise that symbolic interactionists do not attend to the permanence of the categories themselves as referents for identity and practice. This is largely because interactionism remains somewhat ahistorical and so does not address the social construction of categories and practices as indicative of social hierarchies and power relationships which have developed through time. In this sense it is not a useful way of explaining the paradoxes of our sexual identities (Weeks 1996), particularly the dimension of our identities which is historically specific and yet contingent on our identification. Since I have used Weeks' paradoxes as an illustration of the relationship between subjectivity and social categories, I suggest that there needs to be a more detailed consideration of subjectivity than I have managed in this chapter.

In particular, the hierarchical construction of sexual categories and subjectivities needs to be acknowledged as a manifestation of power. This issue, and the problematic account of structures may suggest that interactionism is, after all, not the best way forward as a basis for a theory of political subjectivity which takes account of power relationships. However, the various derivatives of interactionism have retained a concern with the self as process and the importance of meaning to human action, whilst incorporating an analysis of power. Ken Plummer's work on sexual stories demonstrates such an approach (1995), focusing as it does on both the cultural and interpersonal sources of both meaning and identity and how these embody and reflect power relationships. Another such approach is demonstrated in the work of Dorothy Smith (1988) who develops a feminist position derived from interactionism and phenomenology but also acknowledges that social relations construct the context-specific sites of interaction. Smith argues that 'social relations in this sense do not exist in an abstract formal space organised purely conceptually, but as determinate actual processes' (1988: 135). I will return to both Plummer's and Smith's perspectives in the more detailed consideration of the process of achieving sexuality conducted in the next chapter, but I foreground them here simply to emphasise that there are interactionist derived approaches which retain the idea of subjectivity as process whilst locating that process within social power relationships.

The concern with subjectivity as process has also been an important part of the approach to sexuality demonstrated in the more fashionable perspective of Queer theory. Derived from the Foucauldian perspective on the creation of the sexual subject through juridical and constitutive power, and also influenced by deconstructionist literary analyses, the Queer project attempts to combine the sensitivities of a historical, discursive perspective on social categories and power with an emphasis on subjectivity as a contingent and multidimensional process (Butler 1990a, 1991; Seidman 1996). Indeed, it is the post-structuralist approach to subjectivity, exemplified in Queer theory, which has provided the departure point for many of the current explorations of the possibilities of a politics of difference. Queer theory developed in part as a reaction to the problems of an exclusive and homogenous homosexual identity which was apparent in both gay and lesbian politics during the 1970s and 1980s.[6]

The beginnings of an explicitly social constructionist perspective on sexuality are hard to pinpoint (Vance 1989), but the emphasis within the various interactionist and labelling theory approaches on the social construction of the gay or lesbian identity (Boswell 1980, 1992; Foucault 1980; Weeks 1977, 1989) tended to merely reinforce the focus on those identities as socially oppressed (Seidman 1996) without bringing into question the legitimacy and/or effectiveness of those identities for political strategies. It was really only in the late 1980s that an explicitly Queer body of work developed and it was distinct because it emphasised the deconstruction of sexual and political identities. In this sense, Queer developed as an attack on the positivist epistemology of essentialist sexuality.

Queer theorists took their cue from Foucault's thesis on power operating through essentialist discourses to constitute regimes of knowledge around sexuality and sociosexual identities. This analysis suggested that the goal of Queer theorists should be to deconstruct the hierarchical ordering and binary categories of sexuality, and thus to contest and resist the legitimacy of the essentialist discourse. Furthermore, the influence of linguistic theory, in the shape of the semiological thesis on the polarity of signs which influenced Lacan, served to reinforce the

Understanding sexual subjectivity

relativist epistemology of Queer theory and the focus on the construction of the binary, polar, categories of sexuality (Butler 1991).[7] It is the emphasis on power as constitutive of sexual identities and hierarchies which is perhaps the most important contribution of Foucault's work to the sociology of sexuality. In this sense, the Queer approach to sexuality suggests that we may explain the paradox of a historical and yet intimate construction of sexual subjectivity as an effect of the operation of power in society. Moreover, in its aim of deconstruction and resistance, this perspective has the potential to meet the third criteria of a transformative theory of sexual subjectivity which interactionism lacks.

However, the Queer enterprise is not without some of the difficulties faced by those working from an interactionist position. In particular, the theorisation of the relationship between subjectivity and structures, or rather discourses, is as problematic for social analysis here as in the interactionist approach.[8] Subjectivity is regarded as the constituted effect of various intersecting discourses, that is to say that multiple discourses produce a sense of social identity and subjectivity, and this construction of self shifts over time depending on which discourses are available. In this sense, Queer theory is no different from interactionism in that both emphasise the multifaceted and contingent nature of the self as a process of identity construction. However, distinctions arise between the two perspectives on the one hand because of the explicit connection between power, discourse and subjectivity made in Queer theory, and also because some Queer theorists resort to using Lacanian psychoanalysis in order to discuss the intricacies of meaning and process in the self (see Butler 1993; and the discussions by Fuss 1991).

Drawing on the work of Foucault, Queer theorists suggest that where there is power, there is also the possibility of resistance. Thus, the constitutive effect of power operating through discourses is not only to produce subjects – as organised constructions of identity – but also to produce resistance, since these subjects necessarily exclude the 'other' by de-emphasising other identity components which are not privileged or suited to the particular intersection of discourses being deployed. For example, in gay and lesbian politics in the USA during the 1970s, the assertion of an exclusive and homogenous 'ethnic' homosexual identity submerged differences of class, race and gender which were then reasserted by those so excluded, resulting in part in the development of Queer theory itself and an associated change in the political identities mobilised in lesbian and gay politics from 'ethnic' to 'queer'.

Of course, this view of the self as multifaceted and contingent echoes the interactionist perspective on subjectivity as a process. Furthermore, Queer theory contains an implicit acceptance of the agency of the subject, since identity constructs are unstable and are transformed and renegotiated within multiple discourses. Perhaps the most sophisticated development of this position appears in the work of Judith Butler, who emphasises gender as 'performativity' – what we actually do to reiterate, reinscribe and potentially, to destabilise and transgress the normative binary constructs of gender (1990a, 1990b, 1991). It is not difficult to see the ways in which a Queer perspective may be used to explain the process of achieving sexuality. There are problems with the connections made between power, subjectivity, agency and discourses and I will deal with these in depth in the subsequent chapters. However, it is important to grasp at this point that whilst Queer theory does offer a radical view of the link between subjectivity and power, there are elements of the perspective which echo the much older work produced in the sociological approaches to the sexual self found in interactionism and associated feminist theorisations (Stein and Plummer 1996; Plummer 1995).

Queer, however, has a distinctly political edge to it and it is worth reiterating the political context to my ongoing sociological discussion before we move on to the next chapter. Much of the political focus in Queer theory has been to problematise the implicit construction of the political subject: as unitary, male, white, heterosexual, able-bodied. The central argument has been that social location and subjectivity profoundly affect political subjectivity and thus the political subject cannot be regarded as an unencumbered or suprasocial actor. In terms of social and cultural diversity, it is the term 'difference' that has come to characterise the present debate. Those theorists wrestling with the various problems of reconciling difference with democratic individualism have agreed on the whole that we need a non-essentialist understanding of political subjectivity as multifaceted, contingent. There is a widespread recognition that the self is socially constructed and is negotiated and defined in relation to others and in the context of dominant categories of identity and social structures. As the basis for a politics of sexual difference, we need a social understanding of sexual subjectivity. I have argued elsewhere (Rahman 1998) that the individualist conceptualisation of rights collapses all too easily into an essentialist construction of subjectivity, and that this serves to reinforce oppressive essentialist understandings of sexuality. An alternative to both sexual and political essentialism must be found if we are to overcome the subordination of lesbians and gays.

Queer theorists have expanded and developed the original

Understanding sexual subjectivity

Foucauldian perspective on power and they are now engaged in the illumination of the discursive construction of dissident sexual identities, as both contingent and forged through the political struggle of appropriating dominant discourses for themselves (Butler 1990a, 1991; see also the edition of *Differences* edited by de Lauretis 1991; Meyer (ed.) 1994; Stychin 1995). Projects such as Queer have, however, too often narrowed the focus of investigation exclusively to the discursively constituted self, without locating the self within social structures. The self is too often seen as the constituted effect of discourses without an explication of what that process means in terms of agency, subjectivity and practices. Despite their resolutely anti-essentialist credentials, Queer theorists are actually rather reticent on the question of how subjectivity is formed and processed in relation to social structures or formations. Moreover, both Queer and interactionist perspectives imply a fluidity of subjectivity afforded by either an active self or the multiplicity of discourses, and both characterisations seem to ignore the material relationships, social processes and structural conditions within which sexual subjectivity is achieved. Again, the importance of social structures in creating patterned ways for the self to exist is underplayed. One way of thinking about the fluidity of subjectivity and its location within social relations is to draw on Mead's conceptualisation of the self as differentiated between the 'me' and the 'I'. I would like to suggest that in many ways subjectivity is only ever achieved in certain conditions and times – the 'I' is only momentarily coherent, whilst the me is a process of self-understanding and self-location. Both in terms of our own process of conceptualising our 'self' and in terms of the categories with which we identify or are allocated to by wider social forces, we achieve a sense of subjectivity.[9] In the following chapter, I intend to explore a way of theorising this process which combines the sociological insights of interactionism with the political aims of Queer theory.

NOTES

1. Although Abelove has argued that Freud did not support the pathologisation of homosexuality within clinical practice which developed with the use of his theories in the early part of the twentieth century (1993).
2. Semiology was developed through its application to more than language – Barthes applied it to the text in cultural studies (1957) and Levi-Strauss to kinship patterns and cultural myths (1978).
3. Queer theorists are the oddest of this strand since Foucault describes

psychoanalysis as part and parcel of the 'regimes of truth' which construct sexuality.

4. As Blumer argues, symbolic interactionism 'is able to cover the full range of the generic forms of human association. It embraces equally well such relationships as co-operation, conflict, domination, exploitation, consensus, disagreement, closely knit identification and indifferent concern for one another' (1966: 13). For just such a comprehensive application, see Cohen and Taylor, 1976.

5. However, put another way, you could argue that the lesser social and economic independence of women suggests that the process of becoming lesbian is actually much more of a deviance from the traditional role of women than becoming gay is for men. See Wittig 1992, Whisman 1996, Jackson 1996b, Richardson 1996.

6. The development of commercial subcultures tended to produce a minority rights and assimilationist agenda which excluded differences of race, class and gender within these communities, especially in the US. I deal with this issue of differences in Chapter 5, but for a good discussion see Seidman, 1996, and de Lauretis' introduction to the Queer theory edition of *Differences*, 1991.

7. For a detailed reminder see the section on Lacan and Language earlier in this chapter.

8. I will discuss the use of the concept of discourse in more depth in the next chapter but for the moment I want to concentrate on the issue of subjectivity in Queer theory.

9. Brake (1982) introduces the idea of achieved gender, arguing that sexual behaviour and identity are crucial factors in the allocation of appropriate gendered identity. Whilst I agree with this, I am also using the notion of 'achieving sexuality' simply to emphasise the conditions and actions required to identify with and inhabit sexual categories – the processes by which we become or are interpellated as sexual.

Chapter 3

SEXUAL SUBJECTIVITY IN SOCIAL CONTEXT

INTRODUCTION: LIVING WITHIN HISTORY

My aim in this chapter is to continue to develop a sociological account of sexual subjectivity upon which a reconceptualised political subjectivity can be constructed. I begin the attempt to integrate sociological and political ideas by expanding on the discussion conducted in the previous chapter; specifically by considering the structural context to sexual subjectivity. It is the lack of such a context which undermines the potential of both interactionist and Queer perspectives as a basis for political activity. As argued in the preceding chapters, we need to bring in a more sociological understanding which acknowledges that human agency occurs within historically specific conditions. As Marx put it: 'It is not the consciousness of men that determines their existence, but their social existence that determines their consciousness' (1982: 37). I am not advocating a return to structuralist Marxist characterisations of subjectivity as the wholly determined function of social relations – in the vein of Althusser (1971), for example – but I am simply using this classic formulation in order to emphasise themes which run throughout this chapter.

The first reason for using Marx is to provide – in these post-structuralist times – a reminder to us that theorising the relationship between the structural forces of a specific historical era and the lives and actions of those whom these forces affect has been a perennial problem for sociological theory. Interactionism and Queer theory are perspectives which seem to emphasise agency over structure, and so require a corrective which allows us to acknowledge that sexualities as social constructions are not simply a product of interaction or discursive location, but they are also an indication of the fact that we live within history – within historically specific categories of identity, frameworks of thought and practices of law and social convention (Weeks 1996). Although the first wave of sociological perspectives on sexuality detailed the social factors which led to the development of homosexual identity, the associated formation of subjectivity was not dealt with in any integrated manner (Seidman 1996; Watney 1980). An understanding of sexual subjectivity as socially constructed is the unfinished business of the sociology of sexuality. Even though the issue of subjectivity did preoccupy symbolic interactionists, the problem of relating experience and identity to social structures has never been adequately theorised because the location of the self within hierarchies of social categories and desires is not comprehensively explained. In his recent work, Ken Plummer continues to wrestle with this problem in interactionist thought by turning to the concept of narratives or 'sexual stories' (Plummer 1995). He draws on interactionism, ethnomethodology, phenomenology and feminist work in all of these traditions (see for example: Haug *et al.* 1987; Smith 1988; Stanley and Wise 1983; Steedman 1986). The focus on the agent in these approaches has been tempered by a recognition that the reflexive construction of self occurs within structured contexts and with reference to structurally dominant ways of thinking about identity.

Plummer's work is more explicitly concerned with the structural production of narratives. He suggests that the conditions for telling sexual stories are dependent on the dimensions of power in the social world since these stories cannot always be heard and nor are they always available across time and cultures (1995). Both Plummer's work and associated feminist work on narratives, memory, biography and autobiography (Stanley 1992) begin to suggest ways in which subjectivity may be linked to structural conditions. Plummer goes on to argue that the proliferation of sexual stories in the late modern world suggest the possibility of what he calls 'intimate citizenship' – a concern with moral and political questions surrounding intimate life and the recognition of differences within this sphere. This leads me on to my second reason for quoting Marx. Marx's theories were explicitly political: he argued that material relations should be the focus of political activity in order to overthrow the oppressive class system. The above quotation is part of a broader section dealing with the characterisation of consciousness and its function in repressing the working classes. A Marxist perspective reminds us not only that social conditions are potentially susceptible to

Sexual subjectivity in social context

political interventions, but also that the self should be understood in the context of general social conditions – thus a sociological theorisation of sexual subjectivity is crucial for organising political goals and strategies. The problems with attempting to provide such a perspective on sexual subjectivity are my third reason for using a quotation from Marx to begin my discussion. The main division between structuralist and post-structuralist theorists of social life has been centred on the move away from Marxist explanations – which focused on the material realm – towards post-modernist perspectives, which focus on the cultural.[1] Add to this debate the implicitly anti-structuralist perspective of interactionism and you have a brew which suggests major difficulties will arise out of any attempt to integrate various perspectives on sexual subjectivity. Moreover, this will have inevitable consequences for the overall aim of my study – the attempt to use sociological theories to provide a departure point for political activity – since the political questions cannot be resolved if there is no consensus on the relative importance of the material and cultural realms.

This can be left for the moment to lie as a thread throughout the remainder of my discussion, but it is one which I will pick up in the final chapter. Let me return to the first point about integrating structure and subjectivity in current theorisations of sexuality. What strikes me is the similarity between Plummer's interactionist concerns and the preoccupations of Queer theorists in the realm of subjectivity. Queer theory is a perspective which is similarly anti-essentialist, with an emphasis on subjectivity as a process of achieving identity which is never complete and is, therefore, open to transformation (Seidman 1996). Plummer has moved towards a position which accepts many of the premises of Queer theory, although he is also critical of the lack of sociological underpinnings to the Queer perspective (Plummer 1995; Stein and Plummer 1996). However, part of the attraction of Queer theory for those working within sociology is precisely the emphasis placed on the social construction of sexuality. Queer theorists are committed to destabilising the notion of an essential sexual identity and the binary categories which regulate, discipline and produce sexual subjects. In Queer theory and in the related Foucauldian sociohistorical approaches (such as Weeks' perspective on the paradoxes of identity, 1996), and in the engagement between interactionism and politics (Plummer 1995), there is an explicit recognition that perspectives on the self need to be related to a reformulated conceptualisation of the political subject. In this sense, social theories of sexuality are already convergent with radical democratic theorists – a convergence which will be discussed in greater detail in the final chapter. Before that discussion can take place, I want to explore the lack of a structural context in sociological approaches to sexual subjectivity.

It is the idea of the self as process which I think is the most useful insight of both interactionism and post-modernism. For this reason, I have characterised sexual subjectivity as 'achieved' subjectivity. I am using the notion of achieving sexuality in order to help us to think about the ways in which we engage in the process of constructing our 'selves' and also the ways in which we mobilise a construction of identity in order to take action.[2] The self as process has become the orthodox approach in the analysis of social identity in late modernity – a focus on what Giddens has called the 'reflexive project of the self' (1991a). Furthermore, as Evans (1993) and others have suggested (Epstein 1992; Heath 1982), this construction of the self is anchored to and filtered through an essentialist understanding of sexual identity – sexuality and gender are seen as the immutable and permanent 'truth' of our identities (Giddens 1991a, 1992; Nixon 1996; Weeks 1996). Sexuality and gender are often also allocated to us by others with reference to essentialist conventions of morality and gendered behaviour and identity. Being queerbashed is perhaps the most stark example of an occasion when we are allocated a social identity (queer = deviant = legitimate target of violence) in conditions which we do not control.

Since both the allocation of sexual identity and the reflexive construction of our sexual identities are underpinned by hierarchical social relationships and historically specific conditions and contexts, I will argue that interactionist and post-modernist theories become problematic when the emphasis turns to the conditions in which sexuality is achieved, in large part because they lack an integrated structural emphasis. This inevitably creates problems for theorising political identity, given that political activity is conducted within a network of institutions, practices and spheres which are themselves highly structured and reflect the structural divisions within democratic societies along dimensions of class, race, gender and sexuality. I will suggest that political aims need to be directed at the conditions which sustain the essentialist construction of sexuality and, moreover, that our political identities and presence need to reinforce this emphasis on sexuality as a hierarchical social construction and a set of social processes.

After an introductory discussion of the issues around structure, agency and the self which need to be addressed in the consideration of sexual subjectivity, I begin a review of structural accounts of sexuality which covers both historical and materialist perspectives (Adam 1985; Evans 1993; Greenberg and Bystryn 1984). Drawing particularly on the work of David Evans, I argue that these perspectives illustrate the importance of the material basis both to sexual categories and the process through which we develop our subjectivities. In Evans' analysis of consumption, other perspectives on the self (Giddens 1991a) and feminist investigations into the construction of sexual identities (Hollway 1984; Whisman 1996), there is a more or less explicit notion that we reflexively construct our sexual identities. This leads me to discuss the issue of structure and agency as the theme which relates subjectivity to structural conditions and structural categories of sexual identity. I return to the paradoxes of identity introduced by Weeks (1996) as a way of thinking my way through these issues. Central to the dynamic of these paradoxes is the dominance of the essentialist paradigm both as a means of legitimising hierarchical social categories and as the framework for the construction of subjectivity. I suggest that the benefit of a structural analysis is that it allows us to think of essentialism as a paradigm which reflects gendered power relationships in the social world. This critical approach to the sexual order is absent in symbolic interactionism but it is taken up by those working with narratives and feminist standpoint theorising and it is also central to the analysis put forward by Queer theorists.

Although those theorising the relationship between structures, ideologies and subjectivity have turned to the use of discourses, scripts or narratives, I will argue that the problems associated with the older structuralist concept of ideology have not been fully resolved through the use of these newer concepts. I suggest that we need to understand the structural contexts within which we achieve sexuality and the effects and social practices which these entail. I argue that there is a structurally grounded dimension to the construction of subjectivity, whereby the effects of essentialism exist within and are negotiated through material relationships and social practices. Moreover, essentialism serves as a convenient shorthand for the rationalisation of strategic human action and so it must be challenged with a sociological account of action which illuminates the relationships between structures, ideologies or discourses and consciousness and subjectivity.

STRUCTURE, AGENCY AND THE SELF

Any theorisation of the conditions for achieving sexuality at the level of the self must incorporate the influence of structural conditions. At one level, this is simply a matter of context, acknowledging that there are different realms of social analysis. The dualism of structure and agency does not necessarily invalidate any theorisation which cannot integrate the two levels. In the study of sexuality, to describe and theorise sexual selves and careers is a distinct enterprise from theorising the structural institutions, relationships and practices which underpin the categories which those selves inhabit. In this sense, the sociohistorical structural analysis of sexual categories can be regarded as an explanation of how sexuality has come to be understood as essential to our selves through the influence of 'expert' knowledges, and also how the current hierarchical organisation of sexuality – in terms of both gender and categories of sexual identity – has emerged in conjunction with bureaucratic and material developments in Western societies. Structural analyses provide the background to how and why sexuality is the basis of social identity.

However, the other implication of structural approaches is that social conditions and ideological formations also underpin the ways in which we achieve our sexual identities; how we engage in sexual practices and negotiate sexual careers at the level of the self. For example, in current Western culture, we can only identify in binary terms – as male or female and so as gay, lesbian or straight or indeed, as bisexual. Furthermore, this identification signals to others how to interact with us and governs our interaction with them in terms of how we relate sexually; where we go to socialise, how we flirt, use our bodies, dance, walk, and ultimately, who we are likely to have sexual encounters with. Theorising this relationship between structure and the self involves a consideration of many issues and one way of negotiating our way through these issues is to return to the four paradoxes of sexual identity which Jeffrey Weeks (1996) describes as central to the construction of sexuality and which I used to organise my discussion in Chapter 2.[3] The paradoxes of identity bring to the fore the relationship between subjectivity and social structure because they address the various ways in which our sense of self is indicative of sociostructural conditions of sexuality. In this sense, I want to draw out the tensions between essentialist understandings of subjectivity as natural, eternal and immutable, and the construction of our sexual selves as markers of our location within historically produced social categories, hierarchies of power and modes of identification and subjectification.

The pre-eminent factor which underwrites the process of achieving sexuality at the level of subjectivity has been the development of specific forms of 'expert' knowledge around sexuality which are premised on sexual and psychological essentialism (Foucault 1980; Weeks 1989). Material relationships and general social interaction and practices combine with essentialist ideas in the realm of gender and sexuality to create structured social contexts in which sexuality and gender are embodied. We cannot escape gender or sexual identity: we are compelled to be male or female, homosexual or heterosexual. The relationship between essentialist conceptualisations and sexual subjectivity has been theorised through the use of a variety of conceptual tools, ranging from ideology, discourse, narratives, sexual stories (Plummer 1995), dominant accounts (Whisman 1996) and, of course, sexual scripts (Gagnon and Simon 1974). Each admits essentialism as the socially dominant form of knowledge but none of these analytical devices evinces a structural understanding of essentialism, either in terms of the effects of the deployment of knowledge or in the material and social conditions which underpin the production and deployment of this knowledge.

Within structural perspectives, this link between structure, subjectivity and action has traditionally been theorised through the concept of ideology. In the realm of sexuality, we need to think about how essentialism affects our reflexive understanding of identity and the ways in which we mobilise that identity. Ideology is a problematic device in this realm of analysis, often collapsing the structure/agency relationship into a determinist equation which denies any possibility of self-aware subjectivity and effective agency. However, tracing the relationship between cultural formations of knowledge and practice on the one hand, and the construction of subjectivity on the other has remained a difficult task for theorists of sexuality. Nonetheless, I would argue that there is a way forward through this theoretical debate which is suggested by the direction of sociological perspectives on sexuality. To be specific, I suggest that the idea of subjectivity as process – which is the most important insight of sociological views of sexuality – can only be explained in terms of the reflexive construction of self. The intersecting effects of social power and social hierarchies not only affect subjectivity in terms of creating limits and opportunities for agency, but also in the sense that subjectivity is constructed as multidimensional. For an individual to produce agency – taken to mean the combination of strategy and intention (Hay 1995) – out of such a multifaceted social existence suggests that the self is engaged in a constant reconstruction and reordering of subjectivity, with the aim of mobilising the huge variety of experience and purpose into a sense of coherent identity on which to base the strategy and intention for social action.

This immediately suggests that self-awareness and the possibility of effective agency must be central criteria in any development of a viable theory of sexual subjectivity. Therefore, the following discussion of structural conditions, essentialism and subjectivity will be underpinned by the assumption that reflexivity is a key feature of the process through which we achieve sexuality. Structural conditions must therefore be connected to subjectivity in an analysis which does not dictate a determinist relationship between structure, culture and the self. I will argue that many of the structural conditions discussed in the following section have derivative social practices which are embedded both institutionally and in everyday interaction. Thus subjectivity is not determined through structural location or constructed simply by structural forces, but rather it is reflexively constructed through interaction and articulation with structure and culture. In this way, I will attempt to develop a position whereby I argue that there are structured social and material conditions for the self which provide the context for the interaction and construction of subjectivity.

WHY SOCIAL STRUCTURES AREN'T 'SEXY'

When we achieve and deploy a sense of sexuality, we are evidently constructing and processing a sense of subjectivity with reference to various social identities, their associated social practices and the cultural ideas which explain and connect identity with conduct. The progress of young men and women in our culture still follows the general path of gendered identity preceding sexual identity and, although there may be more awareness and tolerance of homosexuality (although this is probably more generally true of Britain than the USA), most young adults conform to gendered heterosexual patterns of relationships and adopt and learn to inhabit these categories of sexual identity. At this level of social analysis it is correct to say that we are dealing with the formation of sexuality as social structure since these categories of identity and modes of appropriate behaviour have a permanence beyond individual action. Although there are a few specifically structural accounts of sexuality, most of the research has been developed from specifically anti-structuralist or indeed, post-structuralist perspectives. Those investigating categories of sexuality from a socio-historical perspective have tended to rely on the Foucauldian concept of discourse when describing underpinning social forces, rather than relying on any explicitly structural framework of analysis (see Boswell 1992; Foucault 1980; Boswell 1992; Ramazanoglu

Sexual subjectivity in social context 89

1993; Weeks 1989). Even explicitly structural accounts of sexuality tend to focus on social identity rather than on the associated production of subjectivity although feminist critiques of the institutionalisation of heterosexuality are more sensitive to the distinction between social and self-identity (Rich 1980). Contemporary research into heterosexuality is much more adept at linking subjectivity to structural conditions and discourses (Holland *et al.* 1998) but this is still a vastly under-researched area.

Whilst Foucault (1980) puts forward a post-structuralist argument with regards to the operation of power and the creation of sexuality, the subsequent use of his perspective by others takes more account of the impact of gender and class divisions as structural factors (Weeks 1977, 1989). However, there is no thorough consideration of how these structures affect agency through the production of subjectivity. For example, Weeks (1989) argues that changing class and patriarchal relations in the nineteenth century produced the gender specific notions of sexuality enshrined in the 'domestic ideology' (Davidoff and Hall 1987; Hall 1982) but he does not develop an account of how these materially based changes come to be translated into individual subjectivity although he is keen to argue that individual sexual identity is constructed with reference to these structural transformations. Part of the reluctance to engage with structures is, it seems, a consequence of the perennial structure/agency divide. The inevitable prejudice of any structural theory is to under-theorise agency and subjectivity whereas agent-focused theories underplay the importance of social structures. As so often in social theory, these approaches operate at two levels of analysis and remain unintegrated.[4]

There are of course considerations of structure in social constructionist accounts of sexuality. Interactionists consider the importance of culture (Plummer 1975) and other social scripts and identities such as gender (Gagnon and Simon 1974). The institutionalisation of heterosexuality, the existence of gender divisions and the dominant understanding of sexual identity as innate are all cited by interactionists as aspects of the scripts through which we learn appropriate sexual behaviour and incorporate sexual knowledge and experience into our sense of self. Yet, as argued in the previous chapter, there is a reluctance to theorise social structures as underpinning conventional conduct and social meaning, a reluctance which can only be remedied if scripts are understood as the product of contextually embedded structural relationships and social practices if they are to afford any analytical purchase on sexuality.

The Foucauldian approach demonstrates a similar reluctance which, to be fair, is inevitable in a perspective which has come to be understood as an exemplary post-structuralist view of the social world. Foucault regards the development and deployment of sexuality solely as an effect of power: 'power mechanisms that functioned in such a way that discourse on sex . . . became essential' (Foucault 1980: 23). In effect, Foucault ascribes subject status to power. The possibility of agency for individuals disappears because subjectivity is wholly constituted through discourse: there is no meaningful concept of extra-discursive existence which means that agency is, to a large degree, no longer a self-aware or reflexive property but rather a predictable result of discursive location. As Evans puts it, 'Foucault's emphasis on complete subjectivity brings his analysis into direct confrontation with the most basic sociological equation; social structure plus social consciousness equals social action' (1993: 20). However, this reading of Foucault has been contested, especially by Judith Butler in her development of his ideas (1993: 1–16) and also because of his later work on 'practices' and 'technologies of the self' in which Foucault elaborates on potential strategies for resisting dominant discourses – a recovery of the idea of effective and reflexive agency (Foucault 1990; Simons 1995). I will discuss this issue in more detail in Chapter 4, but for the moment I want to concentrate on Foucault's conceptualisation of power which underpins his ideas about discourse and the later elaboration of 'practices' of resistance.

Since Foucault sees power as 'a heterogeneous ensemble of power relations operating at the micro-level of society' (Sawicki 1991:230), it is difficult to explain patterns, consolidation or shifts in the manifestations of power. If power is not a resource which derives from hierarchical social relationships, such as class or patriarchy, it becomes difficult to explain the connections between the existence of power and the differential access to it (Ramazanoglu 1993). For example, non-egalitarian relationships between men and women are reflected in the hierarchy of sexualities which Foucault describes (1980), but these inequalities are never explicitly accepted as constitutive of that sexual hierarchy (Seidler 1989) or as important dimensions to the diffusion of power within that hierarchy. This bottom-up analysis of power is a radical perspective on power relations at the micro-level of society but the link between the micro-level and institutionalised oppression or structured inequality is not easy to trace (Ramazanoglu and Holland 1993; Ransom 1993).

In both interactionism and the Foucauldian approach the link between social structure, essentialist understandings and sexual subjectivity is under-theorised because of the lack of a recourse to any structural emphasis within these perspectives. In some senses, it is simply not fashionable to talk of social structures because the very turn towards interpretative and post-structuralist sociology which focused on the realm of human sexuality is part of a wider shift in attitudes and intellectual debates which have rendered 'social structures' as an outmoded concept. Social structures are not a key concept in either of the theories discussed thus far but I would argue that – for any full sociological understanding – we need to think about the fit and interdependence between social structures, social meaning and subjectivity. Before I go on to discuss this relationship in detail, I will consider whether there are any useful links to be made between structural analyses of sexuality and the conditions for achieving sexual subjectivity which are implicit in both scripts and discourses.

STRUCTURAL CONDITIONS AND SEXUALITY

Structural accounts of sexuality tend to focus on male homosexuality, both in the sense of excluding lesbians and in the sense that the development and treatment of gay identities is often used as an indicator of the complementary construction of heterosexuality and the underpinning divisions of masculinity and femininity in the society and period under discussion. Lesbians are often subsumed under the category of women, which makes sense only insofar as the development of lesbian identities has been dependent on the degree of sexual and material autonomy available to women (see Adam 1985; Evans 1993; Weeks 1989). However, lesbians constitute a social category distinct from both the generic 'woman' and the generic 'homosexual'. Whilst some of the structural factors underpinning the emergence of lesbianism and male homosexuality are the same, the context and impact of these factors is different for each identity (see Faderman 1981; Smith-Rosenberg 1975, 1990). Furthermore, there are considerable differences of experience and theoretical emphasis between lesbians and heterosexual women, highlighted by recent feminist debates on the relationship between sexuality and gender (Jackson and Scott 1996; Richardson 1996).

The focus on male homosexuality does, however, serve to illustrate the general trajectory of the development of the essentialist understanding of sexuality. Foucault's (1980) historical work provides just such an analysis, and the link between both male and female homosexuality and wider cultural changes is also made in Gagnon and Simon's interactionist study (1974). Structural accounts of sexuality share this emphasis but are weighted towards a more traditional materialist perspective. For example, Adam (1985) suggests that the change in kinship structures brought about by industrialisation contributed to the formation of gay identities. The separation of work and home and the emergence of male-only spaces for work and socialisation produced the opportunities for same-sex interaction and afforded the development of specifically homosexual spaces. Underlying this change was mass urbanisation and the emergent separation of men and women into the industrial and domestic spheres. Adam suggests that the development of state bureaucratic procedures – again, necessary to deal with the effects and conditions of capitalism – provided more direct and institutionalised methods for the regulation of sexuality. This argument is developed more thoroughly by Greenberg and Bystryn (1984) who argue that those working within state organisation had more resources to pursue 'deviants', through the criminal justice system, and through medical and educational institutions, and that this policing of the deviant went hand in hand with the institutionalised state support for monogamous heterosexuality, through marriage, restrictions on female wage labour and morality campaigns. Greenberg and Bystryn see bureaucratisation as the form of impersonal and extended social control necessary for the initial stages of capitalism, and as having a reinforcing effect on the changes in population migration and kinship organisation which occurred during these periods.

Another direct effect of capitalism which both they and Adam (1985) discuss is the emphasis on competition. Early capitalists fostered the need for strong competition between each other for funds and markets and between waged labourers for jobs. Of course, this meant competition between men, and both Greenberg and Bystryn (1984) and Adam (1985) suggest that this atmosphere of competitiveness precluded intimacy and emotional ties between men, shifting the source of these relationships to the domestic realm and thus the burden on to women. The increase in gendered divisions of paid and unpaid labour, which characterised the early development of capitalism, served to reinforce the increasing emphasis on sexual difference which underpinned the newly emergent understandings of masculinity and femininity during the Victorian period (Jackson 1992). The advancing material and social divisions between the genders during this era was underwritten by the conceptualisation of biological and emotional differences; masculinity untroubled by emotional feelings and in control of physical ones, complemented by a femininity untroubled by sexual urges but wholly subordinate to biological and emotional forces (Davidoff and Hall 1987; Hall 1982; Jackson and Scott 1997; Weeks 1989).

It is, however, important to bear in mind the differential effects of these structural forces on different classes, and to recognise the convergence of material relations with other cultural factors during this period, particularly religion and the advance of professional status within the medical profession. It is clear that the domestic ideology and the gendered division of rationality and emotionality did not have a uniform impact throughout all classes (Davidoff and Hall 1987; Hall 1982, 1992; Seidler 1989; Weeks 1980) and the working classes in particular were seen as less well developed and less able to achieve the 'civilised' ideals of masculinity and femininity which were promoted within the bourgeois class. For example, although explicit sexual intimacy between men was unacceptable and was policed both institutionally and ideologically, it is clear that physical intimacy has been, and continues to be, a strong feature of some working-class male relationships (Weeks 1977) as well as being a part of many working-class and middle-class relationships between women (Hall 1992; Smith-Rosenberg 1975, 1990).

Furthermore, Protestantism and other austere forms of Christianity were similarly influential on the development of the domestic ideology and other forms of appropriately gendered behaviour, from physical intimacy to specifically sexual behaviour (Boswell 1980, 1992) although, as Connell and Dowsett (1992) have suggested, religious justifications of sexual and gendered essentialism were gradually overtaken by scientific and medical explanations. Most important among these was the development of the idea within the medical profession of the homosexual as a separate psychological 'type'. Although these medical and scientific views developed during the same time as the institutionalisation of capitalism, they were by no means exclusively dependent on material relations. Rather these views served to reinforce the doctrine of sexual difference and heterosexual normativity, both of which were increasingly emphasised as 'natural' explanations of the new settlement in gender divisions brought about by the change in material relationships. In this sense, the characterisation of these views as discourses – frameworks of explanation (Foucault 1980; Weeks 1989) – acknowledges their contribution to the formation of our current understanding of sexuality as related to but not determined by material relationships, with certain discourses becoming hegemonic in their effect (Sawicki 1991).

The accounts of sexuality dealt with hitherto point to material conditions and religious–cultural modes of reasoning which have underpinned the emergence and development of the current dominant understanding of sexuality and the social practices and divisions which are associated with this essentialist framework. Perhaps the best account of contemporary structural characteristics is provided by David Evans in his work on the material construction of sexualities (1993).[5] He argues that since late-twentieth century capitalist systems rely upon the notion that consumption will provide self-fulfilment, it is reasonable to investigate the consumerist and thus material construction of sexualities given that sexuality is seen as a central to the identity of the self and therefore a major dimension of self-fulfilment. Yet again the focus is on male homosexuality (although he does deal briefly with women, transsexuals, transvestites and children as sexual subjects and objects) and he details the various ways in which gay identities have become the epitome of consumerist individualism, with the gay social world organised around commercial spaces and the gay identity produced and sustained through 'lifestyle' (meaning consumer) choices.

Evans (1993) connects the importance of continued capitalist accumulation to the decriminalisation of homosexuality; gays, and to a lesser extent lesbians, have become 'free', but only within certain spaces within which the main way of achieving a sense of sexual identity has been through leisure activities and consumption. In making this connection between material relations and the construction of gay identity, Evans reiterates the structural foundations of the sexual realm and begins to suggest the importance of the reflexive construction of subjectivity. Although he relies on a characterisation of sexuality as script and discourse, he does not however focus on the ways in which such an understanding of subjectivity can be integrated with material relationships and institutionalised social conventions, regulations and conditions. Furthermore, I want to reiterate the importance of gender divisions in the discussion of structural factors and sexuality since gender is the connecting lens between material relationships and their impact on homosexuality and heterosexuality. Sensitivity to gender divisions is crucial in any analysis which focuses on the material construction of sexuality. Although gender divisions are based on an exploitative material relationship between the social groups of men and women (Delphy and Leonard 1992), this dynamic is manifested differentially across classes, cultures, races and religions: the differential effects of class, particularly when seen in intersection with race, culture and religion, produce a variety of gender constructions which feed into the derivative constructions of sexualities. Moreover, it is important to grasp that gender divisions are

Sexual subjectivity in social context

constitutive of masculinity, femininity and the hierarchical ordering of sexualities (Butler 1993; Delphy 1993). Even within an exclusively homosexual subculture, gender is not only evidently present as a distinction between gay men and lesbians but in fact gender is socially constitutive of what it means to be lesbian or gay. The simplest example is the division between gay men and lesbians in the 'homosexual' commercial scene: the material advantages of men, in terms of higher wages, are enjoyed by gay men and this has led to a commercial scene focused on gay male consumers.[6]

It is interesting, and perhaps not surprising, to note that the structural accounts of sexuality deal with many of the same social relationships and conditions which are mentioned or implied in interactionist or Foucauldian analyses. What is less clear is how these structural conditions can be integrated into either the subject-focused accounts of sexuality to be found in interactionism or the discursive analysis of Foucauldian or Queer theorists. Taking interactionism first, Gagnon and Simon (1974) discuss a combination of material and cultural factors when discussing the increasing sexualisation of society: post-Second World War affluence and the increasing emphasis on consumption as indicative of social location and identity; the rise of counter-cultural ideas from the New Left; and the associated social movements of women's liberation and gay liberation, which brought intimate relationships into the political sphere. More recently mass communications, the emphasis on consumption and the self, the importance of youth culture and the development of cultural intermediaries who encourage the expression of identity through sexuality have provided the conditions for the emergence of particular 'sexual stories' (Plummer 1995): it is clear that many of these narratives emerge from a combination of the effects of structural material relationships and related social conditions within capitalist society.

It is evident that Queer theorists would not admit extra-discursive social structures or forces, but I suggest that the term 'discursive formations' – used to describe the coalescence of social practices, relationships and ideas within a discourse – refers to structural conditions and relationships (Butler 1993; Finlayson 1998: 91–3; Foucault 1980, 1989). It seems that structural theorists are, on the whole, simply much more explicit about the impact of material relations on the social conditions, practices and relationships which sustain the construction of sexual identities. However, central to the integration of interactionism and a structural account (whether that is specifically materialist or not) is the connection between structure and agency, or rather, historical conditions and subjectivity. We live within history, not above or outside it, but how do we make sense of our lives within social conditions? In common with the great tradition of structural explanations, none of those discussed above considers subjectivity to any great degree, although a logical starting point is to consider the concept and role of ideology as the traditional way of explaining how structural forces provide the conditions for the (sexual) self.

ESSENTIALISM AS IDEOLOGY AND DISCOURSE

The founding arguments for ideology were developed by Marx and Weber. Marx regarded ideology as the set of cultural ideas which reflected the dominant position of the ruling class and, crucially, legitimised and reproduced that position as natural or inevitable (see for example Marx 1954 or Giddens and Held 1982). Marx suggested that 'the mode of production of material life conditions the general processes of social, political and intellectual life' (1982: 37). Weber takes a less determinist view of ideology, arguing that the culturally ideological realm of social life can have an independent existence from the material base of society. His position on ideology is central to his argument about the elective affinity between the Protestant ethic and the values of competitive capitalism: Weber argues that the convergence of these two ideologies was crucial to the initial development of capitalism in the Protestant states of the time (1976). Both positions have subsequently been developed and refined by other theorists and it is fair to say that the implicit functionalism of Marxist accounts has been refined by the critiques of Weberians who emphasise the progressive independence of culture. It is not difficult to integrate the structuralist explanations of sexuality with either Marxian or Weberian concepts of ideology. Both Adam (1985) and Greenberg and Bystryn (1984) argue that the expansion of bureaucratic rationalisation into social life – necessary for capitalist development – contributed to the regulation and classification of sexuality, through both state and wider cultural practices. Specifically, the development of 'expert' knowledges around sexuality in the medical and natural sciences underpinned the essentialist understanding of sexuality which emerged over this period.

As Arnold Davidson (1992) argues, the particular form of psychological essentialism which is dominant today is the result of a paradigm shift in ways of thinking about the origins and practice of sexual desires and identity. It seems that essentialism can be thought of as an ideology since it is enshrined within cultural ideas and practices and serves to legitimise and mystify the oppression of heterosexual women, lesbians and gays as the inevitable consequence of a natural biological and moral order. Ideology is also constructed and promoted by specific social groups within institutions and cultural arenas and again, it is relatively simple to describe such cultural specialists in the field of sexuality: the family, the medical and legal professions, education professionals, media professionals and religious leaders. There is, however, an implicit understanding in traditional Marxist and Weberian accounts that one unified ideology will come to dominate the culture. This follows from the logic of the ideology as an exclusive resource for the dominant group in society. This perspective is particularly problematic when considering sexuality. As a dominant and unified ideology, it is difficult to explain what interests sexual essentialism serves. Although it is easy to suggest that essentialist understandings of sexuality serve patriarchal domination in that they legitimise the current male-dominated order of desire and identity, it is also apparent that the construction of sexualities is not manifested uniformly throughout the intersections of different social relationships. As Weeks says in his discussion of capitalism and sexuality: 'Concepts of sexuality are not only culturally specific but are also class and gender specific' (Weeks 1980: 15). Frank Mort (1980) also points out that sexuality is regulated and stratified in a differentiated manner and argues for an analysis of specific conjunctures rather than a grand universal theory.

In some senses this characterisation of essentialism as an ideology is sustainable as long as we understand that it is simply an analytic device allowing us to argue that essentialism can be mobilised to serve the interests of a patriarchal and heterosexual social order. However, since the dominance of men is crosscut with other social hierarchies – primarily of race, class and sexuality – it is not accurate to say that essentialism is an ideology in the traditional sense since that would imply that these sets of ideas and practices are an exclusive resource for one unified social group. What I think is more accurate to say is that what underpins the way in which we think about sexuality is the concept of an essential self. The essentialist understanding of sexual subjectivity was part of the broader philosophical shift towards a modernist construction of an essential, autonomous and coherent self, reinforced by the epistemological shift in science which transformed the understanding of sexuality from its characterisation as a sin into part of the 'natural' and necessary functioning of the body (Davidson 1992). In this sense, it is the idea of an innate self – part metaphysical and part embodied – which is the dominant conceptual framework, one manifestation of which is the way we think about sexuality. Essentialism is an ideology which serves the status quo in whatever realm it is deployed. Who that status quo benefits is, however, not reducible to one social grouping. Furthermore, while one dimension of this set of ideas developed in interaction with changing class and sexual divisions to consolidate an essentialist model of sexuality, it has also been mobilised to explain a variety of social divisions other than those of sexuality. Essentialism is a resource which is used to explain hierarchies of gender and race and, in the past, those of class. Thus it does not simply serve as a unified ideology which reflects the dominance of one social group, but rather the essentialist ideology has many dimensions which have served the interests of the status of medical and scientific professions, men over women, white Westerners over non-whites (Guillaumin 1995), and latterly, gay groups against heterosexual moralists (Epstein 1992; Evans 1993).

It is inaccurate to characterise essentialism as an ideology which is exclusively dominant or consistently unified throughout the cultural realm. To some extent, this analytical position echoes neo-Weberian concepts of ideology (see for example Abercrombie, Hill and Turner 1980) and also reflects the less unified sense in which current concepts are used in discussions of sexuality, be those terms discourse, narratives or scripts. It is still possible, however, to characterise the framework of psychological essentialism as ideological in its effects. Most important of the associated ideological effects is legitimisation through mystification: social hierarchies are seen as natural and therefore sexual categories become inevitable divisions between immutable and exclusive types of people, outwith the reach of social and political intervention.

What strikes me is that the characterisation of essentialism as ideological is similar to the conceptualisation and effects of discourse: both terms describe a set of ideas which provide explanations that both exclude alternative understandings and legitimise their own 'regime of truth'. Discourse has become a more popular concept than ideology in the characterisation of essentialism: Foucault (1980) introduced the term in his description of the historical development of the essentialist construction of sexuality and the term has become commonly used by most theorists, from interactionists through to Queer theorists. In her use of discourse to analyse male sexual violence, Wendy Hollway argues that the power of a discourse derives from its hegemonic effect (Hollway 1981; Sawicki 1991) and although discourses are conceptually distinct from the more narrow term of ideology (Howarth 1995), hegemonic discourses do have ideological effects in that they are dominant forms of knowledge which exclude alternative modes of explanation.

As a central component in the construction of sexuality, essentialism must be considered as operating ideologically, whether this is thought of in terms of discourse or the less unified (perhaps neo-Weberian) concept of ideology. This is to suggest that any perspective must account for the ideological effects of essentialism, not only as a social resource for understanding the phenomena of sexuality, but also as the framework for the construction of self-identity.

CONSTRUCTING OUR 'ESSENTIAL' SELVES

The ideological effects of essentialism can help to account for the issues raised by the first two paradoxes of identity that Weeks characterises as symptomatic of the construction of sexuality: why individuals see themselves as essentially sexually orientated even though this seems an unlikely explanation of sexual careers; and how our personal identities indicate our social location within hierarchies of sexuality (Weeks 1996). At this level of analysis, an apparently personal sexual identity is actually a social identity achieved through the framework of essentialism. However, the characterisation of essentialism as ideological explains why certain categories and discourses exist, but not how we identify with them. In this sense, we still need to think about the latter two paradoxes: how our identities are historically specific and yet contingent on our identification, and the related paradox of how we use them as 'necessary' fictions.

I suggest that these two paradoxes lead us to consider the problem of structure and agency; specifically, how the ideological effects of essentialist constructions recruit us into historically specific social categories and how this affects our construction of self-identity. This relationship between structure and agency has at its heart the question of identification; how we locate ourselves within social categories and why we apparently need to do so.[7] The critique of ideology and discourse suggests that the relationship between structures and the self must be conceived of in broader terms than the traditional structural emphasis on culture as constitutive of consciousness through ideology. Essentialism may operate ideologically, but it is not reducible to specific structural forces such as class or gender divisions. It may seem that the description of essentialist discourse as ideological simply returns us to the premise that ideological effects create a false consciousness. This view of subjectivity is explicit in the original concept of ideology, drawn from Marx's thesis that ideology mystifies and legitimises conditions of material domination in those subjects it affects. Such an argument in the realm of sexuality would lead to a conclusion that sexual identity is determined for us by the dominant categories and discourses of explanation available to us. Of course, in a historical sense you could argue that this is true. Gay men and lesbians could not have identified as 'homosexual' until the advent of the current essentialist sexual framework which provided these categories and the underpinning rationale of immutable sexual desires. Nowadays, when we say that we are gay or lesbian, we are engaging in at least three modes of identification: that of positioning ourselves with the discourse of essentialist sexual categories, that of signalling our likely course of action in potentially sexual interaction, and that of identifying our subjectivities with our sexual actions – sexuality becomes ontological 'truth'. However, the notion of a structurally determined consciousness removes any possibility of self-awareness and thus any possibility of effective agency. Although we identify as sexual within a historically specific framework over which we have no individual control, it is highly problematic to suggest that we are 'duped' as to the nature of our real conditions of existence. Is our sexual consciousness merely a false understanding of our 'selves'?

Laclau has argued – like Althusser before him (1971) – that the notion of a 'false' consciousness implies that there is some essential human identity which is misrepresented through the distortion of ideology (1991). If we accept that the ideological effect of the discourse of sexual essentialism is to create a 'false' consciousness, then we must also accept that there is an essential 'truth' of human sexual identity behind this ideological colonisation of the self. However, this is clearly a contradiction, since sexual essentialism cannot mystify or misrepresent sexual essentialism. If it is not an essential human identity which is displaced by the ideological effects of essentialism, then what exactly is? The only logical answer to the question is that there is no essential human sexuality behind the ideological construction of an essential sexuality. As I have said above, the notion of an essential human subject underpins most frameworks of thought around the self and conjures up a construction of subjectivity which is both unitary and static. Critical social theorists have shown that social identities are multiple and often contradictory as well as being a process of development rather than a fixed essence (ibid.), and this is particularly true in the realm of sexuality, illustrated by the vast body of research on sexual identities and careers (Gagnon and Simon 1974; Plummer 1975, 1995; Whisman 1996). The important distinction to make is that while the essentialist construction of sexuality is problematic, this does not preclude the notion of a stable sense of sexual identity which is incorporated into subjectivity. I would therefore suggest that it is the process of the development of subjectivity which is mystified by any ideological effect of essentialism rather than any essential ontological 'truth'. In this sense, I reject any notion of false consciousness: the ideological effect on subjectivity does not produce an illusion but rather, as Laclau puts it (following Althusser), the ideological is the misrecognition of the self as fixed meanings and identities rather than differences and process (1991). We narrow our reflexive gaze to the identity which we inhabit, giving us a sense of fixity, of permanence and, most crucially, of reference for social action. Essentialist understandings of self allow us to narrate action without dealing with either the complexities of deciding on action at the level of subjectivity or the social inequalities and divisions which our actions inevitably embody and sustain.

I would argue that in the realm of sexual subjectivity, the primary ideological effect of essentialism is to mystify the structural and social characteristics of the divisions of gender and sexual identities, and consequently to veil the social relationships, practices and contexts which create and sustain sexual identity. This emphasises the point that Giddens makes about ideology, that it should not be seen as mystifying any essential truth but mystifying certain social relationships of power and domination (1991b).

It may seem that even in this formulation, the understanding of the effects of the discourse of sexuality is still that it constructs subjects as somehow 'false'. I would argue against this interpretation, since the critical development of ideology by those theorists mentioned above does not suggest that the subject is 'duped' as to their own nature, but rather that the subject is duped as to the social construction of their 'nature'. The issue is not the integrity or validity of a sexual subject, but the fact that the reasons for being identified and identifying as a sexual subject are hidden, misrecognised and misunderstood. Within the current sexual order, essentialist constructions are the dominant resource available for the 'reflexive project of the self' (Giddens 1991a): our sense of self and the related opportunities for agency are woven into an essentialist gendered matrix which tells us first what we should do by who we are and second, in a spectacular circle of reasoning, who we are by what we have chosen to do. Sexual subjectivity *per se* is not an illusion: most people develop a stable sense of sexual identity but are not aware that it is socially constructed rather than naturally formed. Indeed, Althusser's development of ideology positions the subject as a central concept (1971). He suggests that the subject category functions as the constitutive power of ideology: ideology 'hails' or 'interpellates' individuals by providing subject categories with which those individuals identify and thus locate themselves within. Moreover, this only happens because ideological constructions make allusions to the experience and perception of subjects. We are 'always-already' subjects in terms of having experience and identity in various dimensions and thus we are recruited or interpellated through ideological constructions which recognise this and make allusion to it.

In this sense, it is easy to understand why the ideological effect of sexual essentialism so readily resonates with subjectivity. The discourse of sexuality rests upon the division of gender and before we are sexual, we are 'always-already' gendered in a heterosexual matrix of identity which carries its own logic of sexual desire for the 'opposite' gender (Gagnon and Simon 1974). In this sense, we are ripe for interpellation because we have had real or imagined experiences of ourselves as sexual before we come to identify with a specific sexual identity, and the process of interpellation alludes specifically to gendered desires. Of course this is most obviously true of those developing homosexual careers and identities – think back to Ken Plummer's work on the stages of the homosexual coming-out process (1975) – but heterosexuals are interpellated as well through the equation of gender and desire (Hollway 1984). The point about the ideological impact of essentialism is that it alludes to sexual desire as the sole marker of sexual identity. In this way, interpellation resonates with our 'always-already' status as 'correctly' or inversely gendered, but through interpellation we are transformed into social identities with a position on the sexual/moral hierarchy and a more specific location with the matrix of gender. Of course, the ideological effect of essentialist discourse means that these social locations are taken as reflections of a natural order, and crucially, our sexual selves are misrecognised as innate and immutable desires instead of as a process of development of sexual experience and identity.

Although I have relied on Althusser's reformulation of ideology and its effects, I want to make explicit my rejection of the determinist bias in Althusser's form of structuralist Marxism (and his reliance on Lacanian ideas of the symbolic construction of subjectivity). What is useful in Althusser's work is the critical emphasis on ideology as a representation of the relationship of individuals to their real conditions of existence and its effects in constituting us as subjects (1971). It is this emphasis which has been taken up by those developing the concept of ideology and applying it to the politics of difference (Laclau 1991; Laclau and Mouffe 1985, 1987) and it is these aspects of the ideological which I have used to describe the effects of essentialist discourse.

I suggest that this perspective on ideology helps to explain the third and fourth of Weeks' paradoxes of identity, provided that we retain the premise of a reflexive subject. Essentialism, as the discourse of sexuality, has ideological effects which entail that the power relationships which underpin sexual identities are hidden and thus sexual subjectivity is misunderstood as a fixed essence. Subjectivity is not therefore a 'false' construction of consciousness but a misrecognition of the processes which have contributed to the formation of subjectivity. Moreover, subjectivity is constructed through an identification with ideological categories of subject status which exist as the locations into which subjects are recruited. This suggests a way in which we can understand how our sexualities are historical identities – subject categories which outlast individual lifecycles – which are given substance by our interpellation within them. As argued above, this interpellation relies upon gendered sexual desires as the resonant experience which leads us into the sociohistorical categories of essentialism.

Once located within ideological categories, it is easy to see how the framework of explanation – the discourse of essentialist sexuality – leads us to construct our subjectivities as immutable and eternal. Our sexualities become misrecognised as immutable and eternal and this understanding pervades our sense of subjectivity; we construct the fiction of a sexual essence. By explaining Weeks' fourth paradox in this manner, I reiterate that our construction of sexual subjectivity is not 'false' in any sense but rather that our perception of how this construction is achieved is a 'fiction'. Two points become important in following this line of argument. The first is that we, as subjects, seem to need the 'fiction' of an essential sexual self. Weeks (1996) suggests that our identification with the historical fictions of eternal, essential, sexual identities is necessary because we need an identity around which to organise politically. I accept this aspect of our need for our sexualities but I would like to emphasise again the importance of our recruitment into or identification with historically specific identities – what Althusser called interpellation. Interpellation succeeds by creating experiential resonance between individual context and ideological or discursive categories.

Therefore, we move into categories – construct our 'selves' as essential – because there is some resonance between how we may perceive ourselves (usually in terms of gendered sexual desire) and the social locations with which we are presented. Thus, we have to consider how far the fictions of sexualities are necessary for our sense of self as much as for a political identity.

The second important point is that the line of reasoning running through the arguments thus far suggests a reflexive understanding and construction of subjectivity: identifying with ideological or discursive categories; incorporating these into our sense of self; using these identities as necessary fictions – each discussion suggests an understanding of subjectivity as self-aware. In his discussion of the 'subject', Althusser (1971) tried to retain the notion of a reflexivity through his emphasis on subjectivity as defined and constructed by material social practices and ideas.[8] However, his reliance on the base–superstructure model of material relationships still suggested that subjectivity was ultimately determined by socioeconomic structure. Althusser has been criticised for actually under-theorising or disregarding subjectivity rather than providing a new insight into it but I would suggest that this criticism only holds up insofar as Althusser's analysis is focused on the state and class relations. As has been demonstrated above, sexuality cannot be reduced to such a one-dimensional or dominant thesis type of explanation and neither can it be regarded as exclusively dependent on material relationships. Therefore, it is possible to focus on his specific points about ideology *per se* and to apply this analysis to the discourse of sexuality. Althusser's characterisation of ideology suggests a material existence of the framework of thought within social practices and institutionalised ideas and, more specifically, within what Althusser terms the ideological state apparatuses (ISAs) – the predominantly private sphere of organisations which reinforce the dominant cultural ideas of the ruling group. We can thus retain an idea of subjectivity constructed through the material social practices derived from ideology and embedded in social institutions and conventions. For example, we encounter the most influential ISA early in life: we go to school and are so drawn into the ideology of the self, being an individual rather than a family member; we are divided by gender in school and subsequently, sexuality is policed at adolescence whilst at the same time being reproduced through sex education and peer group discussions. It is during this period that homophobia first develops and becomes another way of marking out 'misfits' in the classroom and playground. The ideology of an essential heterosexual sexuality is thus sustained and produced through social practices and joint interaction.

Hitherto my discussion suggests the ways in which we may work towards a viable theory of sexual subjectivity which is both structurally grounded and yet leaves room for effective agency. The recent use of the concept of narratives of self takes up the reflexive construction of subjectivity through social practices and has gone some way to theorising subjectivity as produced by narratives which are in turn produced by the interplay of structural, cultural and political forces (see Plummer's work on sexual stories 1995; Smith 1988; Stanley 1992). I have suggested that we identify with sexual categories in a reflexive process which results in large part from the ideological effects of essentialism. The emphasis on social practices which is implicit in interactionism but explicit in Smith's approach (1988) also serves to reinforce the links between structural conditions and relationships and the construction of subjectivity. I have also suggested that the rejection of the notion of a false consciousness allows space for an understanding of reflexive subjectivity. In this sense, I am arguing that we are actively engaged in constructing our sexual selves but that we must do so in structured social contexts which are produced through social divisions, hierarchies and inequalities. The link between structural forces and subjectivity has been made through the characterisation of the essentialist discourse as ideological in its effects and physical in its existence. I will turn now to detailing the interaction between social practices and ideas and subjectivity.

MATERIALITY, AGENCY AND THE NEED FOR SEXUAL IDENTITY

My discussion of structural conditions, essentialism and subjectivity has been underpinned by the assumption that self-awareness and the possibility of effective agency must be a central component of a viable theory of sexual subjectivity. I have argued that structural conditions do not construct subjectivity through a determinist relationship between structure, culture and the self but rather that structural hierarchies and conditions of sexuality are legitimised by and embedded within the social practices and ideological effects of essentialist discourse, and the specific material relationships which underpin sexuality. However, I want to consider in some detail the impact on subjectivity of the derivative social practices of both essentialist ideological effects and these other structural conditions. In this way, I will attempt to develop a position whereby I argue that there are structured conditions for the self which provide the context for the interaction and construction of subjectivity.

The direction of my perspective on sexuality casts subjectivity as a process, constructed through a combination of social meanings, practices, identities and relationships. Whilst our reflexive construction of self must always be in large part a momentary abstraction at the point of taking action or simply engaging in reflection, I also want to suggest that our subjectivities are in large part defined by what we do: practices of the self as well as simply perceptions of our self. This perspective draws on the materiality of Smith's interactionism (1988) but it also derives from both Althusserian and Foucauldian ideas about materiality.

Althusser argued that ideology has a material existence (1971), suggesting that ideology was embedded within and embodied by the practices, ideas and rules of those organisations and institutions which he regarded as ideological state apparatuses. Leaving aside the focus on ISAs, I have argued that it is appropriate to apply this analysis of ideology to broader social arenas in the case of sexuality. Essentialist constructions and the associated practices of sexuality are embedded within social organisations such as state institutions and policies, laws, media, the family, schools, and through the common cultural practices associated with pursuing a sexual career. An extreme example of the repressive ideological operationalisation, or materialisation, of essentialism is a current proposal in China to outlaw sex outside marriage, both as a defence of marriage and an encouragement to it in a period when many marriages are breaking up and fewer people are getting married. Crucially, Althusser suggests that the material existence of ideology governs the ways in which we can construct subjectivity: we are defined by how we are interpellated and how we take action derives from this sense of how we see ourselves and the associated appropriate social practices which govern this social category.

In the realm of sexuality, many of these practices may be direct ideological effects of essentialist understandings: for example, desiring the opposite sex because one has been allocated a gender and thus engaging in practices appropriate to this gendered orientation – dress, mannerisms, emotional engagement, sexual assertiveness. However, the structural underpinnings to sexuality also dictate their own material conditions within which essentialism is sustained and through which sexuality is achieved. Most important among these is the materialist analysis of the construction of sexual identity, put forward by Evans (1993), since this form of consumer capitalism now pervades much of the social world. For example, the divisions in leisure space confine gays and lesbians to particular pubs and clubs (and there are further subdivisions between genders). The notion of an exclusive gay or lesbian identity is thus reinforced by physical location and emotional/sexual engagement within these spaces and practices. Rather than view subjectivity as some kind of abstraction, I am suggesting that we start to think about it as a process of deployment and action. In this sense, I think that we can begin to think of the practices and meanings that derive from essentialism and our location within time and space as opportunities or constraints on action. We move along the web of the social world – our subjectivities are formed not just through location but through movement, action and development along various dimensions of this social web.

It is at this point that some of Foucault's later ideas about sexuality become useful. Foucault suggested that there were 'arts of existence' – conduct and codes of behaviour – which governed the construction of sexual subjectivity in conjunction with the dominant discourse of sexuality (1990). The arts or technologies can be understood as the social practices and ideas with which we interact in the reflexive construction of subjectivity. In many ways this is a similar perspective to Althusser's conceptualisation of the materiality of ideology. I would argue, however, that Foucault's perspective helps us to focus more on the practices of the self, on subjectivity as a reflexive process. Althusser's formulation continues to emphasise the materiality of ideology without explicitly describing the interaction of consciousness or subjectivity with these material practices. It is a minor distinction, but taken in conjunction with the less determinist concept of discourse, I think it is somewhat easier to understand the materiality of the self and its potential for agency by thinking in terms of 'material' practices of the self, since Foucault emphasises that we actively take up these practices.

The issues thrown up by technologies of the self have been taken up by some Queer theorists in their theorisation of subjectivity. However, I have implicitly demonstrated that the post-modernist premises of Queer are, after all, not really such a revelation, since interactionists and feminist standpoint theorists have been engaged in an explication of the self as social process for far longer than Queer has been around. One of the more specific problems with Queer theory is the lack of emphasis placed on social practices. This last point is of course another way of characterising the immateriality of a discursive perspective which refuses to acknowledge structures as constitutive of particular ideological frameworks and social practices and relationships. If the retort is that every social action and relationship needs to be understood as discursively constructed because we negotiate the world through the interpretation of social meaning, one can simply point to the symbolic interactionism of Mead (1967), Blumer (1966) and Gagnon and Simon (1974) as an example of similar ideas which predate the concept of discourse. Indeed, many theorists have drawn out the parallels between scripts, narratives and discourses as concepts which describe the same constructions of social meaning.

Some feminist researchers have moreover talked about the ways in which we locate ourselves within discourses as a means of social and self identification (see Hollway's work on heterosexual discourses 1984; and Whisman's account of lesbian and gay identification, 1996). These perspectives on discourse suggest that subjectivity is produced in interaction with discourses: we identify with certain discursive locations because they are the main resource in the negotiation of social and self identity. Indeed, this is the core of the argument put forward in the Queer theorisation of subjectivity (see Butler 1990a, 1991, 1993; Fuss 1991) and it draws on Foucault's ideas about the physical practices which contribute to the construction and perception of subjectivity. In the development of her notion of gender performativity, Judith Butler expands her discussion of the subject as one which is produced, constructed and regulated through the reiterative practices of heteronormativity – the hegemonic set of discourses on gender and sexuality (1993) – although she tends to rely on psychoanalytic precepts at various stages of her argument. However, I would suggest that Butler may be read as suggesting that subjectivity is a process of reiterative performance which is, in large part, governed and constructed through social practices.

Whichever theoretical heritage is emphasised – interactionism, structuralism or post-modernism – it is clear that you can argue for a sense of materiality underpinning the process through which subjectivity is constructed. Since the materiality of subjectivity implies that certain repeated acts and practices construct subjectivity, and so that experiential learning is part of the process of subjectivity, it is relatively easy to see how this theorisation of subjectivity requires both self-awareness (for reflexive understanding and experiential learning) and the potential for effective agency (the possibility of changing practices based on experience).

It may seem contradictory, but rejecting the idea of the essential subject allows for the notion of effective agency in subjectivity. The notion of an essential subjectivity implies a fixed identity which does not change or develop: it is both unified and static. The process of negotiating the social world is not therefore important as an influence on sexual subjectivity since subjectivity will not change or develop or be affected by different opportunities or the accumulations of different experiences. For lesbians and gays, this means that we will always be understood as deviant since that is how the essentialist discourse casts us. There is, therefore, no scope for the effective agency of the subject, since this essentialist construction of subjectivity, and more importantly, the associated oppressive discourse of sexuality, cannot be disturbed, challenged or undermined by our actions.

Since the social formation of sexual subjectivity is misrecognised and mystified through the ideological impact of essentialism, we are left only with essentialist understandings of self as the framework for social action. The rejection of an essential subjectivity removes these constraints on the agency of the subject. However, the materiality of the discourse of sexuality suggests that we construct subjectivity through an experiential and reiterative process of engagement with the social world as meaning and practice. This action, whether in terms of the ways in which we negotiate sexual careers, or in terms of the ways we identify as sexual, is not unified, predictable or reducible simply to ideological effects. The sites of interaction with social practices are the sites for the potential transformation of our subjectivities and the ideologies or discourses within which we are located. The relationship between structure and agency is not determinist or simply focused on the agent, but rather the conditions and practices which derive from structural relationships provide the interactive context for subjectivity and agency.

This perspective is echoed in most of the recent theoretical work on structure and agency. In his comprehensive review of the directions of this debate, Colin Hay suggests that there is an increasing understanding of agency and structure as interactive rather than discrete; two parts of the same dynamic rather than separate social phenomena (Hay 1995). When Hay describes strategy as the selection of objectives and the means to achieve them, and intention as action based on the knowledge of conditions, both imply an experiential process wherein agents learn how to act in different and similar situations based on an analysis of past encounters. Thus the subject is reflexively self-aware and interacts with the social world rather than being determined by it. Again, I suggest that this view of agency echoes much interactionist thought, specifically the experiential process emphasised by Mead (1967) and Blumer (1966) and the development of these perspectives by Smith (1988) and the post-modernists who have taken on board the materiality of the self (Butler 1993).

In the realm of sexuality, this allows us a way of thinking about the process of achieving sexuality as one which is self-aware but governed by certain essentialist scripts, discourses or narratives which are ideological in that they mystify and legitimise the social relationships and hierarchies of sexual identity. Essentialist constructions also provide the social categories to which we are allocated or identify with. Again, this can be thought of as an interactive process, not simply structurally determined but intentionally achieved as well. For example, the construction of subjectivity through gender divisions allocates us to one of two social groups (and this is done initially by others for us when we are born) but it also then provides a fundamental reference point for the subsequent development of other dimensions of subjectivity such as sexuality. We are recruited into social categories and then reinforce those very categories by identifying with them and learning to adopt the expected social practices.

The discussion of agency and materiality brings me to my final point about sexual subjectivity. The characterisation of agency suggests that in order to engage in social action, we must have a strategic reflexive understanding of our self-identity which we use to select goals and practices. Since subjectivity is composed of many different social identifications and different material practices and ideas, it is easy to see how this conjures up a notion of subjectivity which is a fluid process and multifaceted. How is it that we can select goals and practices out of such a variety of opportunities? How can we produce effective agency out of such a compendium of identities and locations?

It is clear that the imposition of the essentialist version of a coherent eternal and exclusive sexual identity denies the multiple differences of actual experience. However, this is not simply an imposition on the self, but an active engagement of subjectivity with the material practices of the essentialist discourse of sexuality. We take the essentialist discourse on board in terms of our own constructions of self and we use it as a 'necessary fiction'. However, none of the sociological approaches to sexuality really attempts to explain the need for a coherent sense of self, and therefore why essentialism is so attractive a resource in our reflexive construction of self.

I would suggest that the construction and mobilisation of a sense of coherent identity is necessary to signal both our resonance with allocated social categories and our identification to the others with whom we interact. Viewing subjectivity as a social process means that it is produced through our negotiation of the social web, and I suggest that moving between social groups – along the web, if you like – requires strategy and intention – agency – which in turn requires an ability to reflexively perceive and project one's self as having a past, present and future that has some intelligible, coherent purpose. Moreover, I think that this suggests that we have an understanding of core components to our subjectivity – such as gender and sexuality – which may well shift over time or in relative importance, but are seen as stable points in the negotiation of social life and identity. It is not that these are essential qualities, but more often than not, they are reflexively understood as stable and core components of selfhood. We need to impose a sense of coherent identity, however unstable or temporary it may be, precisely because subjectivity is a social construction: we learn who we are by defining ourselves in relation to other social identities and locations and by engaging in associated social practices. We need to take action in the social world, and this action is based on mobilising an intelligible construction of our subjectivities which integrates past and present and projects a future path which makes sense of our self-identity. It is in this sense that we can explain Weeks' fourth paradox: we mobilise coherent constructions of identity as 'necessary' fictions because we need them to move through the social world.

This view of subjectivity is particularly evident in the realm of sexual identity. Gender identity is integrated into subjectivity at a relatively early age in childhood, and it is this sense of our selves which acts as the determinant for future sexual behaviour and identity. In a world of gender divisions and essentialist reasoning, the expected path of our sexual careers is governed by the cross-sex matrix: we expect to become sexual according to these frameworks and practices of gender. When homosexual men or women describe feeling 'different' from other boys or girls, the construction of self in which they are engaged is underpinned by gender divisions. In this sense, homosexuality is the inevitable social identity available to those uncomfortable with ascribed gender identities. Furthermore, the sexual careers of those who have achieved any sexual identity remain governed by structural conditions which reinforce the exclusivity of essentialist categories of identity. Thus there are straight scenes and gay scenes, lesbian scenes. Even though the individuals within these sexual spaces are from a variety of sociosexual groups, the sexual interaction remains predominantly determined by the reflexive understanding of sexuality which actors have. In this sense, our sexualities are necessary fictions; identities which we incorporate into our sense of selves as a basis for social action.

CONCLUSION: QUERYING SEXUAL AND POLITICAL SUBJECTIVITY

I have tried to draw together the sometimes disparate implications of various sociological approaches to sexual subjectivity. In describing sexuality as a reflexive narrative process constructed through social practices, I have taken up the themes developed within interactionism, Queer theory and specifically Foucauldian thought, and placed these theorisations within a structural context. I have attempted to construct a theory of sexual subjectivity which admits reflexivity and thus the potential for transformative agency, while at the same time being structurally grounded and aware of the resonance of essentialist ideas.

In this sense, I am trying to think about sexual subjectivity as a process of achieving sexuality on a number of different levels:

- Social–psychological – achieving a core and stable sense of sexual identity anchored to gendered identity and divisions. The sense of stability is reinforced every time we are expected to mobilise or foreground a gendered sexual identity; which leads onto:
- Social process – sexuality as identity is used as a referent for agency. It becomes a core quality in this way and is not therefore an essential characteristic but rather a filter for social action. This sense of achieving sexuality echoes the emphasis within Mead's ideas on the 'me' and 'I' as distinct components of the self's journey through the social process as well as the Queer inclination to performativity as an analytical concept. Sexual subjectivity is reiteratively achieved through the process of engagement with social practices, relationships and discourses.
- Social investment – subjectivity is multidimensional because we use interpersonal interaction to locate ourselves within social relationships and hierarchies; to position ourselves within frameworks of meaning. Subjectivity is therefore meaningful only in relation to others: we are boys or girls, sons or daughters, husbands, wives, partners, mothers, fathers, siblings and so on. We have to invest our selfhood with these meanings because we can only define ourselves by what we mean to others. Sexuality becomes a key theme in all forms of social investment, either explicitly or implicitly, simply because it is used as shorthand for a core identity. Of course, this is true at the social interaction level precisely because sexual identities also have social significance.

- Social significance – although this links to the sociopsychological sense of achieving sexuality, we must also be aware that we are interpellated into sexual identities as often as we actively identify with them; indeed it would be difficult to separate the two processes in everyday social interaction. Achieving sexuality is therefore also a process which has important meaning for us as individuals but also illuminates the social significance of sexual and gendered identity categories. It is at this level that we can begin to explore the structured meanings and effects of sexual identities and categories and discourses.

I suggest that thinking about sexual subjectivity as achieved sexuality allows us to consider both structural factors and reflexive action, whilst accepting the central role of social meaning in conditioning material contexts and agency in the social process. I am not trying to put forward this grounded interactionist perspective on achieving sexuality as another meta-narrative to supersede all the theories that have gone before. I am simply suggesting that this perspective takes forward our ability to theorise sexual subjectivity in a way which allows us to be sensitive both to the need for and deployment of a core sense of sexual identity, and the structural existence of the essentialist discourse.

I therefore reject the 'hyperactive' interpretation of subjectivity which characterises criticisms of both post-modernist and interactionist views. I suggest that there is in fact a core sense of identity within reflexive understandings of self which is actually necessary for the production of agency and is, therefore, similarly necessary to any analysis of the relationship between structure, agency and subjectivity. Thus, the actual process through which we achieve a construction of sexual subjectivity resonates with essentialist discourse and moreover, this discourse becomes the shorthand for explaining identity and organising strategies and intentions as agency. This characterisation of the mobilisation of a core sense of identity provides a theorisation of sexual subjectivity which, while being anti-essentialist, also resonates with the ways in which the essentialist discourse constructs our understandings of self.

In these two aspects, my development of sociological views of sexuality meets the first two criteria which I put forward in the last chapter as necessary for a politically viable sociological theorisation of sexuality.[9] At first, it may be less apparent whether the third criterion – the potential for social and political transformation – is contained in the direction which I have taken. I suggested in the introduction to this chapter that we had to aim for a gay and lesbian politics which focused on the conditions which sustain essentialism and to develop a political identity which reinforced this emphasis on social relationships and practices as constitutive of sexuality. The focus on conditions is already the business of much of the politics of lesbian and gay campaigns and organisations but a clearer emphasis on the processes of achieving sexuality should help to reinforce the socially constructed nature of our oppression. Problems remain when political activity is implicitly or explicitly anchored in an essentialist political identity because then we reinforce the essentialist discourse on one dimension by our very attempts to contest its effects (Rahman and Jackson 1997). It is clear that we need to work out a reconceptualised political identity as part and parcel of the wider engagement with the conditions which oppress us as 'deviant' sexualities.

This point brings me back to the third criterion mentioned above. I suggest that my position – in terms of an emphasis on social practices and processes as constitutive of sexual subjectivity which, in turn, provides a stable and core referent for social action – encourages a focus on political identity as representative of experience and location rather than as a mere reflection of innate characteristics. Political identity can be reconceptualised as an identity which is indicative of a social process – achieving sexuality – rather than read off as an indicator of a 'natural' and/or 'minority' status. Such a grounded interactionist perspective may seem unpromising as a basis for political activity but in large part this is simply because the interactionist inheritance is focused more on descriptive theorisation rather than transformative potential. It is in the realm of the political where Queer theory really does contribute something distinct to considerations of sexuality. As a predominantly relativist theoretical enterprise, the Queer project contains explicit attempts to deconstruct the hegemonic discourses of heteronormativity and to replace it with a recognition of differences as socially produced. In many ways, Queer theory is avowedly about reconceptualising political identity (de Lauretis 1991). I have already suggested that many of the fundamental premises of Queer theory are in accordance with the grounded interactionist perspective I have developed in this chapter. What I want to go on to discuss in detail is the potential for using Queer to reconceptualise political identity while retaining the emphasis on sociostructural conditions, agency and reflexivity, which I have suggested are central to viable political identities and strategies.

NOTES

1. Post-structuralism refers to theories of society which claim that the structuralist theories found in classical sociology are no longer appropriate for describing or analysing contemporary social conditions. These conditions are said to indicate a world which is post-modern, that is no longer divided along the dimension of class or organised around the precepts of rationalism and positivism which characterised the economy and cultures of Western societies during the period since industrialisation (loosely termed modernity). Hence, post-structuralist theories are brought to bear on post-modern societies and conditions, but post-modernism is often used interchangeably with post-structuralism when referring to these contemporary social theories.
2. Although there may seem to be an analytical connection in the Parsonian distinction between an ascribed or intrinsic condition and one that is achieved through performance, I am simply using the term 'achieved' to focus attention on the social process of constructing a sexual identity.
3. 1. Sexual identity assumes fixity and uniformity while confirming the reality of unfixity, diversity and difference... 2. Identities are deeply personal but tell us about multiple social belongings.... 3. Sexual identities are simultaneously historical and contingent... 4. Sexual identities are fictions but necessary fictions...' (Weeks 1996: 88–98).
4. For a brief review of feminist approaches, see Jackson and Scott's introduction to their reader (1996).
5. For a materialist account of gender divisions and sexuality it is worth looking at the work of Delphy and Leonard (1992), Christine Delphy (1993), Colette Guillaumin (1995) and Stevi Jackson (1996a, 1996b).
6. For accounts of British lesbian and gay histories and difficulties with the straight world and gay world, see the collection by Cant and Hemmings, 1988. For the impact on Queer theory, see Seidman's introduction to his collection (1996), and the edition of *Differences*, vol. 3, no. 2, Summer 1991.
7. As mentioned before, some Queer theorists resort to Lacanian psychoanalysis at this point (see discussions of this by Butler 1993, 1994; Fuss 1991, 1994) but I have already made clear my resistance to such an interpretation of subjectivity.
8. His use of the term 'material' existence is in the sense of 'physical' rather than describing a materialist basis to ideology. I will try to refer to physical social practices or simply social practices and use material only in the Marxist sense of describing economic relationships but I will be discussing materiality in the sense in which Althusser, Foucault and Smith use it – as a term to characterise the physical processes of action and interaction as the basis for perceptions of self and others.
9. The three criteria introduced in Chapter 2 were as follows: a viable theory of sexual subjectivity should resonate with people's understandings of self; it needs to be anti-essentialist so that the moral divisions of essentialism are challenged and third, any politically viable theorisation needs to contain a transformative potential.

Chapter 4

QUE(E?)RYING POLITICAL IDENTITY

INTRODUCTION: IDENTITY POLITICS AND THE POLITICS OF IDENTITY

Hitherto I have conducted a predominantly sociological theoretical discussion in which I have argued for the rejection of the moral and epistemological consequences of the essentialist paradigm. I have, however, also been trying to suggest that lesbian and gay politics is not simply about illuminating an academic critique of the social construction of sexuality, and the resulting legal and social policies. I have suggested that a politics of lesbian and gay liberation must also engage with democratic structures precisely because essentialism also underpins both the construction of political identity and, in conjunction with specifically sexual essentialist ideas of morality and gender, the broader construction of social and political citizenship. In these two final chapters, I want to begin an exploration of how we might translate sociological perspectives on sexual subjectivity into the more practical realms of political identity and political strategy. In the broadest sense, my discussion thus far has already marked out the need to reject essentialist moral divisions and to reintegrate sexual politics with the politics of gender. This position provides a reference point for political aims and for strategies in the sense that gay and lesbian liberation must involve a displacement of the essentialist paradigm and, furthermore, this must be accomplished without recourse to essentialist versions of identity, gender and sexuality. Whilst I will address specific political strategies in Chapter 5, it is first necessary to bring a sociological critique to bear on 'identity' politics since it is this form of engagement which predominantly characterises current lesbian and gay politics in the representative democracies of the West (Epstein 1992; Gamson 1996).

Que(e?)rying political identity

At the beginning of Chapter 3, I argued that democratic practice operates on the assumption that political identity is, to a large extent, a reflection of ontological 'truth' – a sense of being, if you will. The most sophisticated exploration of this sense of sexual/political identity is to be found in Queer theory, but I am wary of fully endorsing the Queer approach to sexual politics. I have two doubts: first, the Queer emphasis on deconstructing identity can be read as denying the experiences and problems of those for whom sexual identity is central to their lives, thus creating further tensions between political aims and political strategies. I am thinking here of the gay men who have had to deal with the devastation wreaked by the AIDS epidemic and for whom it has literally been a matter of life and death to be recognised politically as gay men. I am also thinking of the majority of lesbians and gays who live their lives in ordinary towns and cities, removed from the fashions of metropolitan intellectual debates, and who conduct their sexual and emotional relationships with a strong sense of their lesbian or gay identity. For most of these people, as indeed for any 'minority' group, political identity is supposed to represent their experiences and existence. This leads me to my second doubt about Queer: the structured contexts in which identities are constructed and deployed is often de-emphasised within Queer theory, which again makes it difficult to argue for a stable sense of sexual or political identity. I would suggest that this does not resonate with the majority of lesbians and gays to whom the discourse is largely, although not exclusively, addressed.

However, these tensions between political aims, identities and strategies are common to most politics of the marginalised and oppressed and I therefore engage in a general discussion of these tensions in relation to 'identity' politics before moving on to Queer theory. The broad aim of Queer theory is to resist and eventually displace the heteronormative discourse (Halperin 1995) and with this overall goal I have no argument. However, I am not convinced that the translation of post-structuralist thought into modernist constructions of political identity and strategy can be achieved – mainly because, I argue, we do not live in post-modern conditions. Given this position, and the avowedly marginal location of the Queer sensibility, I will suggest that the construction of viable political identities should entail querying essentialism rather than adopting a strictly Queer rejection of identity politics. However, I attempt to draw parallels between the Queer attempt to illuminate and destabilise the heteronormative politics which underpin sexual identities and my own development of a materially inflected interactionist approach to subjectivity.

I suggest that an interactionist understanding of sexual subjectivity – which is grounded in the material conditions and social practices through which our intimate lives are experienced and our sexual identities achieved – allows us to deploy sexual/political identities, not as necessary fictions[1] which reinforce essentialist discourse, but rather as necessary, sociopolitical identities which emphasise the social significance and construction of sexuality and thus de-emphasise naturalist ideas about morality and gender. Although I remain unsure what such a political identity might actually look like, I conclude with a discussion of the contexts in which political identity is deployed, suggesting that since our political identities become meaningful within democratic discourse and practices, we need to focus on the forms of strategic engagement with democracy in order to better understand the vision of a reconceptualised sexual/political identity.

SEXUAL SUBJECTIVITY AS A BASIS FOR POLITICAL IDENTITY

By characterising the sexual self as an achieved sense of subjectivity, I have emphasised not only the structural contexts but also the social processes through which we construct our sexualities. Social change is thus possible through political interventions in the legal and democratic processes which underpin essentialist constructions of sexuality and morality. Because sexual subjectivities are also achieved as socially significant identities, the experiences and treatment of those who are thus interpellated forms a basis for both the construction of selfhood and related political organisation and expression. A reconfigured sociological version of sexual subjectivity has the potential to underpin a representative and advocative sense of political identity. Sexual subjectivity is also a process of achieving a sexual identity and mobilising that sense of identity within social contexts. Since the sexual self is primarily a social self, subjectivity is therefore inherently political because it is a reflection of the multiple dimensions of the social world and thus collective sociopolitical action can be focused on revolution, resistance, reform, protest, agenda setting, or influence over decision-making and policy formulation, implementation and review.

I began this study with an assertion that gay and lesbian politics has not been terribly successful in the West – not even 'a piss-ant civil rights bill' in the United States as one of Larry Kramer's characters puts it rather more colourfully in his play *The Normal Heart* – and certainly a long way from equivalent social rights even in the more progressive West – the social democratic states of Scandinavia. This is not to say, however, that there has been no progress whatsoever. The initial wave of decriminalisation in both the UK and some parts of the USA allowed for the political and social organisation of homosexuals. Moreover, the more politicised groups became an audience ready for the revolutionary social constructionist ideas about sexuality and gender developed within second-wave feminism and subsequently taken up within Gay Liberation. Cultural and political visibility has had a positive effect on countless individuals by creating conditions for the process of 'coming out' (Cant and Hemmings 1988; Gomez 1995; Maupin 1995) and in the provision of spaces for leisure activities organised around the pursuit of sex and the construction of sexuality as a lifestyle. Moreover, the explosion of a confident, visible and commercially viable gay and lesbian presence resulted in some vigorous community building in large urban areas where gay 'ghettos' have developed (Epstein 1992; Seidman 1996), helping to consolidate a sense of distinct group identity.

Legal and social reform has either followed the development of gay and lesbian subcultures or has at least been brought on to the agenda by political activity from within these communities. The rise of homosexual visibility, concerns about the role of the family in modern societies and issues surrounding women's equality have all served to keep sexuality centre-stage in the cultural and political life of the West. In one sense, this has meant that the very existence of homosexuality and individual homosexuals within the public, social and cultural realm is no longer either a shock or a matter for an immediate oppressive reaction. For example, in the UK not only is the fact that there is an openly gay Secretary of State for Culture, Media and Sport an unremarkable feature in contemporary political life, but it seems almost impossible to peruse cinema, television, radio, popular music or the print media without engaging with issues surrounding sexuality in general, homosexuality in particular and particular homosexuals.[2] I am not suggesting that visibility and cultural presence makes for social and civil equality. However, there has been an identifiable increase in gay and lesbian political activity which has stemmed from decriminalisation, the development of commercial scenes and the impact of the AIDS crisis.

Women's sexual behaviour and lesbian and gay sexual acts have been the basis of political discussion and intervention since the nineteenth century, but it is only in this century, with the advent of second-wave feminism and gay liberation in the late 1960s, that sexuality as a social identity became the basis of progressive political movements along with the various forms of lesbian and/or gay political organisation. With this more contemporary emergence of sexual politics has come a sense of political identity and a set of political aims and strategies. Many commentators have noted that the history of homosexual politics has given rise to many different forms of political activity and identity, from the reform-minded assimilationist homophile movements of the 1950s through the revolutionary rhetoric of Gay Liberation and back to the discrete 'minority' basis of the rights-based politics of the present[3] (Altman 1971/1993; Evans 1993; Gomez 1995).

I am not suggesting that understandings of the political significance of sexuality and the sexual self have not been transformed during this period, but rather that this transformation has not gone far enough in terms of illuminating the sexual self as social and therefore political. Gay and lesbian social and political organisations talk about equality and argue that our sexual concerns are human rights concerns, but we rarely address the ways in which we are socially constructed and positioned as deviant; gays and lesbians are understood as traitors to our genders, and therefore traitors to institutionalised heterosexuality or what Queer theorists call heteronormativity. Moreover, the social construction of sexuality has not been simply mapped on to political structures and practice but is, I suggest, largely intertwined with them. Political identity is too often taken as representative of an essential nature or attribute within democratic processes. This assumption of political essentialism combines with and reinforces the oppressive essentialist understanding of sexuality thus rendering invisible the social conditions and relationships which need to be the focus of political engagement. It is these conditions which have been the structural foundations of the development of modern homosexual identity since the time of Gay Liberation (Adam 1985; Evans 1993), resulting in a distinct homosexual (predominantly gay male) subculture which in turn has produced an ethnic/essentialist version of political identity (Altman 1971/1993; Epstein 1992; Weeks 1996). We must therefore engage with the essentialist paradigm along the dimensions of both sexuality and democratic practice in order to resolve the tensions between political aims, strategies and identities.

THE ODD RELATIONSHIP BETWEEN POLITICS AND IDENTITY

I have argued that we need to displace essentialisms of sexuality and representation but I recognise that we also need to retain sociosexual identities as focal points, both for illuminating our different experiences and for our claims to our integrity as legitimate representatives of an oppressed social group. As Joshua Gamson suggests in his discussion of Queer theory (1996), institutional politics in democratic systems requires a collective character or identity, both as a basis for political action and for targeting public policy: thus the use of a quasi-ethnic sense of identity makes sense in certain political circumstances.[4] Democratic political representation can therefore be understood as 'standing for' a social group in the sense of belonging to that group and symbolising their experiences and demands – what Pitkin has termed respectively 'descriptive' and 'symbolic' representation (Pitkin 1967). However, as Pitkin suggests, both the symbolic and descriptive elements of representation may create an assumption that representatives are comprehensive embodiments of their social group; a criticism which underpins contemporary debates within feminism and lesbian and gay political theory on the 'risk of essence' (Fuss 1989; Weeks 1996; Young 1989).

I am trying to think my way into a political identity and form of representation which reflects social process and context and, moreover, both the contingency and stability of subjectivity – thereby incorporating 'the personal as political' without reducing the political to some personal or essential/natural attribute. The key problem in such a challenge is how to avoid identity politics becoming a politics which indicates essential (and thus presocial) differences which would in turn render political action futile. This is the 'dilemma of difference' which bedevils political organisation by groups who seek to emphasise the social causes of oppression but, by organising politically, may seem to reinforce a perception of their essential distinctness or difference from the 'norm' (Phillips 1993; Young 1989). As a response to this dilemma, and to the apparent deconstruction of identity as a basis for representation evinced within post-structuralist theories of gender and sexuality,[5] there has been a discussion of the extent to which essentialist versions of identity can be used for strategic political purposes (Butler 1992; Epstein 1992; Fuss 1989; Mouffe 1992; Weeks 1996).

The case for strategic essentialism may appear to be a seductive argument, drawing as it does on the fact that most people do identify their sexualities as essential qualities. An essentialist version of identity may well serve a tactical purpose by allowing us to argue for our inclusion in the descriptive and symbolic aspects of representation. However, an attachment to the essentialist discourse raises important political problems. Any essentialist arguments confirm the current social hierarchy which can only reinforce the moral and social dominance of compulsory heterosexuality. Tactical use of essentialism can only thus undermine the overall aim of achieving social equality for lesbians and gays. The promotion of this form of identity serves as a pervasive cultural resource which gays and lesbians may use to construct their own senses of identity, thus compounding the misunderstanding of the self as an essential sexual self and further mystifying the social processes and significance which construct homosexuality as deviant. It is important to understand the interdependent relationship between political identities and subjectivity. In their study of gay political movements and subcultures in Western Europe, Kriesi *et al.* suggest that a political movement not only needs to project an identity which resonates with the life experiences of those it represents, but also that the two arenas affect each other (1995). Thus they illustrate how the commercialisation of gay subculture has led to a depoliticisation of gay identity in some countries, with the emphasis shifting to the fulfilment of personal desires and attainment of individual rights rather than the political and social reforms or revolutions needed to secure the deconstruction of heterosexual privilege.

Moreover, Evans (1993) suggests that the commercialisation of male homosexual subcultures has led increasingly to an individualised sense of gayness, whereby gay identity is constructed and defined through consumption practices which are legitimised by essentialist ideas about innate desires and self-fulfilment. Such a self-perception on the part of gay men renders invisible the social construction of sexuality and so produces an audience susceptible to the political individualism of liberalism. In such a social context, political perspectives will therefore inevitably be focused on individual rights and other remedies which secure the protection of an intrinsically different group in society who are in a sexual, cultural and numerical minority. As both Evans and Gamson (1996) suggest, this quasi-ethnic model of gay politics reaffirms essentialist divisions and categories since it relies on an exclusive and immutable version of sexualities.

Institutionalised politics in Western liberal democracies forces us to confront the odd nature of the relationship between politics and identity.

Que(e?)rying political identity

If we seek to deconstruct essentialist identities, do we leave ourselves without political locations from which to articulate our experiences and, crucially, do we delegitimise any form of representative political identity as impossibly essentialist and thus inevitably exclusionary? Just as I have rejected the use of essentialism as a basis for understanding sexuality, I think so too can essentialism be rejected as a basis for democratic politics. This does not mean that we cannot adopt a political location from which to speak, advocate and represent. However, we need to rethink how we deploy political identities in order to reinforce the understanding of them as socially oppressed groups rather than representative of a 'naturally' deviant group.

I suggest in the next chapter that institutionalised group representation is one means of providing a means of influence and access for lesbians and gays. The proposals go a long way to smoothing out the tensions between political aims and political identity because the principle behind them challenges the liberal democratic fetishisation of the individual as the exclusive focus of political action and policy. In short, the essentialism of democratic individualism can be challenged through alternative means of political representation and policy targeting. This will help to reinforce the idea that political presence is a mechanism to provide a perspective on experience and conditions rather than simply an individualised vote. The problem of how to pluralise participation within the group itself is one that remains a crucial one if we are not to produce a false sense of homogeneity in the act of representation. However, these issues are best left to my discussion of practical strategies which takes place in Chapter 5, particularly because it is through exploring political strategies that we will gain a better understanding of what forms of identity are needed within specific contexts. For the purposes of my discussion here, it is sufficient to concentrate on the fact that the relationship between politics and identity is certainly odd, or rather ironic, in that we need to organise around a sexual identity in order to secure the overthrow of the forces which make that identity sociopolitically significant, just like the politics of class and more pertinently, the politics of gender (Delphy 1984, 1994; Jackson 1996b). Perhaps this fact should be taken as a reminder that politics is a process as well, just as social life is, but distinct in that institutionalised political structures and procedures lead more often to the reification of the categories and identities of the people involved, and thus the naturalisation of social divisions and oppressive discourses. Before I turn to the more pragmatic translation of sociological identity into political practice, I will discuss the currently dominant form of sexual political theory which is loosely termed as 'Queer'.

THE QUEER RELATIONSHIP BETWEEN POLITICS AND IDENTITY

The attraction of neo-essentialism is perhaps largely based on the weight which nature carries in moral discourses leading to an attempt to use nature as a container for cultural and social differences. This approach has been particularly prevalent in the USA, in large part because much of the contemporary research into biological explanations for homosexuality has provided a 'scientific' point of access into a political culture in which the protection against discrimination is constitutionally guaranteed as long as discrimination is focused on an 'immutable' (natural) attribute. Moreover, the promotion of such 'ethnic' group interests is a common political bargaining practice in the pursuit of votes, particularly when that group is geographically concentrated or financially powerful, as indeed some of the urban gay and lesbian communities have become.[6]

Queer theorists are attempting to deal with the questions raised by those from different races, cultures and classes who have criticised the false universality of identity, experience and aims that derived from a homogenous representative idea of 'women' or 'gay' or 'lesbian'. The work of Butler and other Queer theorists has extended the interrogation of the social construction of gender and sexuality in marked contrast to the essentialist explanations to which many gays and some lesbians and feminists (re)turned in their attempts to seek out a politically intelligible basis for their demands (Seidman 1996).

The heritage of Queer theory can be traced to Foucault's thesis on the ubiquitous operation of power and the related effects of discourse in constituting social identities, subjectivity and the pattern of social relationships (Epstein 1996; Halperin 1995; Seidman 1996; Stein and Plummer 1996). Queer theorists concentrate on contesting identities by illuminating their discursive production. As David Halperin (1995) suggests, it is the work of Michel Foucault and subsequent theorists that has provided the loose theoretical framework for the post-emancipation politics of gay and lesbian activism – characterised as Queer. This politics is still largely an intellectual exercise in translating the theory into attempts to contest traditional political processes and identities and which emphasises and celebrates the marginalised location of those identities as sites of potentially productive and destabilising criticism. This connection between political identity and political goals is central to an understanding of the development and preoccupations of Queer theory.[7]

Foucault's depiction of sexuality as an historically specific object of discourse provided a framework for drawing together the various critiques of assimilationist politics which emerged in the 1970s and 1980s. Although the initial wave of Gay Liberationist politics had included a sociological critique of sexuality, gender and the family (see Evans 1993; Gomez 1995; Watney 1980), the material structural foundations of the 'gay world' (Adam 1985) produced discourses and practices which relied on a semi-ethnic sense of sexual identity which then seemed to reflect the experiences of those living within exclusively gay ghettos. The perception and promotion of ethnicity was also encouraged by the structure of representative politics, predominantly in the USA, and the overall effect was a return to the essentialist ideas about sexuality which had characterised the homophile politics which preceded the era of Gay Liberation. Differences of perspective and experience in terms of race, gender, class and political radicalism emerged within the increasingly commercialised gay ghettos of the 1970s and this dissent converged with similar critiques of homogenous feminist and lesbian politics (Seidman 1996). Thus there was both a cultural context and a community ready for the radical social constructionist ideas put forward by Foucault, at least among intellectuals and activists.

Foucault's thesis allowed a critique of the homogenised and exclusive gay political identities and demands by presenting sexuality itself as an effect of power relationships and therefore suggesting that all sexual identities were problematic productions of power operations, including the much cherished 'gay' and 'lesbian' categories promoted through Gay Liberation. This was, and remains, a radical rejection of the idea that sexual categories are either somehow presocial or that the oppression of the 'perverse' identities is simply the result of a lack of tolerance of natural sexuality in all its diversity. Of course, this latter idea was at the heart of assimilationist, semi-ethnic gay politics and so Foucault's analysis also demands a rejection of this form of liberal political reform whereby what lesbians and gays require is simple tolerance and equal rights with heterosexuals. Foucauldian ideas were taken up by gay, lesbian and feminist intellectuals who were interested in extending the earlier constructionist perspectives found in both symbolic interactionism and feminist analyses and which had served as the blueprint for many 'liberationist' demands. Furthermore, the impact of AIDS in the early 1980s reminded many gays and lesbians that an identity politics based on a semi-ethnic group perception had its limits in a heterosexually ordered world where lesbians and gays were constructed as a social and democratic minority, dependent upon the tradition of liberal tolerance by the heteromoral majority. As Seidman points out (1996), some of those within the lesbian and gay communities sought an extension to essentialist arguments in order to legitimise their existence with the moral weight of nature,[8] but many others, particularly intellectuals and activists within the humanities and sociology, thought is was perhaps time to reinterrogate the social significance and construction of sexuality.[9]

Queer theory developed out of this political and intellectual context, with these thinkers combining contemporary post-structuralist understandings of identity and post-Marxist analyses of political struggle in order to forge a new perspective on both sexual identities and political engagement.[10] In this sense, Queer theory has always been explicitly political in that social identities are regarded as manifestations of power, and the normalisation of these identities into prescribed forms should therefore be resisted in favour of pluralisation or the promotion of differences.[11] Taking their cue from Foucauldian characterisations of power as a relation rather than a resource, lesbian and gay activists and intellectuals reformulated the theoretical rationale behind political activity to suggest that 'the aim of an oppositional politics is therefore not liberation but resistance' (Halperin 1995: 18). Resistance to the discursive practices and meanings of homophobia is what Halperin regards as the proper function of Queer politics: this entails countering the effects of power as it is manifested within essentialist discourses of gender/sexuality or what Queer theorists more commonly call heteronormativity.

Since sexual identities emerged from the operation of power and knowledge through certain dominant discourses, a politics of effective 'liberation' must be concerned with resisting power and its associated discursive effects, which include the idea of an essential 'gay' or 'lesbian' identity. Although Halperin and others such as Butler (1990a, 1993) recognise the need for a political position from which to speak, they reject any characterisation of these political identities as representative of some universal or homogenous homosexual experience or perspective. Thus, the use of the terms 'gay' and 'lesbian' are similarly rejected as too indicative of a quasi-essentialist discourse of sexuality. Instead, we should articulate a discourse of resistance to heteronormativity and acknowledge the potential for political destabilisation which our 'deviance' allows. In short, we should become queers since 'those who knowingly occupy such a marginal location, who assume a de-essentialised identity that is purely positional in character, are properly speaking not gay but queer' (Halperin 1995: 62).

It is difficult to talk of Queer theory and politics within traditional frameworks of political activism or sociological analysis. Queer theorists focus on engagement with and resistance to heteronormativity and its associated practices, but what this entails is often not contextualised in terms of social structures or hierarchies, or indeed the construction of subjectivity and social identity. Halperin (1995) describes the strategies of Queer as threefold in terms of identities, practices and discourses: creative appropriation and resignification; appropriation and theatricalisation to undermine dominant forms of discourse; and exposure and demystification of the same. It is just such strategic purpose with which Judith Butler promotes drag as an important and viable subversion of binary sexual identities and upon which she develops her ideas of 'performativity' as gender production, reiteration and potentially, subversion (1990a, 1991). The exhortation to resist illustrates both Queer's the focus on the micro-social level and also its concern with subversion through the disruption and transgression of normative discourses. It is in this area that the increasingly abstract academic Queer political/social theory still resonates with the activism of Queer politics; transgression of norms of behaviour and subversive parodies of heterosexual conventions have become central to resisting sexual oppression.[12]

The irony is, however, that the presence of Queer activists may have served to enshrine the perception of lesbians and gays as an exclusive group; in this sense the disruption and resistance central to Queer politics has failed to impact upon the dominant discourse of essential political identity and its binary divisions of sexuality. Indeed, as Wilson (1997) and others point out (Gamson 1996; Halperin 1995), queer has become synonymous with lesbian and gay in some activist circles and has, therefore, simply reinscribed the exclusive understanding of sexual identities. Part of the reason for this is simply the context in which Queer actions take place. All too often these are directed at resisting the imposition of heterosexual norms or heteroessentialist morality by the state or another institutionalised authority. The proliferation of the word queer on posters and T-shirts at political events, such as the vigil outside the UK Parliament during the age of consent debate in 1994, and regularly at Pride marches and other smaller scale actions, sets up homosexual activists as queers. This inevitably means that any such action will focus attention on queers as the resistance, and therefore re-emphasises the divisions between lesbians, gays and heterosexuals thus reinscribing the essentialist discourse itself. Moreover, we need to think about the extent to which transgressive behaviour is actually the expected norm for those who are stigmatised as outwith the norms of mainstream (that is, heterosexual, respectable) society. Don't those who regard lesbians and gays as deviants expect us to be revolting, in both senses of the word?

Part of the dilemma of Queer activism is created by the institutionalised procedures of democratic engagement and the need therein for some form of representative identity and, as I have already established in the previous section, this need for an essential political identity is a central dilemma for any politics of social oppression. However, it is also difficult to assess the impact of Queer activism within the cultural and political realms. Although we need to contest heteronormativity, I have suggested that we also need to contest the discourse of essentialism in all its manifestations across both sexuality and democracy. I would argue that we need the analytical purchase of more traditional sociological and political frameworks if we are to determine whether the political engagement and social visibility are actually destabilising 'compulsory' heterosexuality (Rich 1980) and essentialism or are simply reinforcing it through discursive reincorporation. The celebration of marginality is similarly difficult to support within a more structural analysis of social life and political system and so the Queer exhortation to be subversive and transgressive needs to be placed within social contexts whereby it is recognised that most groups or individuals cannot be 'Queer' for fear of consequences which range from social exclusion to violence. Adopting or 'performing' a strategic, marginal position must be recognised as a luxury for most if Queer politics is not to be seen as simply the latest radical chic for those in the know in both academia and broader intellectual circles.

Of course, on a larger scale these points relate to the tension between promoting differences and challenging inequalities in that Queer activism may be illuminating differences and alternative discourses but by doing so also actually reinscribing inequalities because Queer identities are not read or received as anything subversive. Moreover, although Queer theorists have maintained a clear focus on the need to resist the essentialist construction of identity, both in terms of sexuality and political representation, it is this resistance which many find troubling because it is often taken to be a deconstructive attack on the validity of identity.

> I take as central to Queer theory its challenge to what has become the dominant foundational concept of both homophobic and affirmative homosexual theory: the assumption of a unified homosexual identity. I interpret Queer theory as contesting this foundation and therefore the very telos of Western homosexual politics. (Seidman 1996: 11)

This emphasis within Queer theory on deconstructing identity has gone hand in hand with attempts to illuminate and pluralise social differences. However, since Queer theory is dealing in the currency of post-modern relativism, social (and thus political) identity becomes potentially unintelligible: 'With the post-modern rejection of all projects claiming to be universal, the unity of the subject is deconstructed and revealed as plural, fragmentary, and contingent' (Stychin 1995: 20).[13] My worry is that in the Queer relationship between politics and identity, the rigorous anti-essentialist theorisation of social identity takes precedence over any sociological or pragmatic political theorisation of how identities are related to subjectivities and social relationships. This may be a worry which can be seen as a misinterpretation of Queer theory, given that the major Queer theorists are explicit in their call for a focus on the discourses (and thus social relationships and material practices) which constitute identity and subjectivity as heterosexual but Queer theorists themselves are partly to blame for this misunderstanding because, apart from Judith Butler (1992, 1993) and Michel Foucault in his later years (1989, 1990), very few seem to emphasise the point that identities are inevitable effects of discourse and it is thus the latter that is the primary unit of criticism. For example, in the introduction to her collection on Queer political activism, Shane Phelan foregrounds the common theme as identity rather than constitutive effects of discourses and associated practices:

> These many discourses and movements share a profound confrontation with identities, both of persons and of communities. This confrontation is by no means a simple rejection of identity, but is a questioning, a challenge to the ontological and political status of sexuality, race and gender. It emerges both in theoretical writing

that directly addresses identities and in work that genealogizes and/or deconstructs them in practice. (Phelan 1997: 2)

Although Phelan and other Queer theorists are both aware of and emphasise the political aspect to Queer theory (see Fuss's introduction to her 1991 collection for example), it seems to me that the emphasis on deconstructing identities sometimes misguides a reader away from the contributions which a discursive analysis can make and thus removes the political purchase and resonance of a Queer perspective. I have already suggested that we deploy a stable sense of sociosexual identity in order to take action in the social world and that our theorisation of sexual identity must thus take account of this. A reflexive understanding of subjectivity demands an understanding of the self as located within social structures and social practices; formed in interaction with these forces and hierarchies but still able to deploy an extra-situational viewpoint which allows the self to integrate past, present and projected future courses of action. It is not that Queer theorists do not attempt to explain subjectivity in this way, but rather that these attempts make no allowance for the social and material contexts in which subjectivity is formed, relying instead on discourse theory and therefore suggesting that subjectivity is both discursively constituted – which raises the question of whether effective reflexivity can exist – and extremely fragmentary and contingent – which raises the question of whether a stable sense of self-identity can be constructed and deployed to any effect.

This criticism is not meant to deny the beneficial effects that Queer political activism has, but as I have argued above, too often these actions and presences simply reiterate rather than destabilise the essentialist discourse and, as such, are often not accurate reflections of the aspirations of Queer political theory. As I have also argued in conclusion to the previous chapter and in introduction to this chapter, perhaps we should not worry too much about the effects of political presence as long as our political programmes and strategies articulate a non-essentialist version of sexuality and politics. Queer theorists would seem to agree in a broad sense, but while I have been arguing that the Queer relationship between identity and politics is in many ways no more or less problematic than a more traditional representative relationship, we cannot ignore the fundamental problems for political identity which a discourse-based perspective raises in the conceptualisation of power, structures and subjectivity.

POWER, STRUCTURES AND SUBJECTIVITY IN QUEER THEORY

The aim of resisting the essentialist heteronormativity is promoted, both theoretically and politically, through an affirmation of Queerness which, above all, becomes an affirmation of the contingency of identities. While subversion is targeted at the parodic and transgressive imitation and appropriation of 'real' men and 'real' women by those 'unreal', deviant men and women – lesbians and gays, transsexuals, drag queens (Butler 1991; Halperin 1995) – the irony is that we need these 'deviant' identities in order to organise politically and provide a location from which to speak of Queer experience and Queer differences. This 'dilemma of difference' (Young 1989) is not exclusive to Queer theory but is simply part of the dynamic of political organisation and representation within political systems where the difference in question is regarded as a natural or essential attribute.

Resisting heteronormativity is necessary but it is politically problematic if the exclusive focus becomes the deconstruction of those essentialist identities with which most people – straights, gays and lesbians – identify. These cannot be deconstructed without a risk of de-emphasising the fact that they are manifestations of structural social inequalities and divisions; this becomes a more pertinent risk for those who are the oppressed within this hierarchy. The reliance on a discursive analysis of the social world within the Queer perspective evinces a lack of an integrated perspective on subjectivity, social identities and social structures which, somewhat ironically, renders the oppressive elements in the social construction of sexuality difficult to describe and analyse. This in turn brings into question the political efficacy of a Queer perspective in that it is difficult to construct a politics of intervention and resistance if the targets of activity are only vaguely understood or described. Indeed, the theoretical sophistication of Queer academic analysis is very rarely applied to contemporary political activity in a way which makes connections between the two.

I am acutely aware that I am speaking in terms which Foucauldians and Queer theorists will find horribly unfashionable as well as theoretically outmoded (perhaps the two judgements are interdependent as Grant suggests in her critique of the Queer academic enterprise [1996]). My development of a structurally grounded interactionist perspective on the self has much in common with Queer theory and the Foucauldian approach to subjectivity, but I have outlined the understanding that we need of structures and subjectivity for such a theory while including in this theorisation a narrow sense of discourse as ideological in its effects but also material in its existence. At the heart of my scepticism about the more radical interpretation of discourse which is proposed by Foucault, and taken up by Queer theorists, is the shadowy role of power. I can accept that we are all located within and defined by our relevant discursive location, be it academia or a class position: there is no true position from which to observe the structures of social life. Related to this anti-foundationalism (Howarth 1995) is the rejection of metanarratives of social explanation, such as Marxism or patriarchy (Laclau and Mouffe 1987) and I support this rejection of one-dimensional explanations of social life and social inequalities: the intersections and contradictions of race, class, gender and sexuality preclude a focus on one of these social divisions as fundamentally constitutive of the others.

However, although Queer theorists are seeking to disrupt the dominant discourse of sexuality and gender, there is scant emphasis on the structural existence of heteronormativity and its associated social categories and practices and how these construct subjectivity. Much like a traditional interactionist perspective, Queer theorists often focus on the micro-level operations of power and resistance and are thus either silent on the reasons for a discourse becoming dominant or simply unable to theorise the socially structured formation of heteronormativity.[14] I am not trying to suggest a return to structuralism, but rather that social life is structured, and the self is also structured in ways that allow us to talk about the permanence of recurrent interaction, perceptions of subjectivity and social processes. Within Queer, the emphasis lies much more on the contesting identity since subjectivity is constituted through many discourses and therefore open to transformation through the disruption of and resistance to these intersecting discourses. Of course, this begs the question of exactly how the opportunities for disruption and resistance can be provided and expanded at these points of intersection but Queer theorists are too often reluctant to engage in a more traditional discussion of social structures and social practices, preferring the less contextualised language of discourse and cultural practices (Halperin 1995). I understand that Queer political aims are to open up, perhaps ease open, the realm of uncertainty which exists in that space prior to the definite constitution of discourses into formations of acceptable and unacceptable subjects, and particularly to show through imitation and parody that both the subject and its constitutive other are not some essential, natural creation but are indeed, produced in relation to each other. However, we need a more thoughtful application of such strategies to the more mundane politics within which most lesbians and gays are involved and, crucially, to which most lesbians and gays relate. After all, a parodic transgressive performance in drag may not be seem politically relevant to, and may be socially impossible, for most Queer folk.

I have already argued that the focus on power and discourses does not allow those arguing from a Queer or Foucauldian perspective to admit to extra-discursive social structures or hierarchies.[15] The ways in which discourse theorists step around this problem is to talk in terms of discursive formations as the pattern of social practices, relationships and ideas which come together within and between discourses to structure social life. At one level this difference in terminology is not a difference in perspective, given that material relationships, social practices and ideological patterns and concepts are also included in interactionist and materialist perspectives on the social construction of sexuality. Where a problem sometimes arises because many Queer theorists are reluctant to detail the relationship between social structures and the conditions and contexts for the formation and disruption of social identity and subjectivity. Even those using Foucauldian analysis often speak in terms which seem to make no acknowledgement of the permanence and coercive force of certain discourses and the associated discursive effects or formations.[16] This is largely because of Foucault's characterisation of power as a diffuse pattern of relationships operating at the 'micro-level' of social life (Sawicki 1991). Although the radical force of this perspective has sensitised theorists to the ubiquitous existence of power in all social relationships – that power is relational, if you will – the corollary consolidation and permanence of patterns of power has been difficult to integrate into such an analysis, making structured inequalities almost impossible to explain (see for example the critiques in Ramazanoglu's collection, 1993). It becomes similarly difficult to explain, therefore, the differential abilities and opportunities that exist for resistance and subversion.

Moreover, the reluctance to talk in terms of social structures leaves the relationship between discourse, power and subjectivity difficult to theorise. In Foucault's thesis on sexuality, subjectivity is seemingly to be understood simply as a constituted effect of discourse (Evans 1993; Foucault 1980). Despite Foucault's later emphasis on technologies and practices of the self as methods of constructing subjectivity (Bristow 1997: 182–188; Foucault 1990), his explication of how subjects come to take up these practices still lacks any rigorous connection between subjectivity and dominant discourses, emphasising instead the discursive constitution of that subject, leaving us with a woefully under-theorised account of agency and opportunities and mobilisation for action. In the reluctance to theorise the self as an active and reflexive subject, Foucauldian analysts cannot make distinctions between differential effects of power even though the perspective suggests that the self is not monolithic and that the multiplicity of subject positions are the result of power operating through discourses which emerge in 'complex, strategical situations in a particular society' (Foucault 1980: 93). Power cannot simply constitute subjectivity through discourse without an understanding of why power exists or rather, what it means. As Cooper argues: 'Power does not simply exist. It is an explanatory or normative device that highlights and articulates some social situations, decentring others' (1995: 17). Only with such a view of power as an effect of social relationships and hierarchies can we explain the logic behind power creating discourse creating the subject. Without this acceptance of power as an effect of social divisions, power becomes absurdly plural and accessible leaving us with no way of explaining why some subject positions are more imbued with power.

The discursive perspective on subjectivity can explain only that there are historically specific discourses which identify us as subjects: social locations which we inhabit. This position is tenable only in the narrow sense of the ideological effects of discourse, in that various discourses provide a resource for constructing and locating ourselves within the social world. However, despite the acknowledgement of a socially constructed subjectivity as multidimensional (constructed through multiple discourses), the idea of subjectivity as reflexive, as a process if you like, is more difficult to sustain within a discursive framework. How can we have a subject whose subjectivity is constituted through discourse, when this discursive production implies a complete subjection of that agent and therefore no possibility of effective or transformative agency? The way out of this impasse for both Queer and discourse theorists is to argue that when a discourse constitutes subjectivity, that subjectivity is not in any sense a false consciousness (Butler 1993: 4–12; Mouffe 1992). Although this would seem to converge with a grounded interactionist perspective, I maintain that there is a contradiction between an exclusive focus on discursive production of subjectivity and the reflexivity of that subject which would allow for agency. Of course, agency of the subject is vital for the viability of Queer theory, since the emphasis is on the active

Que(e?)rying political identity

disruption and transgression of identities constituted within dominant discourses.

Many Queer theorists simply ignore this contradiction as an argument that is solved by the emphasis on the discursive constitution of the subject, but this line leads all too easily into the determinist cul-de-sac of structuralism. The position which I take has been detailed in Chapter 3 and emphasises that subjectivity is a process which is produced by interaction with discourses and their effects, whereby discourses are seen simply as a set of ideas and social structures and relationships are admitted as distinct but intertwined conditions (or discursive formations if you will). This distinction may seem a minor point but I think that it is vital that we consider whether a Foucauldian view of power and discourse can explain the existence of social structures, hierarchies and ideologies simply within its own frame of reference and still prove politically useful. In the alternative analysis which I have put forward, subjectivity is not determined by discourse, but rather is constructed within its contexts, and thus the operation of power cannot be so overwhelming and pervasive that we are unable to reflect upon its effects. As I suggested in conclusion to the previous chapter, Queer theorists and radical democratic theorists who have taken up an emphasis on the process of interaction with cultural practices characterise agency as materialised sites of opportunity rather than a quality of reflexivity possessed by a subject (Mouffe 1992), and Butler's work on performativity exemplifies this direction (1990a, 1993). However, despite the theoretical appeal of such a reformulation of agency, I will go on to argue that the problem of discursive determination is not necessarily resolved, either within more general perspectives on political identity (Laclau and Mouffe 1987; Mouffe 1992) or within Butler's work and therefore leaves the political efficacy of such a theoretical project open to question.

PERFORMATIVITY, PROCESS AND AGENCY

Judith Butler's work on identity and political efficacy has served as the main reference point for many Queer theorists and, moreover, it provides a contemporaneous development of many of the post-structuralist ideas about political identity used by radical democratic theorists such as Laclau and Mouffe (1985, 1987; Laclau 1991; Mouffe 1992; Phillips 1993; Young 1994). Of central importance is Butler's interrogation of the category of women as a unified subject of feminist political activity (1990a). This deconstruction of women as a universal identity led her to suggest that a gendered subject is produced through the exclusion of other forms of behaviour and identity and becomes naturalised (and thus understood as an essential attribute) through the very discourse which first constitutes gender (naturalism/essentialism) and then purports merely to describe gender and sexual difference. Butler is therefore taking up Foucault's thesis that the operation of power through certain discourses dictates not simply the repression of particular abject subjects but rather that the discourse constitutes abject subjects as the complement to the production of normative subjects. Power is thus relational and productive, generating both the socially acceptable and the unacceptable as part of its dynamic operation. Therefore, a politics based on these discursively constituted identities which are socially deviant – the unacceptable, the abject, such as homosexuals – and, moreover, a politics which takes the discursive category of woman as given, may serve to reinforce the legitimacy of the discourse which has produced the oppression of those inhabiting these categories. Butler is not simply trying to deconstruct the category of woman, but suggesting that the homogenous and stable understanding of such a category serves to reinscribe the binary heterosexual matrix itself: 'Is the construction of the category of women as a coherent and stable subject an unwitting reification of gender relations? And is not such a reification precisely contrary to feminist aims?' (1990a: 5). Butler's answer to this dilemma of difference is to assert the very constructedness and instability of gender identity and, by extension, sexual identity.

In their refusal to accept essentialist categories of identity as ontologically or epistemologically 'true', it may seem that Queer theorists suggest that the deconstruction of identity is the exclusive aim of gay and lesbian and feminist politics because this is the only way to contest and resist heteronormative discourse and its gendered matrix (Butler 1990a, 1991, 1993). As I have said above, this emphasis sits in tension with the need to articulate the problems and experiences of those who inhabit these categories. Queer theorists themselves are aware of both the tension and the perception that they are perhaps too dismissive of pragmatic political engagement (Gamson 1996; Phelan 1997; Wilson 1997). This perception of Queer theory and resistance to it has been reinforced by two other elements: first, Queer theory is derived from Foucauldian theory and as such, suggests that emancipation is not possible because we cannot escape the operation of power. Thus resistance to power is the only hope we have of achieving certain conditions of freedom, wherein we do not escape power but use its productive capacity to construct and deploy a counter-discourse. That this position suggests that power as domination will always exist is one of the reasons why liberal theorists have found it difficult to accept, extrapolating from such an analysis of power that one form of domination can only be usurped by another (Halperin 1995). Moreover, this position suggests that political identities are part of the problem rather than part of the solution – as indeed Butler suggests in the quotation above.

The second element of Queer theory which has made it politically contentious is the way in which theorists explain the process of constructing and deconstructing identity. Again it is Butler's development of the concept of performativity which has provided the basis of a Queer approach to the construction and contestation of identity. To put it very crudely, Butler contests the direction and extent of constructionism itself (see her discussion in *Gender Trouble*, 1990a: 7–13), suggesting that gender should not be thought of as a socially constructed ontology, but rather as a process of reiterative acts which are discursively constructed to constitute a gendered subject (1990a, 1990b, 1991). Gender is therefore not something we are or become through allocation, but rather something that we do: gender is performative achievement rather than expressive behaviour. We are not ontologically male or female, gay or straight, but rather reiteratively, discursively constituted as such through performativity.

This thesis and its subsequent interpretation has caused all sorts of trouble other than Butler's stated aim to 'trouble' the construction and episteme of gender. The resistance to this interpretation of gender is particularly acute within sociological perspectives because Butler's thesis seems to collide (as Foucault's did) with what Evans has called the basic sociological equation of structure plus consciousness equals social action (see Evans' critique of Foucault, chapter 1, 1993). The central problem arises from the discursive approach to gender: Butler is suggesting that gender does not pre-exist discourse but rather that gender identity, and indeed the totality of subjectivity, is achieved only through the process of discursive constitution. At first it might seem that this is not a difficult argument to sustain. If the Queer argument is simply that gendered identities must be understood as existing within certain discourses then this position can be regarded as synonymous with the interactionist argument that human relationships and identities are only constructed and intelligible through frameworks of meaning. However, those who employ the concept of discourse tend towards the argument that subjectivity is itself discursively constituted; that it is, in fact, an effect of discourse. This position has the advantage of being a rigorously anti-essentialist perspective and, in the case of sexuality, it illustrates very well the fact that people understand their gender and sexuality as an essential quality precisely because the essentialist discourse is the dominant framework within which subjectivity is produced and subsequently made intelligible. Again, I would argue that this approach to subjectivity is not problematic if one accepts that we achieve certain states of subjecthood through the conjuncture of discourses which allow us to construct and mobilise a sense of identity. Indeed, this reading of discursive constitution has much in common with a materially grounded interactionist perspective in that in both approaches the emphasis is on social life as a process of reiteration within structures of social meaning and practices. For example, consider Blumer's description of Mead's interactionist position:

> Established patterns of group life exist and persist only through the continued use of the same schemes of interpretation; and such schemes of interpretation are maintained only through their continued confirmation by the defining acts of others. It is highly important to recognise that the established patterns of group life just do not carry on by themselves but are dependent for their continuity on recurrent affirmative definition. Let the interpretations that sustain them be undermined or disrupted by changed definitions from others and the patterns can quickly collapse. (Blumer 1966: 539)

I would suggest that if you substituted discourses for 'schemes of interpretation' and performativity for 'recurrent affirmative definition', you would have the beginnings of a Queer perspective which contains the potential for performative resistance and subversion in the potential for 'changed definitions'. Could Mead be the first real Queer theorist? Unfortunately for theorists trying to get to grips with the vast material on sexuality, apparently not.

The central distinction from interactionism arises in the explanation of agency of a discursively constituted subject. If we think back to Hay's characterisation of agency as strategy and intention (1995) – introduced in the previous chapter – it becomes difficult to theorise the potential for effective agency when subjectivity, and therefore the reflexive capacity to develop strategy and intention, is constituted through discursive production. This perspective contains the implication subjectivity is therefore determined by production through discourses (Evans 1993). This understanding of discursive subjectivity lies behind many of the criticisms of Butler's concept of performativity and the more general employment of the Queer perspective. Butler herself, however, rejects the traditional analytical dichotomy between free will and determinism which, she argues, underpins traditional sociological understandings of structures, consciousness and agency.

> The question of locating 'agency' is usually associated with the viability of the 'subject', where the 'subject' is understood to have some stable existence prior to the cultural field that it negotiates. Or, if the subject is culturally constructed, it is nevertheless vested with an agency, usually figured as the capacity for reflexive meditation, that remains intact regardless of its cultural embeddedness. On such a model, 'culture' and 'discourse' *mire* the subject, but do not constitute that subject. This move to qualify and enmire the pre-existing subject has appeared necessary to establish a point of agency that is not fully *determined* by that culture and discourse. And yet, this kind of reasoning falsely presumes (a) agency can only be established through recourse to a pre-established 'I', even if that 'I' is found in the midst of a discursive convergence, and (b) that to be *constituted* by discourse is to be *determined* by discourse, where determination forecloses the possibility of agency. (Butler 1990: 142)

Butler suggests instead that we should reject the epistemology which sets up the dichotomy between subject and context and recognise that this construction is part of the very apparatus that naturalises the 'I' as subject and the discursive signifying practices which constitute it and its opportunities for agency. Thus, 'the question of *agency* is reformulated as a question of how signification and resignification work' (1990: 144). It may be possible to sustain this line of reasoning from a sociological perspective if we understand that the essentialist discourse provides the dominant organising framework for understanding and explaining sexual subjectivity and therefore we have no choice but to become subjects within this paradigm. We can thus sustain a sociological critique by challenging the epistemology and ontology of essentialism and suggesting a counter-discourse of social construction. However, an interactionist position would still allow for the capacity for reflexive subjectivity which would produce the strategy and intention needed for agency. Butler suggests instead that it is in the experiential process of discursive gender performativity where the potential sites for agency exist, particularly in the possibility of *dis*identification, which may perhaps be understood as changing definitions (within an interactionist context). Although she argues that "to claim that the subject is itself produced in and as a gendered matrix of relations is not to do away with the subject, but only to ask after the conditions of its emergence and operation' (1993: 7) it is difficult to pin down exactly how the conditions may be disrupted or changed so that performative subversive disidentification is possible.

How do we go about disrupting discourses if our subjectivity is already constituted by those very discourses? Is effective agency merely a matter of chance and happenstance or is there a political strategy which we can pursue to deliver it? It is a curious contradiction within Queer theory that one can understand the perspective as structuralist in its emphasis on discourses as the dominant form of social organisation and meaning and thus the exclusive force for the production of subjectivity, and one can also focus on the emphasis that is given to agency through the characterisation of action and process as performativity. To integrate the two interpretations is, however, as difficult as it has been within Foucauldian thought because the use of discourse remains an extremely problematic analytical tool.

I am, in many ways, 'Queered out' by this theoretical debate. Perhaps it ultimately comes down to which analytical framework is most appropriate for the realm which is being investigated. While I think Queer theory has been crucial in sensitising theorists to the epistemological and ontological underpinnings of the subject and agency, the deconstructive challenge implicit in a Queer analysis is difficult to translate into effective political strategies. However, as I have been trying to suggest throughout my critique of Queer theory, the benefits of such a perspective have much in common with sociological traditions such as interactionism and, as such, there is no reason why we cannot take from each tradition in order to construct a more effective and viable understanding of political identity in its different realms. As such, Queer theory may provide us with the overall trajectory of political aims – to deconstruct, resist and displace heteronormativity – but in order to translate this into an intelligible framework of analysis which can be applied to the current social construction of sexuality, both at an individual and structural level, we perhaps need the corrective of a socially material and structurally materialist interactionist context to theorisations about sexuality. The particular advantage of this perspective is that we can account for the

Que(e?)rying political identity

ways in which a core or stable sense of sexuality is constructed and mobilised within the current epistemological framework which permeates not only individual understandings but also political processes and institutions. This still leaves us with the question of how to construct a political identity which is both strategically Queer and tactically interactionist. With this in mind, and as a final interrogation of Queer theory, I will consider the social contexts which Butler proposes in her concept of performativity.

FROM PERFORMATIVITY TO POLITICAL IDENTITY

In her more recent work, Butler attempts to provide the social context to her concept of performativity, both as a response to critics who charged her with overemphasising the opportunities for resistance and as an elaboration of the political implications of her perspective (Butler 1993, introduction). In her original deconstruction of gender identity and formulation of performativity she stated that 'the critical task is, rather, to locate the strategies of subversive repetition enabled by those constructions [of gender], to affirm the local possibilities of intervention through participating in precisely those practices of repetition that constitute identity and, therefore, present the immanent possibility of contesting them' (1990: 147). In her subsequent work in *Bodies That Matter* (1993) she provides a more structural context to performativity by acknowledging that gendered subjects are produced through a process of the materialisation of norms. Performativity is therefore reined in as a concept to include the contexts of interaction and also to describe the process of materialisation itself.[17] Furthermore, she suggests that the materialisation of the regulatory norms of discourses decides performativity as a process of constant citation of these norms, and it is in the constant reiteration and citation of norms that the opportunities for disidentification and thus subversion exist.

The political trajectory of this thesis is much the same as that in *Gender Trouble* but Butler elaborates on the political possibilities of performative transgression. Specifically, she suggests that the constant contesting of identity categories should be at the heart of a democratic political project which is inclusive and representative. It is in this way that she translates the thesis of transgressive performativity into a process of political engagement which constantly resists and challenges the essentialist discourse by contesting identity categories. It is the very construction of these identities which performativity entails, but also potentially undermines, through disidentification, through the opportunities for 'subversive repetitions' and thus disconfirms the validity of essentialist descriptions of both identity and associated experience: 'When some set of descriptions is offered to fill out the content of an identity, the result is inevitably fractious. Such inclusionary descriptions produce inadvertently new sites of contest and a host of resistances, disclaimers and refusals to identify with the terms' (1993: 221). The dilemma of difference in representation cannot be overcome but rather the process of political engagement must be reworked to include the tenets of performativity such that 'To ameliorate and rework this violence [of exclusionary identities], it is necessary to learn a double movement: to invoke the category and, hence, provisionally to institute an identity and at the same time to open the category as a site of permanent political contest' (1993: 222). I would suggest that the link between strategic aims and tactics is still difficult to conceptualise in these terms. The practicalities of group representation are not made any easier by having to be aware of the 'double movement'. Nonetheless, there are mechanisms and proposals which I will discuss in the next chapter that are worth our consideration in terms of providing a forum for social identity. I am not claiming that either an interactionist or Queer perspective can resolve the dilemma of difference which bedevils proposals for representation, but rather that the insights of these sociological perspectives can help us to reconcile strategic aims to pragmatic political representation.

CONCLUSION: TOWARDS POLITICAL STRATEGIES

I called this chapter 'que(e)rying political identity' to signify my reluctance to endorse the Queer perspective on sexual identity because it is not a fully social understanding of sexual subjectivity and its construction through essentialism. I think that we need to challenge the essentialist discourse which underpins both sexuality and democracy rather than simply challenging heteronormativity. Moreover, in the current political climate, we cannot afford to ignore institutional structures and processes in politics – in democratic politics, we still need a collective identity. However, by employing an interactionist perspective on achieving sexuality, I have tried to suggest that the essentialist assumptions underpinning identity can be replaced with a more sociological explanation. The emphasis can therefore be shifted to identity as a social location, defined by structural and sociohistorical conditions as much as by self-identification.

However, as Angelia Wilson points out, translating sophisticated sociological/political/Queer theorisations on identity into pragmatic political strategies is extremely difficult to do (1997). Indeed, this problem is central to my resistance to the Queer exhortation is to resist categories and constantly to transgress their boundaries. If this is our political strategy then we cannot describe or even imagine a common form of political identity which is both stable over time and inclusive of a diversity of experiences and opinions. Identity within Queer becomes almost wholly context-specific and individualistic; a camouflage for cultural guerrillas. Stability is the antithesis of the Queer project.

The irony is of course, that 'Queer' has now become a term which lesbians and gay men use to identify themselves as, well, lesbian and gay. This contemporary, mainstream use of 'Queer' affirms stable, culturally and politically intelligible identities and thus the epistemological and ontological foundations which Queer theory sets out to subvert and replace. Therefore, I argue that we are left only with the aim of querying political identity. A queried conceptualisation of identity must be thought of within its political context or it becomes a meaningless term, or one that is simply reinscribed into the dominant essentialist discourse, as has happened to 'Queer'. I will therefore consider in detail the construction and deployment of identity through various political strategies because it is only within these contexts that we can begin to flesh out forms of identity which can represent experience. These considerations will form the bulk of the next chapter and the main areas of concern will be group representation, citizenship and rights. It is by looking at strategies for effective engagement in these arenas that I hope to define more precisely the form and purpose of a more sociologically informed understanding of political identity.

That is not to say, however, that we cannot draw some conclusions from this chapter. First and foremost, I think that it is evident that we must reject any form of strategic essentialism in any attempts to translate sociological explanations into viable political identities and strategies. We need an alternative discourse which is promoted by all those groups involved in representation, advocacy and action on behalf of oppressed sexualities. I accept that we cannot expect a complex theoretical perspective to make sense to most activists and non-theoreticians, but I think that we can draw out the sociological aspects of people's narratives and expand and explain those using a framework of sociological translation such as the materially grounded interactionism which I have adopted. At the very least, we can find ways of explaining sexualities as important social identities which therefore demand social and political intervention. Providing an alternative 'script' is a fundamental requirement in the fight against the oppressive sexual order which is underpinned by the essentialist natural/moral script or discourse. This is, in large part, the task of any thorough theorisation of sexuality but I am not arguing that a gay and lesbian politics is simply about challenging ideological formations or discourses within society. Our politics requires a thorough sociological rearticulation of sexual subjectivity precisely because it is from such a rationale that we can intervene into debates about the need for our political representation; the need for responsive social policy; the need for the acceptance of social and moral differences. By placing an issue (and its associated practices) into the realm of the social, we immediately make it political.

Moreover, how we construct our sociological alternative discourse will affect the politics which we can subsequently pursue: any residually essentialist versions of identity will, I suggest, limit our political aims and reinforce the oppression which is dictated by essentialism. The social origins of this oppression have been described in the last few chapters; I have illustrated the social conditions, relationships and discourses that need to be challenged and transformed in order to achieve social equality. Moreover, I hope that I have made it clear that categories of sexuality depend upon the preceding division of gender: the preservation of gender divisions is the only consistent theme in the myriad ways in which homosexualities are regulated, oppressed, tolerated and caricatured. As an emancipatory project, the politics of gay and lesbian equality must be connected to the politics of gender equality.[18]

Second in the themes which run through a queried sense of political identity is the need to de-emphasise identity as homogenous or exclusive. We need to find ways of foregrounding identity as process, both in terms of the methods of representation which we seek and in the ways in we articulate our demands, interests and experiences. Moreover, we need to think about how we might make political activism easier so that a wider spectrum of people are involved. I am literally suggesting that we move towards a queried sense and understanding of sexual identity. On the one hand we must accept the centrality of sexuality to most people's sense of individuality (and the salience of individuality itself in late capitalist culture) and yet, on the other hand, construct a theory which queries the essentialist episteme of sexual and political identity. I have tried to demonstrate that many of the 'queries' raised within Queer theory are not original challenges to naturalism but are in fact

Que(e?)rying political identity

part of a wider sociological heritage which predates post-modernist/ post/structuralist theory. The taint of academic fashion is not a sufficient reason for rejecting Queer approaches to identity; it is more that they make it difficult to provide a mobilising force for group political activity. If we think back to Chapter 3, I set out three different criteria which I suggested would be important in developing a viable theory of political and sexual subjectivity, the first of which refers to the potential for the translation of theory into everyday discourse.[19] The grounded interactionist perspective on achieving sexuality has a much greater potential for forming a coherent basis for sociopolitical activity than a strictly Queer version of identity. It is to the arena of the political that I return in my final chapter in order to elaborate on the strategies needed in the deployment of a queried sense of political identity. I suggested in conclusion to the previous chapter that we need to move towards a politics of experience based on a more thorough sociological understanding of sexual subjectivity. I am using the term experience to encapsulate both the experiential social process through which we construct and deploy a sense of sexuality and the related experiences which result from inhabiting structural categories of identity. It is the focus on the experiential which suggests to me a move towards an understanding and deployment of political identity which emphasises social processes and experiences rather than simply representing social groups as unproblematic subcultures with clearly defined and exclusive interests and I will attempt to assess how far current political strategies go towards achieving these aims.

NOTES

1. I have used this phrase from Weeks (1996: 98) before; it forms one of his paradoxes of identity. However, I should make clear that he is not endorsing the use of essentialist identities but rather he is recognising that there is a danger of an essentialist symbolism and interpretation in any deployment of identity.
2. Chris Smith MP has been the Labour Secretary of State since May 1997. Current terrestrial programming (1997–2000) in the UK includes the rather stilted *Gaytime TV* on BBC2 and Channel Four's *Queer Street* programmes and the controversial, popular and acclaimed serial *Queer As Folk*. Regular characters in soaps/serials include Tony and Simon in *EastEnders*, which also features one of the current crop of south Asian gay or lesbian doctors along with the hospital drama *Holby City*; DC Fraser in *Taggart*; Shelley in *Brookside*, Zoe Tate in *Emmerdale*, the gun-toting Dr Maggie Doyle in *ER* (but unfortunately not Dr Carter); Ross's ex-wife and her partner on

Friends; the polymorphously perverse Ferdy on *This Life* (1997) and the lead in *Ellen* (sadly axed in 1998). Pop stars are openly gracious about their gay male and/or lesbian fans, although they are generally less forward about coming out themselves (see Maddison's acerbic critique of the way in which the gay lifestyle magazine *Attitude* deals with this, 1995) although there are honourable contemporary exceptions such as k.d.lang. Movie stars still seem to be reluctant to play gay or lesbian characters with the obvious vanilla exception of Tom Hanks in Oscar-winning mode in *Philadelphia*, or to be open about their own homosexuality, although again, the climate does seem easier in Britain and the rest of Europe than it is in the USA.
3. The difference between the homophile movement and current reformist groups can be characterised as the difference between a psychological and cultural focus. Homophile organisations emphasised innate psychosexual differences coupled with social conformity whereas current arguments tend to draw on a mix of innate sexual differences and ethnic/cultural differences as the basis for an appeal to the discourses of equal citizenship and ethnic/cultural autonomy. Watney 1980, Evans 1993.
4. Of course this debate has raged most fiercely in feminist circles and with particular focus on the implications of post-structuralist theories for understanding women's political identity as legitimately representative of women's experiences (Butler 1992; Fuss 1989; Mouffe 1992).
5. 'It is often said that the deconstruction of essential identities, which is the result of acknowledging the contingency and ambiguity of every identity, renders feminist political action impossible. Many feminists believe that, without seeing women as a coherent identity, we cannot ground the possibility of a feminist political movement in which women could unite as women in order to formulate and pursue specific feminist aims.' (Mouffe 1992: 371)
6. This is the curious contradiction of 'ethnic' gay politics: pursue natural explanations for sexuality (like essentialist explanations for sexual difference) but then use this as a basis for policies which recognise the cultural differences of gay men and women (like minority ethnic policies). Again, nature is used as a container for culture and the social but, as Phelan (1997) suggests, we need to consider whether we are a natural or a 'cultural' minority. A 'natural' explanation of an attribute such as gender or race (as equated with physiological sex) is not enough to guarantee comprehensive social and political equality as has been demonstrated by many feminist critics of gender and racial inequalities (Guillaumin 1995; Guinier 1994; Phillips 1993).
7. For a fuller critique of Queer politics and its relationship with Queer theory see Edwards 1998, Jackson and Scott 1996.
8. The impact of genetic research and research on the brain is particularly important here. For a thorough critique and further reading, see my discussion in Chapter 2.
9. The interaction of gay, lesbian and feminist politics and Foucauldian thought cannot be reduced to a particular period or to particular theorists. The development of Queer theory as a distinct discipline within the academy

Que(e?)rying political identity

is similarly difficult to pinpoint. For more detailed perspectives on these developments, see de Lauretis' introduction to *Differences*, vol. 3, no. 2, 1991, Seidman's introduction to his collection, 1996, Jackson and Scott's introduction to their reader, 1996 and Phelan's introduction to her collection, 1997. Halperin provides a more personalised historical account, 1995. The key difference from earlier constructionist analyses in Foucauldian thought was the concern with the existence of discursive categories as a manifestation of power. This part of Foucault's thesis took somewhat longer to make an impact than the historicisation of sexuality which, appropriately enough, formed the main theme of his *History of Sexuality*, vol. 1, and which was supported by other contemporary research (for example Weeks 1977; Smith-Rosenberg 1975). It seems that the emphasis in these historical analyses was the rejection of essentialism.

10. An equally important influence for some Queer theorists is Lacanian psychoanalysis. Although many use this perspective on sexuality when it comes to theorising subjectivity (see Butler's work, for example, 1991, 1993), I have made clear my resistance to such an explanation of sexual subjectivity (see Chapter 3) and I have suggested an alternative which is sociopsychological (see Chapter 4).

11. 'Difference' – like 'community' – has become one of those terms that is almost always used with a positive connotation and it has a currency within debates of political identity which is almost impossible to ignore. I will engage in a more detailed discussion of the tensions in the next chapter.

12. OutRage are the group most identified with 'Queer' activist politics in the UK and they have been most consistent in staging direct actions to highlight oppression and homophobia. Queer Nation in the USA is now defunct but ACTUP (AIDS Coalition to Unleash Power) continues to engage in direct action to highlight issues surrounding AIDS/HIV and PWA.

13. Stychin is a Queer legal theorist who is engaged in attempts to reconcile the contingent nature of subjectivity and social identity with permanent and inflexible legal policies which are premised on the subject as the bearer of rights. See his book, *Law's Desire*, 1995.

14. Many texts taken to herald the emergence of Queer theory are linguistic/literary enterprises and therefore not focused on the social – see the reader by Abelove *et al.* 1993, *The Lesbian and Gay Studies Reader* and the collection edited by Fuss 1991 for examples of textual Queer analysis. Judith Butler does attempt to address the role of the social but she focuses on 'norms' as a concept of social regulation and as such, reduces the social to cultural patterns of proscription and prescription without developing an analysis of the structural or material existence of these 'norms' (1993, 1998). Michael Warner suggest a material basis to the development of Queer identities but does not provide an elaboration of this relationship (1993).

15. See Chapter 3.

16. Although for an excellent analysis of the normalising effects of heterosexual discourse on social policies, see Carabine 1996.

17. My concern here is not this aspect of her text or the potential for structural analysis which her use of 'norms' introduces (see note 16) but the further

elaboration of the political implications of her perspective.
18. In this context, I use equality in its vaguest and broadest sense to encapsulate the different demands for different laws, public policies and social norms which most lesbians, feminists and gays espouse in the pursuit of qualitatively easier and safer lives.
19. The criteria were as follows: (1) A theory of sexual subjectivity needs to resonate with the understandings of self that people have in order to politicise them; (2) A theory of sexual subjectivity must be anti-naturalist if it is to open up the possibilities of transformation through political activity; (3) A viable theory of subjectivity needs to have a putative framework for sexuality which does not rely on the institutionalisation of heterosexuality or gender divisions. As I have said in the conclusion to Chapter 4, my development of sociological theories of sexual subjectivity meets the first two criteria more convincingly than the third.

Chapter 5

EXPLORING POLITICAL STRATEGIES

INTRODUCTION: DEMOCRACY AND INTERESTS, IDENTITY AND EXPERIENCE

In this chapter I want to focus on the principles underlying effective strategies for articulating a sociological understanding of sexuality within democratic political structures. Although political identity is necessary within democratic polities, I have argued that we need to reconceptualise sexual–democratic identity in order to illuminate the social construction of sexuality (and thus the social basis of the deviant stigmatisation of homosexuality). However, such a translation of sociological ideas into political identities and interventions remains difficult to theorise – and thus translate into practical proposals – unless we begin to explore the strategies of engagement which might give shape to new forms of identity and political processes. The structure of political processes in most Western societies means that we need a representative political identity both as a location from which to articulate our experiences and concerns and as a representation of our 'selves' to the wider political community (Gamson 1996; Weeks 1996) – Pitkin's 'symbolic' and 'descriptive' functions of representation (1967). In the realm of sexuality, I suggest that the problem is that homosexuals need to protect themselves from colluding with oppressive essentialist understandings of it and avoid promoting themselves as a semi-ethnic or natural group in an engagement with the democratic process.

In a cultural and political context in which our very existence is still not wholly legitimate, it is vital that we use our political identities and presence to illustrate that our 'interests' are not simply about demanding special rights for gays and lesbians, but that we share interests with the heterosexual majority in ethical relationships, freedom of expression and behaviour, and family forms. In this chapter I will suggest that our experiences need to be the focus of our aims in representing political 'interests' – emphasising the symbolic aspect of representation over and above the descriptive. In short, we need to use politics to push forward an understanding of sexuality and gender as important sociopolitical questions which concern the whole realm of social interaction and sexual relationships rather than frame lesbian and gay politics as a question of human rights or 'special interests' for a semi-ethnic group. In the first part of this chapter I will therefore deal with the question of how it is that we can represent ourselves and our interests to the wider political community without reaffirming essentialist understandings of sexuality. Underpinning this discussion is the theme of equality versus difference as the basis of strategies for engaging in political processes. Drawing on the parallel debates within feminist social and political theory (Phillips 1993; Young 1989), I will discuss the implications behind arguing either for equality or difference and in doing so I also bring some resolution to the question – posed in the introduction and Chapter 1 – of what we mean by gay liberation or equality. Drawing on my critique of Queer theory in the previous chapter, I suggest that although social equality can be achieved through a recognition of differences – it is the differential experiences of gays and lesbians and the different treatment of them that must be the primary focus – those differences are created through inequalities rather than differences *per se*. Moreover, these differences must be understood as socially produced and socially structured rather than as reflective of some natural or moral division of sex, gender and sexuality.

How do we then achieve equality or liberation in current social and political conditions? Strategies of citizenship have become the mainstay of current political engagement and are used in conjunction with human rights discourses and the deployment of an 'equal rights/universal' gay and lesbian political identity. I suggest that the focus on rights produces an emphasis on legal or policy measures as the exclusive guarantee of social equality rather than an understanding of these advances as simply one limited and relatively abstract indication of formal status under the law. Drawing on some recent discussions about the extension of rights to gays and lesbians, I suggest that we need to conceptualise rights which can become the basis for social equivalence rather than strict formal equality – rights which recognise social differences and inequalities rather than those which are universal and applied equally to all (Rahman

Exploring political strategies 151

1998; Kingdom 1991). Rights can thus be understood as the formal underpinning to equivalent conditions of citizenship and I go on to discuss the different realms of citizenship: legal, political, civil and social and – borrowing from Ken Plummer's ideas (1995) – add the realm of the intimate. Given my discussion of the equality/difference debate, I am critical of the focus on citizenship and equal rights precisely because of the universalist heritage upon which such strategies draw. Moreover, I argue that we need to think about the sexual, gendered construction of citizenship (Carver 1998; Richardson 1998; Walby 1994) and begin to explore ways in which both rights and citizenship can be reconceptualised into differentiated concepts which deliver or underpin social equivalence. Furthermore, as a complement to this formal element of gay and lesbian politics, I suggest that we need to think about pursuing forms of group representation as a way of addressing these failings in rights and citizenship. This has already been suggested by many feminist theorists in their parallel discussions of democratic theory and gender inequalities (Phillips 1993; Young 1989). Moreover, strategies of group representation allow us to consider a conceptualisation of the symbolic aspect of political identity in more detail – such strategies should allow a more practical theorisation of a sociologically astute version of sexual political identity.

To move into the institutionalised political scene is to attempt to consider forms of representation which promote social location and social experiences as a basis for political identity. I engage in a discussion of some historical methods of group representation in order to illustrate that the question of representing difference and diversity is not only complex but has been exercising political thinkers for over two centuries. However, drawing on more recent feminist interventions in this area, I argue that we need to pursue representation within democratic systems in order to pluralise concepts of citizenship, rights and understandings of the social experiences of gays and lesbians. In conclusion I argue that this engagement with democracy does not necessarily entail a replacement of current systems of territorial representation based on individual votes cast, but rather the complement of an addition of some form of deliberative engagement of oppressed groups with political participation, decision making and policy implementation. It is this strategy which I suggest provides the best way forward for developing a queried sense of political identity which challenges the essentialism within sexuality and democracy. However, I acknowledge throughout this chapter that my discussion can only be the beginnings of an exploration of political strategies and so further areas of theorisation and research are left to my overall conclusion which follows this chapter.

ARTICULATING SOCIOLOGY

Before moving to a discussion of differences versus equality and the associated political strategies, I feel that I must address one very obvious point. Could we not, perhaps, merely make sure that all forms of gay and lesbian activism, together with feminist groups, articulated a sociological understanding of both identity and social inequalities? In fact, is this not already the case in the vast majority of political interventions? In truth there is no consistent plea from lesbian, gay, or feminist groups with regards to policies sought or social conditions desired on behalf of their groups. Most of these groups, indeed most social minority groups, ask for equality but the terms and meaning of this equality can vary enormously. What I have suggested throughout this study is that, as a starting point, we need firmly to reject essentialist understandings both within our own communities and in the wider political context. At this level of activism, we need to engage in the process of contesting discourse, and begin to provide alternative discourses or narratives of personal sexual careers which allow space for an emphasis on the social construction of sexuality. Although I have argued that this lack of a sensitive sociological account of subjectivity has been the unfinished business of a sociology of sexuality, I acknowledge that the very existence of contemporary gay and lesbian narratives is a significant advance on the conditions of ten or twenty years ago. It seems clear that gay and lesbian identities and culture are no longer invisible and although many writers have emphasised the material underpinnings to the development of the gay 'world' (Adam 1985; Altman 1980; Weeks 1989), I think it is important to recognise that being publicly present – in popular culture, Gay Pride marches, political campaigns or legal challenges – does contest the understanding of homosexuality as shameful, hidden and secret. Given that all these events happily co-exist within a heterosexually ordered society, my concern is whether this new pluralisation of sexual stories actually contests essentialism as the basis of institutionalised heterosexuality. The illumination of difference is important because those differences (of gay and lesbian lives) have been previously marginalised. But are differences an inevitable challenge to oppression when that oppression is constructed through essentialist psychological and moral frameworks? In this sense, I am suggesting that inequalities between sexual identities are not rooted simply in the dominance of heterosexuality as a social institution, but rather that institutionalised or compulsory heterosexuality (Rich 1980) is an effect of the exploitation which constitutes gender divisions – which are still legitimised with recourse to essentialist discourses of gender and thus sexuality. Historical analyses of the development of the social significance of sexuality are all agreed on this point – that male homosexuality came into being as a social identity as part of the processes which institutionalised a rigid division of gender identities (Delphy and Leonard 1992; McIntosh 1968; Weeks 1989). Does the pluralisation of difference through visibility challenge ideas about the naturalness of gender and sexual divisions – does it allow us to discuss how all sexual relationships have social significance and are to be understood through dimensions of social interaction – that we all achieve our sense of sexuality?

I have argued throughout that it is at the personal level that we need to make new interventions in order to challenge the ideological effects of essentialist discourse. It is clear that individual sexual stories or narratives are permeated with essentialist ideas, even when the speaker is relating a story of change and plasticity in sexual identity (Plummer 1995; Whisman 1996). Moreover, when research illuminates the divisions of power within sexual relationships, and the social boundaries and constraints which construct oppressed gendered and sexual identities, it is clear that we lack alternative discourses which individuals can use to discuss these issues of social construction (Holland et al. 1998). There is, therefore, an urgent need for more empirical research and, while I have been engaged in a theoretical analysis throughout this book, I have tried to remain sensitive to the application of that theory as a tool of empirical analysis. I have already suggested ways in which theorists may begin to translate a structurally grounded interactionist version of subjectivity into an intelligible explanation of the sense of a core and stable sexual identity. In one sense this is a call to theorists and activists to think through ways of translating sociopolitical critiques into new stories which people can use to account for themselves. Research into sexuality is producing a vast diversity of biographies and autobiographies and, as Morgan says, it is important for sociology to bring out the social world in all its complexity and to 'make a difference' (1998). I have already referred to this aspect of sensitising sociological analysis to personal lives and I will return to a discussion of the implications this has for research agendas in the conclusion.[1] However, we also need to challenge the fora in which essentialist discourse is promoted and sustained. We need to change the structural contexts in which narratives are produced; we need to make it easier for people to tell alternative sexual stories (Plummer 1995) and we need to find ways of disseminating such research more widely and translating it more effectively into popular discourses. Taking up this theme, I want to focus on the ways in which we might make a difference through politics and to the political process.

I have argued earlier that the proto-constructionist analysis of sexuality within Gay Liberation (Epstein 1992) failed to take hold at a personal level because there was no similarly astute or sensitive analysis of sexual subjectivity. There is still precious little research into personal histories which makes it beyond academia into general cultural discourses. In order to disseminate versions of diversity and difference, we cannot simply rely upon leakage from academia but we would need transformations in sex education, media representations and, indeed, our own political positions. Since this would inevitably challenge the naturalness of heterosexuality as institution and the essentialism on which it is based, it is doubtful whether this can be achieved without some form of institutionalised advocacy or representation within the political realm of both the state and dominant professional groups such as the law and medicine.

To provide an illumination of the social basis of inequalities will be difficult to achieve without a thoroughgoing critique of gender divisions and the associated moral components to essentialist ideas and practices. Such a critique will be very difficult to operationalise in democratically organised systems where both the state and the majority identify with heterosexuality as a natural and desirable phenomenon. For example, the trajectory of AIDS/HIV policies in both Britain and the United States was initially governed by the essentialist discourse, both in terms of its moral judgements on the deviant nature of penetrative homosexual male sex and in terms of an understanding of 'exclusive' sexual behaviour corresponding to 'exclusive' categories of homosexual and heterosexual (Altman 1986; Aggleton *et al.* 1989, 1990; Schramm-Evans 1990; Weeks 1996). Access to decision making and policy construction and implementation was denied to gay groups, although this later changed in Britain, especially when research demonstrated that there were a significant number of 'men who had sex with men' but did not identify as 'homosexual' (Freeman 1992). However, the access to policy decisions is still not fully institutionalised, and a fierce debate continues about why fewer resources are devoted to gay organisations when they represent one of the most severely affected communities. The example of policies addressing AIDS/HIV raises a number of political questions which serve to illustrate my more general themes. First, I would argue that gay men need a pragmatic form of representation of their experiences in dealing with AIDS/HIV. This cannot be constructed in terms of interest group pressure, but more in terms of constructing and applying policies effectively and meaningfully – access to the processes of decision making and policy implementation would allow both a group-specific experience to be addressed and allow for connections to be made through dialogue with other affected groups.

Second, the belated incorporation of gay groups into consultative procedures surrounding AIDS/HIV issues allowed a partial critique of binary essentialist categories of sexuality and also a critique of disembodied and technical prescriptions for safer sex (Aggleton *et al.* 1989, 1990). At a more general level, what I suggest is that we need to find ways of pluralising the effective deployment of identity with the realms of representation and democratic fora, in order to reiterate at every opportunity that 'identity' is a container for diverse social experiences and behaviour rather than an indication of a monolithic 'natural' group of people. I have already suggested that we need to do this by articulating our experiences of inequality as social. But, even if we have an alternative discourse, even if we are trying to focus our politics on social relationships, how far does this achieve the translation into effective deployment of identity within democratic discourses and structures? This is the question which occupies me for the rest of this chapter, and although I have tried to acknowledge the diversity of gay and lesbian political organisations and perspectives throughout this book, I want to explore how far we can 'articulate sociology' within pragmatic and institutional contexts. To begin this discussion, however, we need first to consider whether we are articulating differences or inequalities in our analysis of sexual divisions and inequalities, and what implications such an emphasis has for the strategic deployment of political identities.

DIFFERENCES OR INEQUALITIES?

I have argued in the section above that we need to keep a focus on resisting essentialist ideas about gender and sexuality if we are to challenge the consequences of those ideas. While it is both impractical and unnecessary for diverse political groupings to adopt one particular version of sociological articulation or identity, it is important that a sociological critique remain a common theme in the realm of sexual politics. However, there is a more specific debate at present about the kind of sociological critique which is appropriate to both gender and sexual politics and this debate centres of the question of whether we should articulate, through interventions and political identities, an analysis of socially constructed inequalities or a promotion of social differences.

The debate about the purpose of the annual Lesbian and Gay Pride march in London signifies the tensions within the various communities which go towards making up the collective of alternative or dissident sexual identities. On the one hand, there are those who argue that the march should become a parade and thus lose all its explicitly political connotations, becoming instead a celebration of the cultural diversity of lesbian, gay, bisexual, transgendered and transsexual identities. This is an argument for illuminating and promoting differences: both differences from the heterosexual norm and between and among all stigmatised sexualities. On the other hand, there are those who resist such a move because they argue that such a visible and large event must retain an annual political theme in order to remind participants, the state and the wider (heterosexual and homosexual) society that social and political equality remains a fantasy for many non-heterosexuals (Simpson 1996; Wilson 1997).[2] Of course this tension is underpinned by debates about the benefits and drawbacks of the commercialisation of Pride and the evident commodification of gay and lesbian lifestyles (Evans 1993; Simpson 1996) but my point is simply to suggest that Pride serves as a major context in which identities are deployed and that there are political implications for the ways in which this deployment occurs.

When we raise concerns about the direction of gay and lesbian scenes and lifestyles, it is not simply a disquiet about rampant consumerism but a profound discomfort with the political goals and strategies which this sort of identity dictates. Put crudely, there is a potential that the simple parade of alternative sexualities will shift the focus from social inequality to social difference, with the implication that the communities which represent themselves at Pride have chosen to do so out of a sense of celebration rather than oppression. Referring to the annual Pride march in London, a heterosexual male friend of mine asked me recently: 'Will you be going to Smug this year?' The problem is therefore not only that our friends may find us self-satisfied in our gay or lesbian identities, but that such an interpretation relies on the perception that there is really nothing wrong with the lives of lesbians, gays, bisexuals and in fact, that we can happily co-exist in equilibrium with institutionalised heterosexuality. Moreover, this shift of focus to social and cultural difference has been compounded by the impact of theoretical work on sexuality from both Queer theorists and those from within feminism who advocate the pluralisation of difference as a way of overcoming social inequality.[3]

How is it that the proliferation and recognition of differences can aid the struggle to overcome social inequality? In her discussion of Nancy Fraser's critique of identity politics, Iris Young reminds us that 'for the movements that Fraser is most concerned with, however, – namely, women's movements, movements of people of colour, gay and lesbian movements, movements of poor and working-class people – a politics of recognition functions more as a means to, or element in, broader ends of social and economic equality, rather than as a distinct goal of justice' (Young 1997: 156). This rationale is sometimes forgotten by those criticising the development of identity and cultural politics. The arguments against a specifically ethnic sense of gay and lesbian identity have been well rehearsed as part of the critique of essentialism (Epstein 1992; Evans 1993; Weeks 1996) and also as part of a general concern within democratic theory that cultural politics does not challenge the economic underpinnings to inequality (Butler 1990a, 1991; Fraser 1997; Phillips 1993). I agree with Young and suggest therefore that the underlying point of identity politics is not simply to promote a recognition of cultural differences and toleration or acceptance of these differences, but that there is also a wider purpose of illuminating group experiences in order to demonstrate social, economic and political inequality. Of course in the case of sexual inequality, either through gender divisions or divisions of sexuality, it is simplistic to suggest that material relations are at the base of every form of social inequality. Sociohistorical researchers on sexuality point out time and again (and somewhat sarcastically in Foucault's case[4]) that essentialism did not develop from capitalist relations but rather in interaction with them (Barrett 1980; Hall 1982, 1992; Jackson 1992b; Weeks 1989). But to articulate a sociological critique of inequalities in the realm of sexuality is not to reduce these inequalities to reflexes of structural factors, but to suggest that sexuality has a social significance which is both complex and constructed through the intersections of many different social hierarchies.

Moreover, as I suggested in the previous chapter, a queried sense of political identity allows us a position from which to articulate such a critique without resorting to essentialist understandings of self or sexual hierarchies. A politics of identity constructed through the essentialist discourse is ultimately fruitless for lesbians and gays, because this discourse does not allow us to put forward any arguments for social equality but instead limits us to the role of a deviant minority in society, regardless of whether that deviance is regarded as naturally occurring or a chosen lifestyle. I am therefore not advocating an acceptance of identity politics as it is currently conceived – as political essentialism – but I do recognise that identity – as political presence (Phillips 1995) – serves a crucial purpose in the articulation of experiences and thus social inequality. We should therefore consider the ways in which we can deploy identity to illuminate our social experiences and the social forces which construct those experiences. There is no point in simply flaunting our cultural difference without a critique of why and how that difference has become and remains socially significant. In its broadest sense, gay and lesbian liberation or resistance must address the inequalities of the social construction of sexuality. I therefore suggest a turn away from an uncritical focus on differences *per se* and a return to a focus on social inequalities as the basis of perceptions and constructions of difference. However, this still leaves the problem of how our identities can be deployed effectively in order to become 'queried' versions of political and sexual essentialism. What strategies and identities allow us to use our socially significant difference to challenge inequalities?

In the case of lesbian and gay political movements, the preoccupation with equal rights and formal civil and legal equality is widespread, particularly in Britain and the USA but also within the more 'liberal' Scandinavian context (Rahman 1998). While each of these countries have very different political structures and cultures, they are all democratic states with the ideal of equal rights, individually ascribed, central to their democratic credentials. At first sight, equal rights strategies must seem the intuitive response to the many inequalities that lesbians and gays suffer. This strategy falls into the pattern of the pursuit of minority protection which is evident in many of these states or, to think of it in another way, the pursuit of the extension of civil and political citizenship to lesbians and gays, underwritten by formal rights. What often occurs in these campaigns is the presentation of a lesbian or gay community through a deployment of identity within the political process but, all too often, that identity is taken to represent a coherent community, thus reinforcing the idea of a discrete, different group within society (Evans 1993; Sinfield 1994). Far more rarely is there a deployment of identity which focuses on the social construction of homosexuality as deviant

Exploring political strategies 159

and thus challenges the social and political institutionalisation of 'compulsory heterosexuality' (Rich 1980).

It is in their critique of the limits and dangers of essentialist identity or ethnic/cultural politics that Queer theorists have suggested a way to work towards the deployment of difference in order to challenge inequality. Although I have stated my reluctance to endorse this perspective, I think it is important to consider the implications of Queer theories for the more institutionalised realm of politics. Queer theorists are explicit about the need for an attack on the dominant hegemonic discourse of heterosexuality. Their theoretical focus has been detailed in the previous chapter but it is important to remind ourselves that, despite the challenge to institutionalised heterosexuality and its associated binary gendered and sexual divisions, the aim of Queer politics is, in fact, not liberation but 'resistance' to the effects of power manifested within the essentialist, heterosexist discourse (Halperin 1995: 18). Thus, despite the understanding of social inequality which is explicit within its critique, Queer theory stands in opposition to traditional political identity because of the emphasis on the deconstruction of these discursive identities (Butler 1990, 1991, 1997; Phelan 1997) and also because of the 'normalising' (deradicalising) effects of institutionalised politics. I have already provided a critique of the relationship between political goals and identity within Queer theory but I want to emphasise again that Queer theorists do not reject reformist political goals or representation *per se*, but rather that they seek to emphasise these political discourses and strategies as effects of power, rather than as a means of liberation from the effects of power. The emphasis thus turns to promoting differences in order to resist and eventually shatter the discourse of heteronormativity and the social effects and institutions it supports. But given the reluctance to engage with traditional democratic structures and identities, what does this leave as the realm of sexual and gender politics?

What this leaves us is an emphasis on expanding the scope for transgressive and subversive performativity in micro-level social interactions. The irony of such an approach is that is locates oppositional politics in the realm of cultural activity and thus, in some senses, reinforces the understanding of lesbian and gay politics as representative of simply a cultural or ethnic/natural difference. Indeed, David Halperin's characterisation of Queer politics suggests a purely cultural deployment of identity with the emphasis on creative appropriation and resignification, appropriation and theatricalisation to undermine dominant forms of discourse, and exposure and demystification of the same (1995). Moreover, Butler's ideas of 'performativity' as gender construction and potential subversion (1990a, 1991) reinforce the grounds for such an interpretation.

Queer activism may illuminate differences and suggesting alternative discourses (Smyth 1992) but whether this serves to destabilise hegemonic heterosexuality is doubtful. Queer parodic performance is not necessarily read or received as anything subversive, either by other lesbians and gays or by those identified as heterosexual (Jackson and Scott 1996; A. Wilson 1997; E. Wilson 1993). Indeed, the likelihood is that the emphasis on challenging our social inequalities with heterosexuals is simply lost in the rush to elaborate and promote differences between and amongst the groups that make up our own sense of community. For example, the vast diversity of sexual desire and identity on parade at any large Pride march may well display differences within the so-called gay and lesbian community but it does little to engage the wider world of homosexuals who do not participate nor does it engage or challenge heterosexuals. I would argue that Pride is an example of how differences can be interpreted simply as another way of signifying deviance, enshrining our difference from a norm without challenging that norm. I am not suggesting that we return to the days when a white gay male and middle-class perspective served as the only perspective of lesbians and gays (Deitcher 1995; Seidman 1996) but I think that within Queer there is a danger that the pluralisation of difference remains uncontextualised – the social significance of those differences is de-emphasised in a pursuit of their celebration. Moreover, to a large extent this is an inevitable consequence of rejecting traditional forms of identity politics as normalising discourses. Queer theorists are champions of using positional identity, but this either becomes an underhand return to 'strategic essentialism' or it tends to ignore that people develop relatively stable senses of identity – the social life-course is a process but not one without either direction or strategy.

Despite my preference for a focus on inequalities rather than merely differences, I am still not exactly sure what a politics of experience – a sociologically grounded deployment of identity – might actually look like within its political contexts. In short, as Angelia Wilson pointedly asks of the Queer attempts to reconceptualise political identity: 'Where is all this getting us?' (1997: 100). We need to think about how we will effectively deploy identity and strategy in order to challenge social inequalities in the realm of sexuality. As I have argued already, one central aim of our

Exploring political strategies 161

strategy must be to deploy identities, not simply to serve difference, but to articulate sociology – to show that deviance is socially constructed and reflects social inequalities. For this to occur it seems that we need to pluralise the fora, and ease the access to them, in which non-heterosexuals can discuss their experiences and have some control or input over decision making. In the rest of this chapter I want to consider specific examples of political strategies as a way of fleshing out a more 'queried' sense of political identity and I begin with a discussion of the political context in which such strategies must operate.

THE CONTEXT OF DEMOCRACY

I have tried to acknowledge throughout this study that there is a diversity to gay and lesbian and feminist politics and, moreover, that each approach has its specific context and legitimacy. I am not therefore denying the benefit of more cultural approaches to sexual politics as adopted in many aspects of gay and lesbian activism but I am unsure as to whether these forms of activity are as effective in challenging both sexual and political essentialism as is hoped. Moreover, I do not think that we can ignore institutionalised forms of political activity precisely because they are also normalising in terms of essentialist understandings of self and sexuality. Since the days of visible gay and lesbian political movements, democracy has also become part of the social construction of sexuality. In Britain and the USA – the twin centres of gay liberation – the context of politics has been a specifically liberal form of representative democracy.

> Liberal democracy appears triumphant and its main modern rival, Marxism, in a state of disarray. Those who have championed alternatives to liberal democracy appear either less confident than ever about these, or are engaged in a process of re-examining their merits in relationship to liberalism, democracy, and other traditions of political and social thought. (Held 1993: 1)

Despite the apparent triumph of democracy in the late twentieth century, we must remain aware that it is a particular model that is now laden with the democratic mantle. Democracy in Western capitalist states is predominantly understood as liberal democracy: in the West the practice of democracy is varied and there are equally varied theoretical justifications and explanations of what democracy is, or should be.[5] However, as my focus has been on gay and lesbian politics in the UK and USA, it is important to set out the settlement of both liberalism and democracy which underpins these states and is increasingly common in other democracies. David Held provides a useful summary of democratic credentials:

> This cluster includes elected government; free and fair elections in which every citizen's vote has an equal weight; a suffrage which embraces all citizens irrespective of race, religion, class, sex and so on; freedom of conscience, information and expression on all public matters broadly defined; the right of all adults to oppose their government and stand for office; and associational autonomy – the right to form independent associations including social movements, interest groups and political parties. (Held 1993: 21)

The form that democracy takes in these states is representative and elitist; for most people participation is limited to voting for a representative and only a minority are involved in political parties. The relationship between the state and civil society is characterised by limits: the state is limited to legitimate spheres of direct influence and civil society is outwith this influence and comprised of individual citizens, families, associations and organisations. Associations and organisations may or may not function as pressure groups or as organised interests, but it is their potential to do so which is seen as the main mode of influence for various social groups within liberal democracies. This ideal of a pluralist society is problematic because the resources to form groups and to gain access to the political agenda and policy process are not, on the whole, guaranteed or underwritten by the state.[6] Therefore, the importance and influence of social groups is dependent on the social relationships, hierarchies and inequalities that determine the material, political and social resources available to them. Rather than engage in a critique of pluralist theory, however, I want to concentrate on the limits of the liberal democratic settlement, both in terms of participation and the divisions between public (state) and private spheres.

Government is by representative means, through the election of members of political parties and so it is obvious that only a minority or elite will be directly involved in agenda setting and decision making. Active political participation is very limited in liberal democracies when compared to the ideas of direct democracy, civic republicanism or some other form of participatory democracy (Held 1993; Phillips 1993). In the bleakest interpretation, representation reduces participation to a choice

Exploring political strategies 163

between either casting a vote every five years or so, or joining the elites who may form the government in the shape of one political party or another.[7] Since, for the majority, representation removes direct control over decision making, two issues become vital in assessing the credentials of this form of democracy: first, who is to represent whom? and second, how effective is representation at delivering the wishes of the represented? I will return to these questions at the end of this section, but first it is important to reiterate that issues of gay and lesbian inequality challenge traditional understandings of legitimate topics of politics.

In a liberal democracy the state is limited to the 'public' arena. This construction of a limited sphere of legitimate state intervention arises from a historical concern with freedom from despotism or autocratic rule and these limits allow for the complementary sphere of 'private' life and civil society. Of course, this implies that the state is the location of politics, becoming in many ways the exclusive arena for collective social decisions and thus implicitly removing the realm of private life from the political and therefore from issues of power, ethics and social justice. Although liberal democratic states have not been consistent in defining a public arena, particularly with the development of welfare states (Lister 1997), there is still an implicit idea that the state does not willingly intervene in family, moral or religious life (Richardson 1998; Walby 1994). In fact, this is a myth: the state has always been an actor in defining concepts of family, sexuality and morality, but the elected representatives often pretend to leave such issues to the 'private' realm of individual freedoms or they argue that they decide on such matters according to their individual consciences (Durham 1991; Richardson 1998). The crucial point for lesbians and gays is that sexual identities are characterised as both natural and indicative of moral status and are thus individualised. This 'essentialist' understanding of sexuality dominates cultural discourse in the West and therefore removes the sexual from the realm of legitimate political activity since sexuality is seen as a natural and immutable quality and the sexual order is understood as similarly natural and thus inevitable and not open to transformation through political activity.[8]

Underpinning the limits on the state and political participation is the focus on the 'individual as the basic unit in democratic life' (Phillips 1993: 114). The individual is both the fundamental unit of participation and the unit of privacy, with rights and protection from arbitrary action by the state ascribed on an individual basis. It is this individualist tendency in liberalism that has come under scrutiny from many democratic and feminist theorists because, as Iris Young puts it, 'this individualist ideology, however, in fact obscures oppression' (Young 1994: 718). Formal political equality, apportioned individually, ignores the social relationships and inequality that creates problems for the individual. Although any demand for representation is made in an individualist polity, the aim of the demand is to overcome inequality which derives from the membership by individuals of a particular, oppressed social group.

The dilemma for lesbians and gays is that sexual oppression is social in origin but political activity is often organised along individualist conceptualisations and practices. This is particularly problematic for lesbians and gays given that we are constructed not only as a numerical minority but also a morally deviant minority. Heterosexuality is the implicit numerical political majority and the institutionalisation of heterosexuality is taken to be the natural norm throughout culture, politics and policy. In the UK, it is unlikely that our political demands will be met in a system where only four homosexuals were elected to Parliament on the government (Labour) side. Not only are these four beholden to the party rather than an agenda for lesbian and gay liberation, but the Labour party's commitments to lesbian and gay freedoms are minimal.[9]

A parallel question has been addressed by feminist political theorists such as Carole Pateman and Anne Phillips, who argue that liberal democratic theory is conceptualised narrowly, focusing on political rights and then ascribing these on an individual basis. In a hierarchically gendered society, political practice derived from a concept of the individual as abstractly equal to all others effectively denies women equality, since it does not address group inequality that is structured socially rather than manifested politically (Phillips 1992).

As yet, no comparable effective analysis has been developed regarding gay and lesbian representation and equality. My aim is to develop an understanding of how lesbians and gays might engage with the democratic process in an attempt to achieve social equality. While much previous work has concentrated on social construction, there has been no detailed consideration of how this construction is reflected in and maintained by the conditions in democratic polities, and furthermore, whether there is a realistic prospect of fundamental social change through democratic processes. Is Clinton's wholesale abandonment of gay and lesbian equality inevitable within democracy? Must we always be understood in democracy as a minority interest group? Or is there a form of political intervention which we can construct and demand which allows us to change the structural conditions which underpin the social construction of sexuality? I move on to discuss

Exploring political strategies

these questions in the sections below, focusing in particular on the strategy of widening citizenship to include lesbians and gays and suggesting that we need to reconsider how effective this is at delivering gay and lesbian equality. Drawing on my argument about differences and inequalities, I suggest that such democratic engagement needs to be undertaken with an explicit articulation of socially structured inequalities of gender and sexuality which lead to the oppression of non-heterosexuals. I then move to a discussion of an alternative strategy which involves addressing the question of who should represent whom and I argue that we need to consider alternative means of political representation if we are to achieve the aim of articulating social inequalities of sexuality. Before that discussion, I want to expand on the point that articulating the social construction of sexuality challenges traditional concepts of legitimate political discussion by politicising the 'private' or intimate realm and, moreover, that exposing this oppression as social also provokes a dilemma of political strategy as well as one of political discourse.

SOCIAL OPPRESSION AND THE DILEMMA OF DIFFERENCE

I have argued throughout this study that contemporary sexual identities are constructed in part through democratic conditions as well as specifically gendered divisions. The social construction of sexuality has been detailed in the earlier chapters and I want to link this construction to the problems of political strategy and identity which are my focus in these later chapters. The suffrage in liberal democracies has come to include all citizens, and obviously this means all gay men and lesbians as well. Gay and lesbian social and political movements can be seen as an expression of the right to associational autonomy.[10] From this it would seem that all is fair and equal for gays and lesbians in the polity; we can organise without restriction and engage in political processes through lobbying, consultation and direct action. In complement to this access to the democratic components of liberal democracy, we may also be able to mobilise the liberal tradition in our support. There is an impeccable liberal case for homosexual equality since liberal democracy is fundamentally limited to the public sphere and sexual relationships are regarded as private activity. Beyond a minimal role of the protection of others from abuse and as a guarantor of private freedoms, sexual behaviour should not, therefore, be a concern of the state.

That this pluralist liberal democratic ideal is a fantasy for lesbians and gays is not in doubt. As abstract individuals, lesbians and gays have equal rights as citizens, but as gay men or lesbians they have no consistent equality with heterosexuals or the abstract ideal of the universal citizen. Thus the state will not question a lesbian's duty to pay income tax since that duty is defined by individual citizenship, but the state may (and overwhelmingly does) question her right to raise children, even her own, since then it is her sexual identity that matters, and being a lesbian is to be part of a deviant minority in Western society. In this example, the social significance of the identity lesbian automatically removes the individual from the category of abstract citizen and constructs her deviant, not only from the sexual and moral order but from accepted gender norms: lesbian parents dare to raise children outwith the patriarchal unit of a heterosexual family (Harne 1984; Rights of Women 1984). Not only does state regulation intrude upon the sexual, personal and family relationships of lesbians and gays but state policies also support and sustain the institutionalisation of heterosexuality (Abbott and Wallace 1992; Carabine 1996; Rich 1986). The condition of individual citizenship is abstract and does not take into account socially significant group identity.

> If we consider liberal democracy as an amalgam of certain key principles from the liberal and democratic traditions, what it takes from liberalism is an abstract individualism which may note the difference between us but says that these differences should not count. At its best, this is a statement of profound egalitarianism that offers all citizens the same legal and political rights, regardless of their wealth, status, race or sex. At its worst, it refuses the pertinence of continuing difference and inequality, pretending for the purposes of argument that we are all of us basically the same.
> (Phillips 1993: 114)

For gays and lesbians, as with women and ethnic minorities, this abstraction presents a problem since it is obvious that the practice in liberal democracies is to take note if you are homosexual and apply specific laws to gays and lesbians. Many gay and lesbian political organisations are concerned with achieving formal legal equality, such as Stonewall's campaign for an equal age of consent for gay men in the UK and the campaign to allow homosexuals to serve in the Armed Forces. In this sense, a large part of lesbian and gay political activity is focused on

Exploring political strategies 167

redressing the balance where laws are applied exclusively to lesbians and gays. In many ways, you can think of this type of activity as an attempt to return homosexuals to the abstract category of citizen by removing the significance of sexuality in the application of law and policy. These attempts are often characterised as the search for human (that is, universal) rights or simple legal equality. Although I am not criticising this dimension of gay and lesbian politics, I would argue that it is a strategy which is necessarily limited by the limits of liberal democracy. Specifically, once these formal legal rights or equalities have been won, we will not achieve the status of the abstract universal citizen because we will still be left with the problem of social oppression as a group constructed through the dominant essentialist social conceptualisation of sexuality.[11] Iris Young has neatly phrased the problem as a 'dilemma of difference':

> Contemporary social movements seeking full inclusion and participation of oppressed and disadvantaged groups now find themselves faced with a dilemma of difference. On the one hand, they must continue to deny that there are any essential differences between men and women, whites and blacks, able-bodied and disabled people that justify denying women, blacks or disabled people the opportunity to do anything that others are free to do or be included in any institution or position. On the other hand, they have often found it necessary to affirm that there are often group-based differences between men and women, whites and blacks, able-bodied and disabled people that make application of a strict principle of equal treatment, especially in competition for positions, unfair because these differences put these groups at a disadvantage.
> (Young 1989: 266)

It is social oppression that constructs many of the groups currently pressing for political representation, and it is for this reason that I suggest that lesbians and gays should join women, ethnic minorities and the disabled (to name some of the groups trying to deal with their difference and inequality) since it is the social construction of sexuality which creates and sustains the oppression of sexual 'minorities'. Most of these groups argue for a wider view of democracy insofar as they seek self-government as groups, more access to decision making and, in some cases, group-specific legislation (Guinier 1994; Phillips 1993; Young 1989). These demands are clearly at odds with the conceptualisation of liberal democracy described above. A central theme in these criticisms of liberal democratic theory and practice is the implication that a much stronger framework of participation is required in order to include diversity within the polity which thus raises the central question of who can and should represent whom. Furthermore, these critics of liberal democracy refute the notion that liberal democratic political activity actually is, or should be, limited to a 'public' sphere. The alternative prescription is that democratic theory and practice needs to engage with the social relationships and hierarchies within society because these forces construct apparently private institutions such as the family and apparently individual qualities such as morality and sexuality. A parallel argument for women illustrates this frustration with liberal democracy:

> For the first time in history, liberal individualism promised women an equal social standing with men as naturally free individuals, but at the same time socio-economic developments ensured that the subordination of wives to husbands continued to be seen as natural, and so outside the domain of democratic theorists or the political struggle to democratise liberalism. (Pateman 1983: 207)

Those that constitute the social category of women clearly need to reconceptualise democracy so that the private sphere of relations within the family and between the genders is seen as a legitimate arena of politics rather than a matter for individual relationships, and so that the constitutive links between these realms and the public spheres – such as the economy for example – are made explicit (Phillips 1993). Indeed, this has been the political aim of many feminist theorists and feminist campaigns. The underlying theoretical rationale is that so-called intimate relations and natural attributes are, in fact, products of social relationships, hierarchies and organisation and are thus socially constructed. Of course, if the personal is seen as political then these arenas of social life become legitimate targets for political intervention. There is a similarly social constructionist position in the critiques formulated of the understanding of sexuality in the West (Foucault 1980; Weeks 1989; and see the collections edited by Jackson and Scott 1996, and Richardson 1996). I argue that gay and lesbian liberation and equality requires a conceptualisation of democracy that allows our politics to confront the incorporation of the essentialist construction of sexuality into both the polity and the wider cultural and civil society. In short, we need a politics focused on social relationships and our social experiences rather than individual attributes, and, moreover, a means of representation which acknowledges group membership as a definitive component of social life rather than abstracting individuals into 'universal' citizens. Before I explore group representation as a means of achieving both sociological articulation and a queried sense of sexual and political identity, I want to deal with strategies of citizenship because they are the mainstay of current gay and lesbian politics and identities. Despite the preceding discussion, I do not intend to dismiss such strategies as inevitably normalising, but rather I want to explore the interdependence of political strategies and set up citizenship rights as the broader context to a more specific call for group representation.

CITIZENSHIP, RIGHTS AND SEXUAL EQUALITY

Within gay and lesbian politics, democratic strategies in use at present tend to focus on discourses of citizenship and human rights. For example, a recent mailing from Stonewall warns that 'the Bill to equalise the age of consent will soon be back in the House of Lords. It is the most fundamental challenge this century for lesbians, gay men and everyone who believes in human rights . . . we want to hand her [Baroness Young, who led the opposition to the amendment in June 1998] the biggest postal petition in Stonewall's history so the Lords cannot ignore the human right to an equal age of consent.' (Stonewall leaflet, London, 1999). Equal rights before the law are understood as the central plank in the construction of equal conditions of citizenship.[12]

Marshall's categorisation of citizenship has been much criticised for being evolutionist and universalist, but the three spheres of civil, political and social citizenship (1950) do allow us to think through the conditions which have been achieved in the pursuit of 'equality'. Walby (1994) argues that citizenship is a gendered concept because the development of the conditions which Marshall and others have discussed have been in a different order for women and have also not been achieved evenly across class and race. She also suggests that the realm of social citizenship has been seen as synonymous with welfare state policies and resources and since these have assumed a heterosexual nuclear family unit, women have been cast as dependent on men rather than autonomous individuals. Furthermore, the interdependence of income benefits and earnings has, on the whole, discriminated against women since their ability to earn is reduced through family care work or extended breaks from work for childcare reasons (Carabine 1996; Lister 1997; Walby 1994).

Given these conditions in women's citizenship and the fact that the construction of sexuality currently entwines women's oppression with that of homosexuals, the question of citizenship is a complex one for lesbians and gays (Richardson 1998). On the whole, we share in the civil and political citizenship of most of our social contemporaries when we are subsumed under the general and abstract category of 'citizen'. There are obvious exceptions and these are in effect when we are identified as 'lesbian' or 'gay' or in any form of a morally or sexually 'perverse' identity. In the realm of social citizenship we are more explicitly regarded as either a deviant minority who are excluded from the decision-making process, or social citizenship is constructed in such a way, linking to some issues in political and civil arenas, as to deliberately exclude us (Carabine 1996; Richardson 1998).

Obviously we need to employ a discourse of political, civil and social equality to facilitate advances for lesbians and gays but, as Carabine (1996) points out, this will inevitably confront the discourse of heteronormativity and so challenge the naturalness and privilege of institutionalised heterosexuality. We need to trouble the abstract conceptualisation and assumption of the universal citizen as heterosexual. For gays and lesbians, as with women and ethnic minorities, this abstraction presents a problem. Specific laws apply to gays and lesbians in both civil and social realms (although perhaps not in specifically political realms) which deny us the conditions in which to achieve full citizenship. However, many gay and lesbian political organisations and campaigns focus on achieving formal equality (witness Stonewall's campaign for an equal age of consent in the UK) but these campaigns rarely challenge social inequality because they rarely confront heteronormativity. The terms of equality being sought are rarely neutral. For example, the age of consent applied only to women when it was first encoded into law in 1885 and there is still no legislation which encodes 'consent' for heterosexual men (Waites 1998). Gay men are therefore seeking a formal equality which encodes the notion of feminine sexuality as passive (they consent to having 'it' done to them). Other examples include the legal recognition of same-sex partnerships and the right to parent. All of these issues are important in that they exclude gays and lesbians, but this is because they are based on a heterosexual model of sexual relationships and family forms. Therefore, the privileges accorded in law are based on normative

Exploring political strategies 171

heterosexuality. Perhaps what we should be arguing for are laws which do not privilege one form of sexual identity over any others; laws which provide equal recognition of our different lives rather than those which use heterosexuality as the benchmark for human rights. The problematic nature of equality is indicative of the second difficulty in pursuing equal rights.

Rights are too often framed as a means of achieving equality with heterosexuals. This can serve to endorse institutions such as the heterosexual family which feminists, lesbians and gays have long questioned. Instead rights are pursued as if equality for lesbians and gays could be accommodated within the existing social order, without significantly undermining heteronormativity. The interwoven relationship of sexuality, morality and liberty is left untroubled by a political agenda which does not question the social construction of sexuality: heterosexual freedoms exist because they occupy the privileged position in the normative order, not because they are the natural, moral human freedoms. We must not mistake heterosexual rights for universal human rights.

Formal equality can too often lead to the continuing enshrinement of social inequalities. The focus on such forms of political activism is understandable, especially given the general withdrawal of the state from social rights symptomatic of financial crises across Western capitalist countries but most acutely seen in the UK and USA (Evans 1993). Indeed, it is these conditions, together with the increasing emphasis on consumer capitalism, which Evans argues has underpinned the development of sexual citizenship – the trade-off whereby he suggests that the freedom of sexual minorities to pursue sexuality within certain spaces and through leisure (consumption activities) dictates that sexual citizenship for these minorities entails material freedoms for a limited access to sociopolitical and civil citizenship. As Evans suggests, a sociological critique of sexuality suggests a need for political engagement with the social conditions which underpin sexuality and so we need to broaden our concept of citizenship away from the merely legal and civil realms and also away from the material freedoms which we enjoy as capitalist consumers.

The recent work in this area uses terms such as sexual or intimate citizenship to describe new forms of regulation (Evans 1993) or new terrains of democratisation (Plummer 1995; Giddens 1992). What is clear is that the discourses of both equality and citizenship carry such moral and popular weight within democracies (Kingdom 1991) that we do need to find points of convergence between a sociological critique of sexual inequalities and political strategies of rights and citizenship. I suggest that we can only do this through a twofold strategy. While we must continue to pursue even the most basic of civil and legal rights, we must also agitate for a realm of dialogue with other communities and the state – the realm of a politics of experiences. Rights discourse enjoys a moral privilege within democracy which we would be foolish to ignore (ibid.), and we share a concern with constitutional enshrinement of rights with many other communities and marginalised groups. At this level, perhaps we must accept that individually ascribed rights will always conflate individual attributes with social conditions, thereby emphasising the protection of a 'minority' or provision of abstract equality rather than equivalent social conditions. I have argued elsewhere that essentialism underpins the discourse of rights through this shift of focus from social conditions to individual significance (Rahman 1998) but I also accept that equal rights provide some basic legal frameworks within which we can seek to expand ideas of who is a valid citizen.

As I have said above, we need to pursue rights which do not assume a natural heterosexual norm or natural gender divisions. Perhaps we would do well to remember that the Equal Rights Amendment to the constitution of the USA has not been approved by enough individual states for its ratification, and legislation varies enormously from state to state (Elman 1996) even though federal legislation – on the whole – promotes gender-neutral approaches to public policy. A natural explanation of an attribute such as gender (as equated with physiological sex) is not, it seems, enough to guarantee comprehensive social and political equality.

In combination with the pursuit of rights, how is it that we can pursue a realm of articulation? One of the ways forward which is suggested by current work is the idea of intimate citizenship (Plummer 1995), which suggests that there is a new and emergent concern with the ethics and politics of relationships, both intimate and sexual. This democratisation of the personal realm (Giddens 1992) confronts the conceptualisation of rights and the state in traditional liberal democracies. Implicit in liberal democracy is the limiting of the state, broadly speaking, to the 'public' arena. This is derived from liberalism's concern with freedom from despotism or autocratic rule, but also merges with the democratic necessity of making collective social decisions. Although liberal democratic states have not been consistent in defining a public arena, particularly with the development of welfare states, there is still an implicit idea that the state does not willingly intervene in family, moral or religious life. This is a myth and particularly so in the regulation of sexual behaviour (Foucault 1980; Weeks 1989, 1977). The state has consistently been involved in defining concepts of family and morality, but its most public face, the elected representatives, often appear to leave such issues to the 'private' realm of individual freedoms.

The articulation of such a realm of citizenship necessarily calls for an engagement of the state with the inequalities which exist currently within that realm. It is perhaps in this way in which the discourses of equality and citizenship can be made to meld with a sociological understanding of the construction of sexuality and the processes of constructing subjectivity. Again, I suggest that to deploy a marginal sexual identity within such a debate requires a politics of experiences which is concerned with dialogue to illuminate the common concerns we share in moral and ethical discourses on relationships and gender inequalities. It is at this point that I think we should begin an exploration of the current ideas surrounding different forms of representation for socially oppressed groups as a complement to more traditional political strategies. Moreover, a discussion of group representation returns us to the theme of political identity and begins to flesh out how identity might be deployed to represent experiences rather than essential sexualities.

REPRESENTING EXPERIENCES

Claims of rights and for representation are based not only on the appeal to democratic discourse of universal citizenship and equality (Young 1989) but also on the assumption that the political subject has some ontological integrity. Thus, the argument so often goes, certain groups need political representation and rights to protect them because they are 'natural minorities' who have immutable characteristics which produce discrimination in the 'majority' community. Radical sexual political identity must therefore reflect a non-essentialist understanding of all aspects of sexuality if we are to overcome the deviant stigma which the essentialist construction of sexuality dictates for lesbians and gays. As I have already engaged in a critique of individualist rights, I want to focus on the means of representation that might facilitate a politics of experience. As discussed in the introduction to this study, it is group representation which is the logical avenue to travel in seeking the inclusion of experiences within the polity in a form which does not necessarily presuppose an essential identity and allows us to focus on social conditions rather than 'natural' effects. Group representation has been a constant source of tension within democratic theory and practice. Along one dimension this is simply the worry of reconciling plural opinions and interests within an existing political system: throughout the history of democracy, the entry of particular groups into the polity through the extension of suffrage has been regarded as potentially destabilising or subversive, particularly in the case of the working classes and women (Hobsbawm 1995). In liberal democracies, however, the expansion of the right to vote has always been allocated to the individual person rather than the social group to which they belong. In this sense, there has never been an explicit attempt to provide a means of representation for social groups as a group. It is this avenue which many contemporary democratic and feminist theorists have been exploring in an attempt to achieve what universal suffrage has largely failed to deliver – an effective means of addressing the social relationships which underpin group inequality.

Group representation therefore raises fundamental questions about representation in democracy, both who is to represent whom and how representation is to prove effective as a means of delivering equality, justice or fair treatment. Given that gays and lesbians are viewed as a distinct group in society, group representation is an obvious avenue to travel in seeking equality, justice or fair treatment. Although gays and lesbians are, on the whole, characterised as deviant and a minority group, it is their claim as an oppressed group that would underpin any demand for political representation. As an extremely diverse social group – at the very least divided by gender – they highlight the questions about representation particularly well. In the following section, I want to consider some methods of group representation which have been employed in various democratic states. Although none of these methods has been adopted for specifically gay or lesbian groups, it is worth considering their potential impact on such constituencies in order to illuminate the problems and issues which underpin the more contemporary debates around democracy and difference which will be my concluding focus.

THE RELEVANCE AND PROBLEMS OF METHODS OF GROUP REPRESENTATION

In this section I will consider various proposals for group representation and their applicability to lesbians and gays; consociationalism, federalism, functionalism and proportional representation. Consociationalism is an explicit attempt to incorporate group representation within liberal democratic structures. Lijphart's description of consociational democracies

Exploring political strategies

gives a full account of the social conditions and political structures which such democracies exhibit (1977) although his account is mainly derived from a consideration of The Netherlands. For my purposes here it is enough to consider the main practices: proportional representation in the executive for all significant groups, a mutual veto for each group, and segmental autonomy over social policy areas.

Lijphart contends that for consociation to work there must be multi-centres of power as well as some overarching loyalty. This would immediately suggest a problem for the representation of women or homosexuals, since both groups potentially challenge the social order, women by seeking to overturn gender divisions and gays and lesbians in seeking to overturn the dominance of a heterosexual norm. This problem illustrates the criticism that consociation is in practice concerned with the pragmatic accommodation of groups that would threaten the stability of the polity if excluded from power. Obviously this characterisation of a social group is difficult to apply to territorially, racially and materially diverse groups such as women, lesbians or gays since they have neither a dominant geographical or cultural base around which to organise nor a single set of issues around which to mobilise politically. Although the same can be said of most racial or ethnic minorities, historical immigration or settlement patterns may have lead to 'ghettoisation' which then provides a geographical basis for territorial representative politics. In truth, this pattern has only developed in large cities in the US and has been helped along by some decisions of the courts when the issue of redistricting political constituencies has arisen.[13] The territorial aspect of consociation is not a viable option for lesbians and gays, and neither would the cultural or political aspect of group characterisation seem to reflect the diversity and differences of opinion within the lesbian and gay communities.[14]

A related problem with consociationalism is that it is an explicitly elitist form of democracy. Although it is possible to argue that logic dictates that representation implies an elite of decision makers, many of the groups pressing for representation advocate a participatory approach to politics (Phillips 1993, 1995). This may not be incompatible with selecting an elite to represent one's group at the very top level of politics, but it does raise the problem of how to represent diversity within a narrow, elite focused system. For example, would one gay man or lesbian be able to reflect the interests of all gays and lesbians, or one woman represent the class, religious and racial diversity of all women? Elites seem even less appealing when you consider studies that have shown that those participating in elite politics from under-represented groups tend to need to achieve the same sociological profile as those who already make up the elite. So women, blacks and poor people need to be well resourced, educated, articulate and implicitly heterosexual; in short they need to be like the white middle-class men already in the elite (see Chapman's 1992 study on women's recruitment into political elites and my similar research, Rahman 1994 and Phillips' arguments, 1995). Therefore, not only is it unlikely that those who are socially oppressed will be able to make it into political elites which are comprised of the socially dominant, but if they do make it in by achieving the appropriate sociological profile, one can legitimately question how well they will then be able to represent those whom they may still resemble, but no longer live as or identify with. On the whole, because the practices of consociationalism are pragmatic ones, there is no clear conceptualisation of democracy or social groups underpinning the principles of consociation. Consociation is therefore not an appropriate conceptualisation of either the condition of gays and lesbians as a social group or their relationship to the social (heterosexual) majority. However, its practical merits should not be ignored: the representation of gays and lesbians within decision-making bodies and the guarantee of a veto would promote lesbian and gay freedoms as would the autonomy over cultural policies, and I will return to these issues later in this discussion; but I turn now to federalism.

As a proposal for group representation, federalism is traditionally identified with territorial representation and therefore the groups it is appropriate for must be territorially gathered. This may well be possible for religious, racial or ethnic minorities but it is dependent on historical patterns of settlement. Moreover, as discussed in the previous section, in the case of women or homosexuals there is no likelihood that a common geographical location will emerge. While it is clear that in some cities and constituencies in the United States, gay and lesbian voters are a significant block and will vote with this in mind, it is also clear that not everybody who is gay or lesbian will vote with that component of their lives as their primary political identity.[15] Moreover, not everybody will be able to move to the Castro in San Francisco or Soho in London, however much it might appeal to them. Gay and lesbian territorial areas are not a realistic prospect and, even if they were, they would be an easily overwhelmed minority in the democratic territorial jigsaw of city, region or state.

Federalism can also be social, however, in the sense of cultural segmental autonomy which is also a feature of consociationalism. In this sense, federalism can be understood as self-government for a group over issues which affect its members directly or exclusively. Shapiro argues for the federal principle linked to the idea of participation:

> If each minority group controlled its own local institutions, that is, controlled its own communities, there would be created 'spaces of freedom' for all, for all minorities could then find justice in one community or another. (Shapiro 1971: 300)

This proposal is not exclusively defined by geographical communities so one could imagine, for example, women controlling an abortion clinic in a particular territorial area. Thus federalism is based on issue, group and area. This principle appeals primarily for the 'spaces of freedom' that would be thus created which echo the autonomy in social policy which is a key feature of consociationalism. This arena of self-government is a key democratic necessity for an oppressed group if they are to have any control over issues that affect them as a group. For gays and lesbians, this could mean the autonomy to enact relationship laws that were not based on the model of heterosexual marriage, for example. For lesbians, it could mean control over reproductive technology. In both these examples, control over social policy would allow differences and diversity to flourish, creating newly legitimate forms of intimate and family relationships. Social federalism, as with consociational cultural autonomy, creates 'spaces of freedom' in which social groups can assert and legitimise their difference. While this proposal may achieve effective political goals, does it overcome the dilemma of difference?

In both of the examples above, you could argue that there is a strong case for reforming all relationship laws, both heterosexual and homosexual, and for giving all women control over reproductive rights and technology. The question thus arises of whether a group-specific autonomy would only further enshrine the divide between sexualities and therefore inadvertently confirm the perception of these categories as reflective of natural divisions and hierarchies. Ultimately, this form of group representation may serve to reinforce the cultural understanding of sexuality which sustains oppression in the first place – Young's dilemma of difference in the realm of political representation.

Furthermore, there is a practical political problem in deciding exactly which group had privilege over which policy area where these areas are contentious or in conflict. An obvious example here is the difficulty gays had in the USA in securing federal funding for AIDS research and care. Although a health issue, AIDS was cast as a 'gay plague' at first (it was initially called Gay-Related Immune Deficiency) and was regarded as a self-inflicted 'lifestyle' disease. The moral judgements associated with gay lifestyles and identities determined that gays lost out on the allocation of resources for AIDS research and care (Altman 1986). Thus, the deviant difference associated with gays marginalises them from the political process. If gay men had had a group input into health policy, it would undoubtedly have furthered the cause of research, care provision and safer sex education. In the UK, the government's reaction to AIDS was similar in rhetoric to the American administration, but gay voluntary organisations were included in consultative policy processes and the medical profession has been characterised as dominating the practicalities of the response from government (Freeman 1992; Moerkerk and Aggleton 1990; Schramm-Evans 1990).

Critics have suggested that it was only the threat of a heterosexual epidemic, in part transmitted by straight men 'who have sex with men', which produced a serious response from the British government (Schramm-Evans 1990; Strong and Berridge 1990). Thus, the characterisation of AIDS as universal, rather than a 'gay issue', achieved the desired results in terms of funding and attention. This universalism has caused its own problems, with argument and counter-argument that gay men have lost out in the competition for resources in care and education despite the fact that the disease still disproportionately affects gay men. Furthermore, the ability of various gay or women's groups to target safer sex education has often been limited by the reluctance of governmental agencies to fund controversial sexual material. In both these issues, the social group of gay men not only has to compete with other, dominant groups, but have also had their cultural differences mobilised against them rather than in support of the need for differentiated treatment.

Federalism in this form also raises the question of group closure: how exactly would people come to locate themselves within a group and to what extent would multiple group membership be an acceptable principle? It is not inconceivable that a multiplicity of group memberships would result in the domination of one group over another, or in fact of the same groups that are dominant now. An obvious solution to this is to restrict significant groups to those that are oppressed and thus disadvantaged. Still, would white gay men not inevitably be advantaged over black gay men and black lesbians? The intersection of differences along various dimensions of social hierarchies make it difficult translate the theoretical desire for illuminating differences into a practical political settlement. Too often, defining group membership along a particular dimension suffocates rather than illuminates differences and thus returns us to a one-dimensional definition of social identity which can reinforce essentialist perceptions and divisions, both in those located within the group and in those excluded by it.

This last point raises the issue of whether it is possible to construct a consensus or a general public good amongst autonomous social groups. Certainly some overarching loyalty and a consensus on the limits of group interest would have to be agreed for any form of cultural federalism or consociation to work but again, this may prove impossible in the case of lesbians and gays, where their differences are regarded as 'deviant'. Would a social or cultural federalism of men and women ever come to an agreement about the gendered distribution of paid and unpaid work? Furthermore, there would also be the problem of the cross-cutting differences mentioned above undermining the construction of political consensus. I think that social federalism can only overcome the dilemma of difference if some form of multiple group membership is allowed, thus removing the implicit assumption that group membership is defined by essential attributes rather than social location. As argued above, this does raise a number of practical problems but I think it has the potential, married with social or cultural autonomy, to provide a forum for political representation which can deliver effective political change.

Functional representation is an allocation of representation primarily through economic location. Although this is derived in part from a Marxist analysis of the need for working-class representation, functionalism is distinct from the Marxist position in that it includes the representation of both bourgeois and professional interests. Perhaps the most developed theory has been put forward by G. D. H. Cole in *Guild Socialism Re-Stated* (reprinted 1980). Cole is concerned primarily with resolving capital and labour power divisions, which were particularly problematic at the time he was writing in the 1930s.

Although economic positions are not appropriate to defining gay and lesbian identity, some of the arguments which Cole makes are relevant to my discussion. The model he proposes provides for group autonomy and participatory democracy in all social sites, based on the argument that effective and legitimate representation must be functional since representing a point of view about a particular issue can only be done by those affected by that issue. Of course Cole is talking about group life-experience and opportunity defined through socioeconomic location. I would suggest that we have again the idea of autonomy for particular social groups running through this proposal. Moreover, underpinning guild socialism, federalism and consocation is the assumption that those affected by a particular social relationship or condition are best placed to bring analysis and experience to bear in developing and changing policy in that area. This is a strong argument for claiming that it does matter who represents whom, although of course it brings us back to the issues of group closure and multifaceted social identity which were discussed above.

Despite developing a strong theoretical framework of how guilds might operate in practice, Cole (1980) does not resolve the question of how competing functional positions of an individual may be categorised and weighted, or indeed how the different groups may be aggregated into a general or common will or purpose. Paul Hirst provides a critique and development of Cole's ideas, arguing that in the late twentieth century, we must look again at some form of functional representation that can reclaim 'social pluralism' for democracy (1986). Hirst calls for a rethinking of the potential of participatory industrial and civil democracy.

Alan Cawson develops this argument and makes a strong case for democratising functional groups, arguing that they are extremely widespread and have more permanent interests than associative interest groups (1983). Certainly many groups excluded from the polity are economically oppressed, and access to control over material resources would be a great help. However, the problem arises again of group closure, in that economic location may be a very limited, and possibly oppressive, part of someone's identity. For gays and lesbians it would seem to be a limited part of a specifically homosexual political identity, and must anyway be crosscut by the gendered division of economic positions as well as class divisions within lesbian and gay subcultures. This is not to deny the importance of the commercial club and bar 'scene' in the gay and, to a lesser extent, lesbian worlds (Altman 1980; Epstein 1992; Mort 1980), or indeed to deny that a large part of homosexual identity is constructed through an engagement with consumption and leisure activities (Evans 1993; Weeks 1996). Rather it is simply to suggest that economic location is not a corollary of sexual identity.

What is perhaps more relevant in Cawson's argument is the notion that different forms of representation should be employed, both in different sites in the polity and across different issues. For instance, he supports individualist representation in issues that are decided on a

Exploring political strategies 181

legal–rational basis such as income tax, for example. However, he suggests that other issues may dictate a form of group representation and I would argue that issues organised around sexual identities fall into this category. Cawson (1983) thus introduces the idea of a differentiated polity which I thinks goes some way to resolving the problem with group closure and multiple group memberships. However, functional representation still raises the issue of definition in terms of appropriate groups; how would appropriate functional groups come to be agreed, and would oppositional groups accept this? For example, much of the opposition to gay and lesbian rights is organised around the argument that these are somehow 'special' rights rather than 'equal' rights. Would heterosexual organisations agree to allow gay and lesbian groups a guaranteed forum of representation that did not include heterosexuals or would a similarly functionalist group of heterosexuals need to be included in the polity?

As well as suffering from some of the same problems as the other proposals for group representation, functionalism also shares the focus on autonomous representation. Moreover, the idea of extending democracy into corporate bodies is an important one and would seem an appropriate method for giving groups some form of access to decision making in arenas where they did not control the policy-making process directly. For example, gay men and lesbians could be given some form of representation on police authorities, health authorities and perhaps even educational boards. Add to this the inclusion of a gay and a lesbian political group in political decision-making fora and a picture emerges of how an inclusive polity might be constructed. Furthermore, Cawson's (1983) suggestion that different means of representation are appropriate across different issues helps us to retain the liberal individualist component of democracy. Before we consider the development of these proposals into a new model for group representation, I want to turn to the issue of voting which is an important aspect of each of the proposals discussed this far.

In all the proposals mentioned above, some mechanism of voting for representation would have to be agreed, whether it be for a consociational elite, a corporate body or a federal assembly. Of course, proportional representation (PR) is the obvious choice for those arguing for a fairer system of democracy but the term is often used loosely to cover a variety of issues and methods. A good review of its many different forms is given by Richard Kuper (1990) who constructs a strong case for PR as the only legitimate choice for those seeking a more representative democracy, but he also makes a point with which I have much sympathy:

'PR is not an end in itself, but one (limited) component of the process of democratising all aspects of social life' (Kuper 1990: 6).

Thus the form of PR chosen will depend on what it is you are trying to achieve. If the aim is to increase the representation of excluded groups in elected assemblies the answer seems to be a party-list system in multimember constituencies, which would increase the chances of more women and more ethnic minorities being elected and should have the same effect on lesbians and gays. However, as Chapman (1992) points out, one should not forget that voter selection is the last hurdle in the process that involves self selection first and then, crucially, party selection. Democratising parties is potentially problematic, as the Labour party has found with the successful legal challenges to its quotas for women. Identifying as a gay or lesbian rights candidate is problematic both with the voters and with the process of party selection. Quotas seem to be the only effective solution to these problems although they are legally difficult to enforce and usually unpopular with the public and party colleagues (Chapman 1992; Rahman 1994).

Another point of concern must be that strict proportionality may not achieve the aim of providing effective group representation if a group is in a permanent minority. This is true for ethnic minorities in the UK and it would also be a problem for gays and lesbians, whose number, though a matter of some statistical debate, is always sufficiently small to ensure that strictly proportional representation in the face of a heterosexual majority would leave us numerically overwhelmed. Furthermore, once elected do all the gay and/or lesbian representatives then form a caucus in the assembly that can override party loyalties, or do they become simply a token symbol of representation for the party? Quotas for queers may just leave us with a visible minority who reinforce the feeling that lesbians and gays are simply a deviant aspect of society and politics.[16]

The only way around the problem of permanent minority status would be the practice of veto for significant groups over the relevant areas of policy. This is practised in consociationalism and would be easily integrated into the other forms of group representation discussed above. However, this practice would fundamentally challenge the notion of the equal weighting of votes which seems so central to the individualist tradition of liberal democracy. It is not inconceivable to adopt this principle for group representation in the areas where it would be appropriate (a veto for women over abortion policy, say) and keep the individual, equally weighted, vote for individualist areas like tax policy. Liberal democracies clearly recognise mutual veto in practice if not in principle: the Security Council of the United Nations is an obvious, if not reassuring, example.

All of these proposals have been tried in one form or another and they each have valuable principles or practices which would further the argument for and practicalities of group representation. On their own, however, they are not catch-all solutions for different groups, and they exhibit many problems. First, these proposals for group representation have not overcome the problem of political elites being unrepresentative of those they represent; each of these proposals necessarily depends on an elite at some stage. This is especially difficult for very diverse, oppressed groups. It seems that even for the working class (who were once excluded from the polity) the presence of one labour or social democratic party is not sufficient to represent the diversity within a shifting class structure. As representation is a key feature of liberal democracy, we must be wary of who our elites are; for gays and lesbians this is extremely problematic, since diversity creates dilemmas of difference within that 'community' as well as in relation to the wider polity. The prescription for avoiding essentialist forms of representation is increased levels of participation (Pateman 1983; Phillips 1993, 1995). This is theoretically possible but practically difficult, and I will discuss some of the problems with participation in the next section.

A second problem is that agreeing the limits of group interest would be difficult. In consociationalism the limits may be too narrow, in federalism they may be too broad. In one sense, these criticisms are really about how far contesting groups can be accommodated within a polity; in short, how plural can decision-making bodies actually be and what are the obstacles to this plurality? Although this relates to the practicalities of participatory democracy it also raises the fundamental question of how effective group representation can be in delivering equality or social justice if a particular group is fundamentally challenging the social order, as many would see gays and lesbians as doing.

A third problem identified is the key one for gays and lesbians; how exactly to define who should be in and who should be out, and then ask if one group can really cover a full identity or should multiple group membership be allowed? In Cole's (1980) vision, the complexity of guild membership in modern societies could pose a real disincentive to participation because multiple group membership would demand a lot of time for political activity and late modernity is characterised by multifaceted social identities (Giddens 1991a). Before this criticism becomes too overwhelming I should make two points. The first is that although it is necessarily a matter of judgement which groups should be represented, it is relatively easy to make distinctions between those oppressed as members of a social group and those who are simply in an associative group to press for a particular interest. Obviously this is not easy if wider society does not accept that your oppression exists and it is crucial that gay and lesbian movements make this case convincingly to the heterosexual majority. We are often characterised as asking for particular, group-specific rights which are then interpreted as 'special rights', as has happened in the United States, both with affirmative action policies and with gay rights ordinances (*The Economist*, 25 June 1996). The second point is that there are prescriptions for the complexity of multiple social group membership in both the call for increased participation and the ideas about differentiated realms of representation. Both of these approaches may, with some development, solve the problem of group closure to some extent while retaining the notion of groups being significant through their exclusion as a group.

I think what is developing in my analysis is a difference between the positive and the negative that can be seen as a difference between principle and practice. The principles of group representation are unproblematic once you have accepted that some social groups are oppressed and that democracy should be a means through which this oppression can be acknowledged, addressed and challenged. The principles of segmental cultural autonomy and of some proportionality in decision-making bodies both push at the limits of liberal democracy in terms of the state and political participation. It is in the practice of these principles that problems arise, with none of the proposals discussed thus far able to resolve both the dilemma of difference and guarantee representation which delivers effective social equality. However, these proposals do push out the limits of liberal democratic thought and practice, and with the notion of differentiated realms and methods of representation, there is a potential for reconciling group membership with the liberal individualist tradition. It is this tension which has occupied many of the theorists working in this field in an attempt to use group representation to address the demands of more contemporary political movements and it is to these discussion that I now turn.

LIBERAL DEMOCRACY PLUS?

Anne Phillips is one of the most influential theorists working on the problems of incorporating groups into the polity.[17] Although her focus has been women, the ideas she has developed apply to a range of excluded groups. What is interesting in her most recent work is that diversity and differences have been recast as being within the liberal tradition of democracy (Phillips 1993, 1995). From this premise she goes on to make a strong argument for a reconceptualisation of politics to include a politics of presence rather than a politics simply concerned with representing ideas. Phillips is suggesting that effective representation can only be achieved by those experienced in the conditions of those they seek to represent. Thus the shared experience of a group becomes an important part of the concept of representation, particularly for groups that experience oppression in the private realm which liberal democracies claim to leave alone and those that have alternative perspectives on social relationships and conditions to the majority or elite (Phillips 1993, 1995).

She then goes on to assess (1995) three different ways in which the relationship between ideas and presence in politics is dealt with: a philosophical resolution, a movement-centred approach, and specifically political mechanisms. She suggests that the first area is undeveloped since it provides no practical theorisation of a way forward. It is in the other two areas that we see problems and opportunities arise for group representation. Among the political mechanisms Phillips mentions are multimember constituencies and other forms of PR. However, she also identifies the problem of essentialist constructions of representation, suggesting that political mechanisms such as PR often rely upon preordained and exclusive social categories. She emphasises the potential for movement-centred politics as a way of overcoming this problem.

In this emphasis, her prescription is in sympathy with Carole Pateman (1983) who also argues for a robustly participatory approach to politics to overcome elitist systems and the problem of elites becoming detached from and unaccountable to those they are supposed to represent. Both of these writers cite the participatory nature of various organisations and campaigns within the women's movement as a positive example of accommodating diversity while representing the group. Gay liberation movements have been similarly described (Birch 1988; Weeks 1989) although these days diversity is represented through a variety of distinct groups rather than within one organisation such as the now defunct Gay Liberation Front. Participation is seen as a key element in proposals for group representation, both as a means of reclaiming presence (experience) as fundamental to effective representation, and as a way of avoiding essentialist constructions of identity.

What seems evident to me, however, is that liberal democratic thought and practice, while potentially containing the concept of difference, cannot give full practical expression to the representation of difference because of the limits of the state and participation which liberalism dictates. The practical proposals for participation and social equality strain the limits of liberal democracy and this suggests to me that group representation cannot merely be liberal democracy plus. There is no practical way of transforming the current pluralist model of interest groups into a form of governance which incorporates social groups and also guarantees these groups effective representation. As Paul Hirst has argued (1986), we do need to reclaim social pluralism for democracy, but in so doing I think that it is inevitable that democracy itself must be reconceptualised away from its liberal inheritance.

An example of such a reconceptualisation is Cohen and Rogers' development of the idea of associative democracy (1992). They argue that the state should become involved in facilitating the formation of secondary associations which should then be involved in democratic governance through policy making and regulation. Where their model differs from current liberal democratic pluralism is their contention that pluralist groups are predominantly middle class, whereas in their model all groups, particularly oppressed ones, should be provided with the resources to participate in governance. Their idea of associative democracy is an attempt to reclaim social pluralism for egalitarian ends. In this sense they concur with the idea put forward by feminist theorists that presence is vital to effective representation and there is an implicit notion that the inclusion of different groups and perspectives will deliver a better form of democratic governance. An important point to bear in mind, of course, is that material resources will still be contested by this method, as Hirst (1986) points out, and also that the state is not a neutral facilitator but contains groups which have their own interests, such as bureaucrats and professional service providers. The details of associative democracy are not important here: what I am trying to illustrate is that any proposal for group representation does indeed go beyond the confines of liberal democracy as it currently operates.

CONCLUSION: GROUPS AND CITIZENS, IDEAS AND PRESENCE

From the discussion of these proposals I think it is clear that group representation requires a form of democracy which is significantly

Exploring political strategies 187

transformed from its current liberal democratic composite. To achieve the conditions of representation posed at the beginning of this chapter, in terms of both effective representation and overcoming the dilemma of difference, we need to think about a variety of issues. First, we need to consider the theoretical rationale for group representation. As I have argued above, once we accept the premise that inequality is primarily organised through divisions in social groups rather than caused by individual natures, it is relatively easy to argue for a form of representation which would facilitate the representation of these groups as a means of achieving social equality. Moreover, the critique of rights in liberalism provides another way in which we can argue for a means of achieving social equality which is denied by a narrow focus on political or civil citizenship.

In the realm of sexuality this precondition has not necessarily been met. The essentialist construction of sexuality which dominates culture and politics in the West does not allow for a social understanding of the formation or significance of sexual identity. I acknowledge that essentialist understandings of sexual identity dictate that we should be oppressed and, in some senses, changing this perception is part of the work that the representation of experiences must do. More pertinent to this discussion of representation is the fact that sexual identities are understood as essential – natural and immutable – and therefore outwith the realm of social or political action and, for gays and lesbians, as permanent, 'deviant' minorities within the democratic system. Therefore, I have suggested that we need a rationale behind group representation which broadens the legitimate scope of politics to include the realm of sexual relationships and behaviour rather than remitting these to the private cultural realm. Moreover, we need a form of representation that does not enshrine minority status but at the same time allows us to speak as 'gays' or 'lesbians'.

This last point has been characterised by Young as the 'dilemma of difference' facing social groups who are seeking political representation (1989). The very act of organising politically as gays or lesbians seems to reinforce the essentialist version of these social identities as natural ones. This conflation of the natural with the social renders invisible the social relationships and hierarchies which construct sexuality and underpin the oppression of heterosexual women, lesbians and gays. And yet to make these issues and social conditions visible within politics requires that we use our experiences and construct a political identity out of that experience. We need political presence in order to articulate alternatives to the heteromoral order. It may be that within democratic structures we need identities to organise around; perhaps the only way of overcoming the dilemma of difference is in the quality of the arguments and the range of alternatives we put forward from our political position.

Although I agree with the argument that we need presence in order to deliver effective political policies and alternatives (Phillips 1995), I also think that presence has little effect without a recognition of the contingency of any social identity and a projection of the social relationships and forces that have created those social identities and thus necessitated their political presence as oppressed groups. It is in this way, through the use of political identity to focus on social conditions and relationships, that the dilemma of difference may eventually be overcome. Bearing in mind the need for an underpinning critical rationale for political presence in order to refute essentialist constructions, we must also consider whether that presence can be constructed in order to refute minority status as well.

It is obvious that social minorities will translate into numerical democratic minorities, but some of the ideas discussed above suggest ways in which we may begin to construct a model of group representation which provides presence while guaranteeing influence despite 'minority' status. Specifically, policy autonomy over relevant areas and mutual vetos in decision-making bodies facilitate the necessary conditions for effective representation. Perhaps the most developed ideas come from Iris Young who has put forward a model that includes many of the positive aspects already discussed:

> I assert then, the following principle: a democratic public, however that is constituted, should provide mechanisms for the effective representation and recognition of the distinct voices and perspectives of those of its constituent groups that are oppressed or disadvantaged within it. Such group representation implies institutional mechanisms and public resources supporting three activities: 1. self-organisation of group members so that they gain a sense of collective empowerment and a reflective understanding of their collective experience and interests in the context of the society; 2. voicing a group's analysis of how social policy proposals affect them and generating policy proposals themselves, in institutionalised contexts where decision makers are obliged to show that they have taken these perspectives into consideration; 3. having veto power over specific policies that affect a group directly – for example,

Exploring political strategies 189

reproductive rights for women or use of reservation lands for American Indians. (Young 1989: 260)

As a model of a more effective democracy this is admirable and, in my view, desirable. It includes the idea that political presence is important in representation as well as simply the presence of abstract ideals. There is also the potential for integrating such mechanisms with current individualised representation; a potential for differentiated representation – group and individual citizenship – which was made more explicit by Cawson (1983). However, although the inclusion of a social group is defined by whether that group is disadvantaged, the issue of group membership is assumed to be by free association and this is common to all of the proposals put forward in the discussion above. Since a robustly participatory politics is seen as one way of avoiding essentialism, by making representatives sensitive and accountable to the diversity of opinion and experience within a particular social group, it is important to enter a caveat about the conditions for voluntary association. Participation has costs and benefits, and for some the costs are prohibitive. For others, there is the fundamental disincentive of perceived irrelevance; could we really rely on all of the relevant people being politicised enough to join a political group, especially in sexual communities which are organised around consumption and leisure activities?

Participation takes time and energy. Bearing this in mind, the key would be to produce an easy way for people to participate and then to ensure that the conditions of participation were as equal as they could be in terms of access to agendas and information about the debate and proposals for action. Finally, you would have to have an agreed method of making decisions. Reaching a consensus is, in theory, the aim and product of participation by all, but this could muffle dissent, especially in face to face encounters. The history of participatory movements also shows that it is fairly easy for a strong character to dominate the meeting and thus to have a disproportionate influence on the outcome of a decision.

> GLF (Gay Liberation Front) felt enormously diverse in culture and ideas. Anyone joined in, with no apparent hierarchy or rules, though of course this could be exploited by the experienced or self-confident who could speak in public and expound their ideas. (Birch 1988: 53)

Participatory democracy has its pitfalls as well as its opportunities. Both the Women's Movement and the Gay Liberation Front in the UK and USA were strongly participatory at first, but eventually fragmented through an inability to reach agreement between the diverse groups involved. The GLF in Britain suffered particularly when the lesbian members left to escape gay male sexism and this pattern was repeated in the USA.[18] To create a properly participatory politics seems an impractical proposition because it would involve a massive change of political culture and the creation of a political framework within which dissent and opportunity were not denied to individuals within a group. Of course this is not to say that constructing participatory groups is impossible, and on one level the problem of ensuring group membership is one which will be resolved and developed through time and experience, as indeed has happened within political parties. However, we have to consider the possibility that group representation may leave the articulation of gay or lesbian perspectives to a self-selected elite, whose members are either already politicised or have the resources to participate. This is better than no representation at all, but it makes the hope of representing difference a slim one.

The problems with participation relate to the question of group closure in that participation may be less likely in one group because it cannot account for the full range of a social and political identity. The complexity of gay and lesbian lifestyles and subcultures makes it difficult to see how much common ground there can be within these communities, if indeed a 'community' exists in any meaningful way. Clearly there is common ground between all gays and lesbians in achieving equal rights but what this means is unclear. Notions of equality dominate democratic discourses to the extent that even most heterosexuals seem to think there should be formal equality, but when this comes down to practicalities there is little consistent support for homosexuals (Liberty 1994). Moreover, the incorporation of differences requires a programme of differentiated or equivalent rights and it is difficult to assess whether these would gain support across a wide social and political spectrum. For example, would gay men be as concerned with reproductive rights as lesbians? Would heterosexual women or lesbians support the libertarian sexual reforms which are demanded by many gay men?

These tensions are the source of much debate both within and between gay and lesbian communities as well as between feminists and gay men. One way forward may be the ideas that Cawson (1983) has introduced about different areas being represented differently. In this way, one could be a group member and an equal citizen; you could have

Exploring political strategies 191

your area of politics as presence and another area where your politics was simply ideas. Of course there would be overlap, and there is a lot of thought that needs to be put into constructing such a polity. However, the idea of difference is increasingly gaining a foothold in social and political policy. Specifically, the idea that a group must have some control over self-definition and policy decisions is becoming more common and being put into practice in a variety of ways. Beyond consultative procedures, there is no formal recognition of the need to include groups as legitimate political actors, and it is in this area that more work needs to be done; I suggest that gays and lesbians must join in this debate with some vigour. I argue that this engagement with democracy does not necessarily entail a replacement of current systems of territorial representation based on individual votes cast, but rather the complement of an addition of some form of deliberative engagement of oppressed groups with political participation, decision making and policy implementation. It is this strategy which I suggest provides the best way forward for developing a queried sense of political identity which challenges the essentialism within sexuality and democracy.

I am aware that these proposals are still utopian in the context of current liberal democratic structures, but I am suggesting that we begin an exploration of representation rather than setting out a specific model of how we might do it. As one strategy in developing a politics of experience, I would argue that this explicit and pragmatic discussion is a development of the more abstract encouragement from Queer theorists and others to engage in developing realms of intimate or Queer citizenship or move towards a politics of radical plural humanism (Plummer 1995; Weeks 1996).

In my discussion of rights, I argued that democratic discourse normalises essentialism when citizenship is thought of simply as equal rights rather than equivalent social conditions. Although group representation potentially broadens the discourse of citizenship to include the sexual or the intimate (Plummer 1995), the problem of how to pluralise participation within the group itself is one that remains a crucial obstacle if we are not to produce a false sense of homogeneity in the act of representation. Political participation is still an elitist activity in Western democracies and has been so for a long time (Carroll 1985; Parry 1969). The history of gay and lesbian political activism has tended to follow this pattern of elitism, although this is less true of those lesbian movements organised around feminist politics. Young's first recommendation – that groups be allowed resources in order to promote organisation and participation – is not one that is terribly reassuring, given that the experience of participatory politics has always been an emotionally costly and politically fractious one. Moreover, dependence on the state for such resources can lead to a clientist relationship where dependence turns into identification and lack of radical critique (Elman 1996).

I am not sure that this obstacle is one that can be overcome: even if resources were provided by an enlightened state, it seems wholly predictable that only the better-educated and higher status members of a community would become involved, since it is those who are already politicised and involved in politics. The situation is somewhat different within gay and lesbian subcultures, especially in relation to issue-specific campaigns such as AIDS funding or supporting lesbian mothers. However, one way forward is the development of a more plural discourse of sexuality. Not only do we need a sociological critique to underpin our experiences of social inequality, but we also need to develop more sensitive accounts of sexual subjectivity which allow spaces for the articulation of inconsistency and differences and, in the more Queer sense, allow us to create articulations which identify us with 'others' who were previously thought not to 'belong' to our political or social location.

The experiences of bisexuality are one obvious point of identification with both 'homosexual' and 'heterosexual' experience and identity. What has always worried me is the fierce disparagement that bisexuals often face from within gay and lesbian communities. While I can sympathise with gut reaction to the heterosexual part of a bisexual career as a potential camouflage for conformity, I think it is more productive to explore the connections between bisexual and homosexual experience, given that this illuminates the inconsistencies in essentialist exclusive or eternal accounts of sexuality. The work being done on the narrative construction of self in the area of sexual identity is an extremely rich vein which we need to tap into more in order to further pluralise and translate sexual stories into political discourses which are potentially open to all in that they provide multiple political positions and identities.

However, even with these reservations, I think that political engagement within democratic structures is worth pursuing, particularly because the very presence of sexually different groups will serve to trouble the notion of conditions of citizenship as conditions of heteronormativity (Richardson 1998). If *we* belong, *you* cannot assume your natural dominance especially when lesbians and gays make demands for equivalent conditions of citizenship as opposed to rights which accrue to an institutionalised form of heterosexuality. Moreover, if this deployment of identity is pursued with a reconceptualised programme of equal rights and/or constitutional reform, we can further uncover the raft of heterosexual privilege that masquerades as human rights. Although I agree with Stonewall's slogan that 'gay rights are human rights' I would feel more comfortable with an addendum which proclaimed that heterosexual rights are not the blueprint for human rights.

The state is of course only one arena of political activism, and I am sure that the progress of lesbian and gay cultural visibility is helping to change perceptions of these identities if not actually challenge heterosexual dominance in society. However, the state is somewhere that we should be too, given its still dominant control over many aspects of social conditions and legal discourses. We need to think more about what form of institutionalisation we can benefit from within the state or associated professional networks. Again, my discussion is merely the departure point for debate but given the unlikelihood of forcing a radical change in representative structures as they currently stand, perhaps we can focus more on agitating for a realm of deliberative representation, where our presence is guaranteed, but focused more on consultation or an exchange of experiences rather than a specific role in producing policy. Again, this perhaps returns us more to the concerns of those who discuss a radical humanist approach to the intimate, and I am not sure how effective such a presence would be when focused on issues such as care, love, respect, and knowledge (Weeks 1996) but it is evident that these issues, which lesbians and gays for so long have had to actually think about, are becoming ever more relevant in a world where heterosexual relationships are more suffused with discourses of equality and where women are forcing such issues into the public realm as matters of importance.

NOTES

1. See the relevant section in the Introduction.
2. This debate is also conducted in the magazine *Gay Times* over various issues but particularly in those published during the months surrounding London's Gay Pride march – see June/July 1997, 1998. In July 1998 the march went ahead despite the collapse of the festival which traditionally follows the march/parade.
3. See my discussion in the previous chapter of the Queer theoretical rationale behind the promotion of differences and the links between theory and contemporary politics.
4. See his elegant swipe at Marxist narrow-mindedness in Chapter 1 – 'We other Victorians' – in *The History of Sexuality*, vol. 1 (1980: 3–13).

5. Democratic systems have been long established in North America and Western Europe but new democracies have also now emerged in Latin America and large swathes of Africa and of course the ex-Soviet republics and Eastern European ex-Communist states. Although most of these states are moving towards some form of liberal democratic settlement in terms of rights and representation, many of them are still fragile in terms of civil society, political institutions and constitutional frameworks. Crucially, there is no overriding consensus within or between these states on the role of the state *vis-à-vis* the economy and civil society. For a good overview see the collection edited by Held 1993.
6. This is different in the social democracies of Scandinavia where institutionalised consultation is often part of the process of decision making. For example, see Elman's critique of this process in relation to feminist politics in Sweden (1996).
7. Joining a political party is a simple task but becoming a representative is not. Research has shown that both within political parties and in single-member simple-plurality constituencies ('first past the post'), the process tends to exclude any candidate perceived as 'unacceptably' different (Chapman 1992). There has been a vast body of criticism of the ways in which parties in democratic systems exclude women and ethnic minorities at each stage of this process of joining the elite. For studies of women's participation see Chapman 1992; Rahman 1994; Sapiro 1982; and for theoretical discussion see Ferguson 1984, and Phillips 1993.
8. My point here is simply that the public/private divide in liberal democracy places sexuality firmly in the realm of private activity and thus outwith legitimate collective social and political action.
9. The four MPs are the Cabinet member Chris Smith and the backbenchers Ben Bradshaw, Angela Eagle and Stephen Twigg, although the Agriculture Secretary, Nick Brown, has recently come out and Lord Waheed Alli of Norbury has been appointed as a Labour peer and is the first openly gay man to take the ermine. The Labour party promised to repeal the infamous Section 28 and allow a free (that is, conscience) vote on lowering the age of consent for gay men to 16 and to review the ban on homosexuals serving in the Armed Forces. The promise to incorporate the European Convention on Human Rights into UK law may also further the cause of certain legal challenges in progress (*New Statesman* May 1997, special edition and *Gay Times* March 1997). As yet, only one of these promises has been fulfilled with the lifting of the ban on gays and lesbians serving in the Armed Forces. The recent second attempt at reducing the age of consent contained in the Sexual Offences (Amendments) Bill passed the Commons in January 1999 and included a new 'abuse of trust' offence which is designed to protect young people who are 16 or over but are also under the supervision or authority of adults. A cross-party committee pointed out that this could allow heterosexuals to 'marry their way out of trouble' given that 16 is the legal age of marriage (*The Guardian* 26th January 1999). Although we are still awaiting the outcome of the age of consent issue in March 2000, the Lords have recently defeated the proposal for the second time but the

Exploring political strategies 195

Government have declared that they will override the Lords to get this reform through. Meanwhile, the repeal of section 28 of the Local Government Act is proceeding precariously and controversially in the Scottish Parliament and should be completed by the summer of 2000.
10. There are of course a variety of political organisations with different aims and preoccupations. Moreover, lesbians have often been involved in autonomous organisations and/or in various feminist movements and organisations.
11. For a thorough critique of equal rights strategies see my discussion of the manifesto for sexual rights put forward by the civil rights organisation Liberty, in Rahman and Jackson 1997.
12. For a variety of perspectives on strategies of rights and citizenship see Carver 1998, Rahman 1998, Waites 1998 (on age of consent), Skidmore 1998 (on Armed Forces in the UK), Bell 1998 (on European Union policy).
13. For a discussion of the practicalities and politics of this issue, see Cain, 1994 and the collection edited by Bush 1984 and Cameron, Epstein and O'Halloran, 1996. For a more theoretical discussion see Cain 1984 and Phillips 1995.
14. The complexities of the relationship between gay subcultures and political movements are discussed by Kriesi *et al.* in chapter 7 of their book on social movements, 1995.
15. Empirical research on this is increasingly available, particularly in the US. See, for example, Button *et al.* 1997 and Rayside 1998.
16. See Rosenblum 1996 for a discussion of proportional representation and lesbian and gay interests in the New York City school board elections. Although this is a much smaller scale focus for PR than I am concerned with, the study raises interesting questions which relate to the problems which I identify.
17. There are various proposals for group representation which the more recent feminist interventions critique and develop. The more recent work of feminists is a more appropriate starting point for my discussion here because they are dealing with gender difference and inequality which underpins sexual inequalities.
18. Furthermore, GLF in the USA suffered a fragmentation which led to the more reform-minded Gay Activists Alliance which was dominated by white, middle-class gay men (Deitcher 1995).

CONCLUSION: LIBERTY OR EQUALITY?

Let me remind the reader that I suggested in the introduction that I would end on a pessimistic note: I embarked on this study in order to untangle some of the questions I had about lesbian and gay politics and my own confusion about the overall aim of equality or liberation politics. Although I have started to unravel threads from this knot of issues, my only firm conclusion is that the convergence of structures of democracy and the material and social construction of sexuality produce an almost irresistible movement towards essentialist sexual and political discourses. Sexual identity is not declining in social significance but to the contrary its salience – for both homosexuals and heterosexuals – remains constant and, moreover, is now constructed through sexual, material and democratic essentialism. My worry is that this direction will only deliver formal, abstract guarantees of liberty – rights ascribed individually – and that this in turn leaves us with little room for social equality: a genuinely equivalent organisation, regulation and acceptance of different genders and sexualities.

In a personal sense, as a gay man, I had hoped to feel more positive after this intellectual journey but I must confess to feeling that the world has changed but the world has not progressed. The enthusiasm for Clinton which I described in the introduction has been tempered by a realisation that rhetoric has not been translated into new forms of politics or even more progressive legislation[1] and although the Labour government in the UK has made some minor attempts at legislative change and policy application in favour of lesbians and gays, these have been largely remitted to individual backbenchers or put on hold.[2] More anecdotally, the social world I inhabit has changed in the sense that

Conclusion 197

there are more bars to go to and more lesbian and gay characters depicted in popular culture but the bars are still 'gay' bars and the rest are 'normal' bars, and culture is still dominated by essentialist portrayals of sexuality and gender. We are still therefore deviant from the norm rather than simply different, but now we are more visibly deviant and social equality still seems a long way off.

I cannot finish on this note of futility, however, and I acknowledge that frustration is part and parcel of producing and disseminating intellectual work. This conclusion is therefore largely an attempt to recover some sense of optimism and to come to terms with the fact that I have not arrived at journey's end but rather at a number of new departure points. Beyond a specific call to think through means of representation, to reconceptualise the ways in which we frame rights and citizenship, and to disseminate more sociological accounts of sexuality and subjectivity, I have no further arguments to make. However, I want to consider how these arguments have addressed the four themes which I laid down in my introduction and which directions need to be considered for further research and thought. The first point that I want to reiterate is that essentialism cannot be part of an effective political strategy for lesbians and gays precisely because such understandings of sexuality and gender legitimises the deviant social significance of homosexualities. Moreover, essentialist ideas about sexual identity converge with the liberal democratic focus on the individual (Phillips 1993) and thus compound the understandings of sexual hierarchies and morality as natural, inevitable and immutable. This renders lesbian and gay politics a politics of minority or special interests with a questionable moral framework which reduces further any ability to articulate a critique of sexual inequalities as issues of social organisation and oppression. However, I also argued that a sociological understanding of sexual subjectivity is necessary if we are to displace essentialist versions of self as the dominant personal and political discourses of sexuality.

This brings me to my second theme: producing a sociological analysis which is resonant with individual and personal lives. It is in this area that sociological research on narratives has much to contribute. Illuminating the diversity and complexity of sexual careers and identities is reason enough as an agenda for such research, but I have also argued that a sociological perspective on the self should help us to understand the perception of the stability of the sexual self and explain the reasons why we feel that we 'need' a stable perception of self and a sense of a core self. I suggested that the very process of social action requires a strategic and intentional engagement on the part of social actors which inevitably produces 'short-hand' rationalisations of the mobilisation and deployment of the different components of our subjectivities which are translated into ideas about a core and stable – or innate/essential – sexual subjectivity. My ideas remain theoretical, however, and I recognise the need to develop more empirical work in this area.

In using my sociological ideas about sexual subjectivity as a basis for rethinking political identity I turned toward the body of work loosely understood as Queer theory, precisely because Queer theorists are attempting to provide both a non-essentialist theorisation of sexual identity and a programme of strategic intervention into the cultural and political realm (Gamson 1996; Wilson 1997). However, I argued that a Queer perspective leaves common experiences of oppression both difficult to explain with reference to structured and materially grounded inequalities of sexuality and gender. I suggest that we should instead develop a thorough sociological understanding of identity which allows us to think through new forms of political representation while acknowledging the structural context to the formation and deployment of sexual and gendered identities.

It is with such a sense of 'queried' political identity that I began my exploration of effective political strategies in the pursuit of lesbian and gay social equality. This forms the final theme of this book and it is in this area that a great deal more thought needs to be undertaken. Although I criticised strategies of citizenship and rights as potentially normalising discourses of essentialism, I have not been able to offer a new vision of political identity, deployment and strategy. However, I did suggest that exploring the potential of methods of group representation for lesbians and gays offers an optimistic departure point for further research. Such debates have become central to political theory over the last few years and while the remit of this book was not to develop a model of political participation, I think that this is one area of thought with which lesbians and gays must engage.

There is perhaps some scope for optimism after all, since there are areas of thought and research that can be explored further to develop democratic frameworks within which the pursuit of lesbian and gay social equality is an easier and more successful task than at present. Moreover, I have tried to illustrate the need for an interdisciplinary analysis of politics in the realm of sexuality and thus have sought to underscore the connections between the social, the political and the personal. And thus I am reminded that intervention is possible through developing a sociological analysis and using that as a basis for political activity. A long and frustrating process it may be, but ultimately this kind of somewhat abstract thinking does have a practical application – we can use our sociological imaginations to 'make a difference' (Morgan 1998). However, in case I now appear to becoming far too optimistic, let me finish by reiterating my underlying concerns.

It is capitalist material relations that underscore my pessimism, particularly in light of David Evans' astute analysis of the ever-expanding material construction of sexualities (1993). The impact of late-modern capitalism and the associated emphasis on consumption has been documented as a fundamental structural condition for the development of gay subcultures, lifestyles and identities (and has conversely explained the relative absence of lesbians from this materially privileged masculine world). Thus the material construction of individuality in late modern capitalist systems has become intertwined with the essentialist discourse of sexuality to the extent that gays and lesbians are identified and identify as an 'ethnic' group; geographically, socially, culturally, sexually and biologically distinct and discrete from heterosexuals (Altman 1971/1993; Epstein 1992). This book has not simply been an overview of the social construction of sexuality, but I have attempted to understand and analyse sexuality as one of the 'fragments of modernity' which constitute the terrain of the social (Frisby 1985). Moreover, the centrality of both the economic and democratic order to the formation of the social during modernity cannot be ignored in any contemporary understanding of sexuality as a social identity – there are not simply 'bodies that matter' (Butler 1993); material relationships which constitute the social matter more.

Gay and lesbian politics must also therefore be concerned with liberation from sexual essentialism and also with liberation from the materially grounded fetishisation of the individual. This is perhaps the more difficult aspect of lesbian and gay politics – indeed any politics concerned with the social significance of so-called 'essential' attributes – given that consumption-orientated material relations and democratic individualist and psychological essentialist discourses are pervasive structural conditions which cannot easily be refuted or overturned by single political interventions or advances. It is these conditions which govern the ways in which we construct our sense of sexual identity and therefore underpin our sense of sexual-political identity. It is perhaps no wonder that in these social conditions the majority of political interventions have been organised around essentialist understandings of sexual identity and have often advocated individualist remedies and protections against homosexual oppression (Rahman and Jackson 1997).

How to elaborate, either through more sensitive narratives or other interactionist analysis, that it is the social construction of sexuality which underpins sexual morality and the formation and treatment of sexual identities in such a material context is difficult to do. Can we only expect sexual citizenship as a trade-off, as Evans suggests, with limited conditions of citizenship underwritten by material consumption and limited to liberal freedoms? Many would argue that political equality and individual liberty are all that we can reasonably expect from society. An extreme position of this sort, anchored in negative liberty, is increasingly the underpinning rationale to gay political activism which converges with much political libertarian theory emerging from the New Right. For example, Andrew Sullivan's text *Virtually Normal* (1995) puts forward the argument that the only reforms necessary for lesbian and gay equality to flourish are the right to marry and serve in the Armed Forces.

This approach, I argue, is virtually nonsense. It emphasises the need to escape from inequality of treatment but it does not acknowledge the social basis of that inequality. If negative liberty had worked for us then we would not be in this position in the first place. It is clear that the social construction of sexuality overrides liberal notions of equal treatment and so it is the social construction of sexuality that must be challenged and deconstructed through democratic processes. In order to do this, we must seek social equality as the ends of democratic equality. Furthermore, since the essentialism consists of moral divisions, we must articulate the morality of our own lives rather than relying on the conditional protection which may or may not be afforded to a group constructed as a moral minority.

As a normative prescription, this is much easier said than done. To locate lesbian and gay politics within a progressive normative theory is a task that I have only begun to undertake here. I have concentrated on one aspect of the task in presenting group representation as an alternative to this silencing of the social determination of inequality. But I suggest that we need to continue to explore the possibilities that sociological analysis creates for reconceptualising political questions if we are not simply to accept a limited form of liberty in place of an expansive and diverse social equality.

NOTES

1. Moreover, given that he has had to stand trial for impeachment, I have had to acknowledge that my political judgement is somewhat suspect.
2. Ann Keen, backbench Labour MP for Brentford and Isleworth, proposed the amendment to the Sexual Offences Act in June 1998 which would have reduced the age of consent for gay men to 16.

BIBLIOGRAPHY

Abbott, P. and Wallace, C. (1992) *The Family and the New Right*. London: Pluto Press.
Abelove, H. (1993) 'Freud: male homosexuality, and the Americans'. In Abelove, H., Barale, M. and Halperin, D. (eds) *Lesbian and Gay Studies Reader*. London: Routledge.
Abelove, H., Barale, M. and Halperin, D. (eds) (1993) *The Lesbian and Gay Studies Reader*. London: Routledge.
Abercrombie, N., Hill, S. and Turner, B. (1980) *The Dominant Ideology Thesis*. London: Allen and Unwin.
Adam, B. (1985) 'Structural foundations of the gay world', *Comparative Studies in Society and History*, vol. 27, pp. 658–71.
Aggleton, P., Davies, P. and Hart, G. (eds) (1989) *AIDS: Social Representations, Social Practices*. London: Falmer Press.
Aggleton, P., Davies, P. and Hart, G. (eds) (1990) *AIDS: Individual, Cultural and Policy Dimensions*. London: Falmer Press.
Almaguer, T. (1991) 'Chicano men: a cartography of homosexual identity and behaviour', *Differences*, vol. 3, no. 2, pp. 75–100.
Althusser, L. (1971) *Lenin and Philosophy and other Essays*. London: New Left Books.
Altman, D. (1971/1993) *Homosexual Oppression and Liberation*. New York: New York University Press.
Altman, D. (1980) 'What changed in the 70s?', chapter 4 in *Homosexuality, Power and Politics*, Gay Left Collective (eds). London: Allison and Busby.
Altman, D. (1986) *Aids and the New Puritanism*. London: Pluto Press.
Angelou, M. (1995) *Collected Poems*. New York: Fontana.
Barrett, M. (1980) *Women's Oppression Today*. London: Verso.
Barthes, R. (1957) *Mythologies*. Paris: Editions du Seuil.
Becker, H. S. (1971) *Sociological Work*. London: Allen Lane.
Bell, M. (1998) 'Sexual orientation and anti-discrimination policy: the European Union.' In Carver, T. and Mottier, V. (eds) *Politics of Sexuality*. London: Routledge.

Benhabib, S. (1992) *Situating the Self: Gender, Community and Postmodernism in Contemporary Ethics*. Oxford: Polity Press.
Birch, K. (1988) 'A community of interests'. In Cant, B. and Hemmings, S. (eds) *Radical Records*. London: Routledge.
Blumer, H. (1966) 'Sociological implications of the thought of G. H. Mead', *American Journal of Sociology*, vol. 71, no. 5, pp. 535–44.
Boswell, J. (1980) *Christianity, Social Tolerance and Homosexuality*. Chicago: University of Chicago Press.
Boswell, J. (1992) 'Concepts, experience and sexuality'. In Stein, E. (ed.) *Forms of Desire*. New York: Routledge.
Brake, M. (1982) *Human Sexual Relations: A Reader*. Harmondsworth: Penguin.
Bristow, J. (1997) *Sexuality*. New York: Routledge.
Bunyan, T. (ed.) (1993) *Statewatching the New Europe*. Nottingham: Russell Press.
Bush, R (ed.) (1984) *The New Black Vote*. San Francisco: Synthesis Publications.
Butler, J. (1990a) *Gender Trouble*. London: Routledge.
Butler, J. (1990b) 'Gender trouble, feminist theory and psychoanalytic discourse'. In Nicholson, L. (ed.) *Feminism/Post-Modernism*. New York: Routledge.
Butler, J. (1991) 'Imitation and gender insubordination'. In Fuss, D. (ed.) *Inside/Out: Lesbian Theories, Gay Theories*. New York: Routledge.
Butler, J. (1992) 'Contingent foundations: feminism and the question of "Postmodernism"'. In Butler, J. and Scott, J. W. (eds) *Feminists Theorise the Political*. New York: Routledge.
Butler, J. (1993) *Bodies That Matter: on the Discursive Limits of 'Sex'*. London: Routledge.
Butler, J. (1998) 'Marxism and the merely cultural', *New Left Review*, no. 227, pp. 33–44.
Button, J. W., Rienzo, B. A., and Wald, K. D. (1997) *Private Lives, Public Conflicts*. Washington, DC: Congressional Quarterly Press.
Cain, B. E. (1984) *The Reapportionment Puzzle*. Berkeley: University of California Press.
Cain, B. E. (1994) 'Racial and ethnic politics'. In Peele, G., Bailey, C. J., Cain, B. and Peters B. G. (eds) *Developments in American Politics* 2. Basingstoke: Macmillan.
Caplan, P. (ed.) (1989) *The Cultural Construction of Sexuality*. London: Routledge.
Cameron, C., Epstein, D. and O'Halloran, S. (1996) 'Do majority-minority districts maximise substantive black representation in Congress?', *American Political Science Review*, vol. 90, no. 4, pp. 794–812.
Cameron, D (1985) *Feminism and Linguistic Theory*. London: Macmillan.
Cant, B. and Hemmings, S. (eds) (1988) *Radical Records: Thirty Years of Lesbian and Gay History*. London: Routledge.
Carabine, J. (1996) 'Heterosexuality and social policy'. In Richardson, D. (ed.) *Theorising Heterosexuality*. Milton Keynes: Open University Press.

Carroll, S. J. (1985) *Women as Candidates in American Politics*. Bloomington: Indiana University Press.

Carver, T. (1998) 'Sexual citizenship: gendered and de-gendered narratives'. In Carver, T. and Mottier, V. (eds) *Politics of Sexuality*. London: Routledge.

Cawson, A. (1983) 'Functional representation and democratic politics: towards a corporatist democracy?' In Duncan, G. (ed.) *Democratic Theory and Practice*. New York: Cambridge University Press.

Chapman, J. (1992) *Politics, Feminism And The Reformation Of Gender*. London: Routledge.

Cohen, J. and Rogers J. (1992) 'Secondary associations and democratic governance', *Politics and Society*, vol. 20, no. 4, pp. 393–472.

Cohen, S. and Taylor, L. (1976) *Escape Attempts: The Theory and Practice of Resistance to Everyday Life*. Harmondsworth: Penguin.

Cole, G. D. H. (1980) *Guild Socialism Re-stated*. New Brunswick: Transaction Books.

Congressional Quarterly, 6 February 1993.

Connell R. W. and Dowsett G. W. (1992) 'The unclean motion of the generative parts: Frameworks in Western thought on sexuality'. In Connell, R. W. and Dowsett, G. W. (eds) *Rethinking Sex: Social Theory and Sexuality Research*. Melbourne: University of Melbourne Press.

Cooper, D. (1995) *Power in Struggle: Feminism, Sexuality and the State*. Milton Keynes: Open University Press.

Cott, N. F. (1978) 'Passionless: an interpretation of Victorian sexual ideology 1790–1850', *Signs*, vol. 4, no. 2.

Cuff, E. C., Sharrock, W. W. and Francis, D. W. (1992) *Perspectives in Sociology*. London: Routledge.

Davidoff, L. and Hall, C. (1987) *Family Fortunes: Men and Women of the English Middle Class 1780–1850*. London: Hutchinson.

Davidson, A. (1992) 'Sex and the emergence of sexuality'. In Stein, E. (ed.) *Forms of Desire*. New York: Routledge.

de Lauretis, T. (1991) Introduction to 'Queer theory: Lesbian and gay sexualities', *Differences*, vol. 3, no. 2, pp. iii–xviii.

de Saussure, F. (1959) *Course in General Linguistics*. New York: Fontana.

Deitcher, D. (ed.) (1995) *Over the Rainbow*. London: Boxtree.

Delphy, C. (1984) *Close to Home: a Materialist Analysis of Women's Oppression*. Translated by Diana Leonard. London: Hutchinson.

Delphy, C. (1993) 'Rethinking sex and gender', *Women's Studies International Forum*, vol. 16, no. 1, pp. 1–9.

Delphy, C. (1994) 'Changing women in a changing Europe: is difference the future for feminism?'. Translated by Diana Leonard. *Women's Studies International Forum*, vol. 27, no. 2, pp. 187–201.

Delphy, C. and Leonard, D. (1992) *Familiar Exploitation*. Cambridge: Polity Press.

Denzin, N. K. (1969) 'Symbolic interaction and Ethnomethodology', *American Sociological Review*, no. 34, pp. 922–34.

Descartes, R. (1986) *Meditations on First Philosophy*. Cambridge: Cambridge University Press.
Dixon, J. (1988) 'Separatism: a look back at anger'. Chapter 7 in Cant, B. and Hemmings, S. (eds) *Radical Records*. London: Routledge.
Dummet, A. and Nicol, A. (1990) *Who Belongs? The Meanings of British Nationality and Immigration Law*. London: Weidenfield and Nicolson.
Durham, M. (1991) *Sex and Politics: The Family and Morality in the Thatcher Years*. London: Macmillan.
Economist, 25 June 1996.
Edwards, T. (1994) *Erotics and Politics*. London: Routledge.
Edwards, T. (1998) 'Queer fears: Against the cultural turn', *Sexualities*, vol. 1, no. 4, pp. 471–4.
Ellis, H. (1942) *Studies in the Psychology of Sex*. New York: Random House, originally published between 1896 and 1928.
Elman, R. A. (1996) *Sexual Subordination and State Intervention: Comparing Sweden and the United States*. Oxford: Berghahn Books.
Epstein, S. (1992) 'Gay politics, ethnic identity'. In Stein, E. (ed.) *Forms of Desire*. New York: Routledge.
Epstein, S. (1996) 'A queer encounter: Sociology and the study of sexuality'. In Seidman, S. (ed.) *Queer Theory/Sociology*. Oxford: Blackwell.
Evans, D. T. (1993) *Sexual Citizenship: The Material Construction of Sexualities*. London: Routledge.
Faderman, L. (1981) *Surpassing the Love of Men*. New York: Morrow.
Fausto-Sterling, A. (1992) *Myths of Gender: Biological Theories about Women and Men*. New York: Basic Books.
Finlayson, A. (1998) 'Sexuality and nationality: gendered discourses of Ireland'. In Carver, T. and Mottier, V. (eds) *Politics of Sexuality*. London: Routledge.
Fletcher, J. (1989) 'Freud and his uses: Psychoanalysis and gay theory'. In Shepherd, S. and Wallis, M. (eds) *Coming on Strong: Gay Politics and Culture*. London: Unwin Hyman.
Foucault, M. (1977) *Madness and Civilisation*. London: Tavistock Press.
Foucault, M. (1977) *Discipline and Punish*. London: Allen Lane.
Foucault, M. (1980) *The History of Sexuality* vol. 1. New York: Vintage.
Foucault, M. (1989) *The Archaeology of Knowledge*. London: Routledge.
Foucault, M. (1990) *The Uses of Pleasure: History of Sexuality*, vol. 2. New York: Vintage.
Fraser, N. (1997) 'A rejoinder to Iris Young', *New Left Review*, no. 223, pp. 126–30.
Freeman, R. (1992) 'The politics of AIDS in Britain and Germany'. In Aggleton, P., Davies, P. and Hart, G. (eds) *AIDS: Rights Risk and Reason*. London: Taylor and Francis.
Freud, S. (1905) *Three Essays on the Theory of Sexuality*.
Freud, S. (1915) *The Unconscious*.
Freud, S. (1925a) *Dissolution of the Oedipus Complex*.

Freud, S. (1925b) *Some Psychical Consequences of the Anatomical Distinction Between the Sexes.*
(All the above taken from Gay 1995, and they are also available in various Penguin collections.)
Frisby, D. (1985) *Fragments of Modernity*. Cambridge: Polity Press.
Fuss, D. (1991) 'Inside/out'. Introduction to Fuss, D. (ed.) *Inside Out: Lesbian Theories, Gay Theories*. New York: Routledge.
Gagnon, J. H. (1973) 'The creation of the sexual in early adolescence'. In Groubard, S. (ed.) *From Twelve to Sixteen*. New York: Norton.
Gagnon, J. H. and Simon, W. (1973) *The Sexual Scene*. New Brunswick: Transaction Books.
Gagnon, J. H. and Simon, W. (1974) *Sexual Conduct*. London: Hutchinson.
Gagnon, J. H., and Simon, W. (1986) 'Sexual scripts: permanence and change', *Archives of Sexual Behaviour*, vol. 15, no. 2, pp. 97–122.
Gamson, J. (1996) 'Must identity movements self-destruct? A queer dilemma'. In Seidman, S. (ed.), *Queer Theory/Sociology*. Oxford: Blackwell.
Guardian, 23 June 1998.
Guardian, 26 January 1999.
Guardian, 27 January 1999.
Gay, P. (1995) *The Freud Reader*. London: Vintage.
Gay Times, March 1997, Millivres Publications, United Kingdom.
Giddens, A. (1979) *Central Problems in Social Theory*. London: Macmillan.
Giddens, A. (1990) *The Consequences of Modernity*. Cambridge: Polity Press.
Giddens, A. (1991a) *Modernity and Self Identity: Self and Society in the Late Modern Age*. Cambridge: Polity Press.
Giddens, A. (1991b) 'Four theses on ideology'. In *Ideology and Power in the Age of Lenin in Ruins*, special edition of *The Canadian Journal of Politics and Social Theory*, vol. 15, nos. 1, 2 and 3, pp. 21–3.
Giddens, A. (1992) *The Transformation of Intimacy*. Cambridge: Polity Press.
Giddens, A. and Held, D. (eds) (1982) *Classes, Power and Conflict*. Berkeley: University of California Press.
Gilligan, C. (1982) *In a Different Voice: Psychological Theory and Women's Development*. London: Harvard University Press.
Gomez, J. (1995) 'Out of the past'. Chapter 1 in Deitcher, D. (ed.) *Over The Rainbow: Lesbian and Gay Politics in America since Stonewall*. London: Boxtree.
Grant, C. (1996) 'Queer theorrhea (and what it all might mean for feminists)'. Reading 2.8 in Jackson, S. and Scott, S. (eds) *Feminism and Sexuality: A Reader*. Edinburgh: Edinburgh University Press.
Greenberg, D. F. and Bystryn, M. H. (1984) 'Capitalism, bureaucracy and male homosexuality', *Contemporary Crimes: Crimes, Law and Social Policy*, no. 8, pp. 33–56.
Guillaumin, C. (1995) *Racism, Sexism, Power and Ideology*. London: Routledge.
Guinier, L. (1994) *The Tyranny of the Majority: Fundamental Fairness in Representative Democracy*. New York: The Free Press.
Hall, C. (1982) 'The butcher, the baker, the candlestick maker: the shop and

Bibliography

the family in the industrial revolution'. In Whitelegg et al. (eds) *The Changing Experience of Women*. Oxford: Martin Robertson.

Hall, C. (1992) *White, Male and Middle-Class: Explorations in Feminism and History*. Cambridge: Polity Press.

Halperin, D. M. (1995) *Saint Foucault: Towards a Gay Hagiography*. New York: Oxford University Press.

Harne, L. (1984) 'Lesbian custody and the new myth of the father', *Trouble and Strife*, no. 3, pp. 12–14.

Haug, F. et al. (1987) *Female Sexualisation*. London: Verso.

Hay, C. (1995) 'Structure and agency'. In March, D. and Stoker, G. (eds) *Theory and Methods in Political Science*. Basingstoke: Macmillan.

Heath, S. (1982) *The Sexual Fix*. London: Macmillan.

Held, D. (1993) 'Democracy: From city-states to a cosmopolitan order?' In Held, D. (ed.) *Prospects for Democracy*. Cambridge: Polity Press.

Herdt, G. H. (ed.) (1982) *Rituals of Manhood*. Berkeley: University of California Press.

Hirst, P. (1986) *Law, Socialism and Democracy*. London: Allen and Unwin.

Hobsbawm, E. (1995) *The Age of Capital*. London: Weidenfield and Nicolson.

Holland, J., Ramazanoglu, C., Sharpe, S. and Thomson, R. (1998) *The Male in the Head*. London: Tuffnell Press.

Hollway, W. (1981) '"I just wanted to kill a woman." Why? The Ripper and male sexuality', *Feminist Review*, no. 9, pp. 33–40.

Hollway, W. (1984) 'Gender difference and the production of subjectivity'. In Henriques, J., Hollway, W., Urwin, C., Venn, C., and Walkeraine, V. (eds) *Changing The Subject*. London: Methuen.

Howarth, D. (1995) 'Discourse theory'. In March, D. and Stoker, G. (eds) *Theory and Methods in Political Science*. Basingstoke: Macmillan.

Irigaray, L. (1985) *This Sex Which is not One*. Ithaca, NY: Cornell University Press.

Irigaray, L. (1981) 'This sex which is not one', *New French Feminisms*, pp. 99–106.

Jackson, M. (1989) 'Facts of life? or the eroticisation of women's oppression? Sexology and the social construction of heterosexuality'. In Caplan, P. (ed.) *The Cultural Construction of Sexuality*. London: Routledge.

Jackson, M. (1994) *The Real Facts of Life: Feminism and the Politics of Sexuality c. 1850–1940*. London: Taylor and Francis.

Jackson, S. (1978) 'On the social construction of female sexuality', *Explorations in Feminism*, no. 4. London: Women's Research and Resources Centre Publications.

Jackson, S. (1983) 'The Desire for Freud', *Trouble and Strife*, no. 1, pp. 32–41.

Jackson, S. (1990) 'Demons and innocents: Western ideas on children's sexuality in historical perspective'. In Perry, M. E. (ed.) *Handbook of Sexology* vol. 7: *Childhood and Adolescent Sexology*. Oxford: Elsevier Science.

Jackson, S. (1992a) 'The amazing deconstructing woman', *Trouble and Strife*, vol. 25, pp. 25–31.

Jackson, S. (1992b) 'Towards a historical sociology of housework', *Women's Studies International Forum*, vol. 15, no. 2, pp. 153–72.
Jackson, S. (1993) 'Even sociologists fall in love: An exploration of the sociology of emotions', *Sociology*, vol. 27, no. 2, pp. 201–20.
Jackson, S. (1994) 'Theorising heterosexuality: Gender, power and pleasure', *Strathclyde Papers on Sociology and Social Policy*, no. 2. Glasgow: University of Strathclyde.
Jackson, S. (1995) 'Gender and heterosexuality: A materialist feminist analysis'. In Maynard, M. and Purvis, J. (eds) *(Hetero) sexual Politics*. London: Taylor and Francis.
Jackson, S. (1996a) *Christine Delphy*. London: Sage.
Jackson, S. (1996b) 'Heterosexuality and feminist theory'. In Richardson, D. (ed.) *Theorising Heterosexuality*. Milton Keynes: Open University Press.
Jackson, S. and Scott, S. (1996) 'Sexual skirmishes and feminist factions'. Introduction to Jackson, S. and Scott, S. (eds) *Feminism and Sexuality: A Reader*. Edinburgh: Edinburgh University Press.
Jackson, S., and Scott, S. (1997) 'Gut reactions to matters of the heart: reflections on rationality, irrationality and sexuality', *Sociological Review*, vol. 45, no. 4, pp. 551–75.
Jonasdottir, A. G. (1988) 'On the concept of interest, women's interests and the limitations of interest theory'. In Jones, J. and Jonasdottir, A. G. (eds) *The Political Interests of Gender*. London: Sage.
Kennedy, H. (1997) 'Karl Heinrich Ulrichs, first theorist of homosexuality'. In Rosario, V. (ed.) *Science and Homosexualities*. London: Routledge.
Kingdom, E. (1991) *What's Wrong with Rights? Problems for Feminist Politics of Law*. Edinburgh: Edinburgh University Press.
Kinsey, A., et al. (1948) *Sexual Behaviour in the Human Male*. Philadelphia: W. B. Saunders.
Kinsey, A., et al. (1953) *Sexual Behaviour in the Human Female*. Philadelphia: W. B. Saunders.
Krafft-Ebbing, R. von (1931) *Psychopathia Sexualis*. Brooklyn: Physicians and Surgeons Book Co. (originally published in 1886).
Kriesi, H., Koopmans, R., Dyvendak, J. W. and Giugni, M. G. (1995) *New Social Movements in Western Europe*. London: University College London Press.
Kuper, R. (1990) *Electing for Democracy: Proportional Representation and the Left*. London: Socialist Society.
Lacan, J. (1975) *Le Seminaire XX Encore*. Editions du Seuil. Also available in translation by Alan Sheridan, *Ecrits: A Selection*. London: Tavistock, 1977.
Laclau, E. (1991) 'The impossibility of society'. In *Ideology and Power in the Age of Lenin in Ruins*, special edition of *The Canadian Journal of Politics and Social Theory*, vol. 15, nos. 1, 2 and 3, pp. 24–6.
Laclau, E. and Mouffe, C. (1985) *Hegemony and Socialist Strategy*. London: Verso.
Laclau, E. and Mouffe, C. (1987) 'Post-Marxism without apologies', *New Left Review*, no. 166, pp. 79–106.

Lacqueur, T. (1990) *Making Sex: Body and Sex from the Greeks to Freud*. Cambridge, MA: Harvard University Press.
Le Vay, S. (1993) *The Sexual Brain*. Cambridge, MA: MIT Press.
Levi-Strauss, C. (1978) *Meaning and Myth*. London: Routledge.
Liberty (1994) *Sexuality and the State: Human Rights Violations Against Lesbians, Gays, Bisexuals and Transgendered people*. London: National Council for Civil Liberties.
Lijphart, A. (1977) *Democracy in Plural Societies*. New Haven: Yale University Press.
Lister, R. (1997) *Citizenship: Feminist Perspectives*. Basingstoke: Macmillan.
Macionis, J. and Plummer, K. (1998) *Sociology: A Global Introduction*. Hemel Hempstead: Prentice Hall Europe.
Mackinnon, C. A. (1989) *Towards a Feminist Theory of the State*. Cambridge, MA: Harvard University Press.
Maddison, S. (1995) 'A queered pitch', *Red Pepper*, February, p. 27.
Marshall, T. H. (1950) *Citizenship and Social Class*. Cambridge: Cambridge University Press.
Marx, K. (1954) *Capital*, vol. 1. London: Lawrence and Wishart.
Marx, K. (1982) 'Selections'. In Giddens, A. and Held, D. (eds) *Classes, Power and Conflict*. Berkeley: University of California Press.
Mathieu, N-C. (1996) 'Sexual, sexed and sex-class identities'. In Adkins, L. and Leonard, D. (eds) *Sex In Question*. London: Taylor and Francis.
Matza, D. (1969) *Becoming Deviant*. New Jersey: Prentice Hall.
Maupin, A. (1995) Foreword in Deitcher, D. (ed.) *Over The Rainbow: Lesbian and Gay Politics in America since Stonewall*. London: Boxtree.
McCall, G. J. and Simmons, J. C. (1966) *Identities and Interactions: An Examination of Human Associations in Everyday Life*. London: Macmillan.
McIntosh, M. (1968) 'The homosexual role', *Social Problems*, no. 16, pp. 182–91.
Mead, G. H. (1967) *Mind, Self and Society*. Chicago: University of Chicago Press.
Meyer, M. (ed.), (1994) *The Politics and Poetics of Camp*. New York: Routledge.
Miegs, A. (1990) 'Multiple gender ideologies and statuses'. In Sandey, P. R. and Gooderoyd, R. G. (eds) *Beyond the Second Sex*. Philadelphia: University of Pennsylvania Press.
Mills, C. W. (1970) *The Sociological Imagination*. Harmondsworth: Penguin.
Mitchell, J. (1974) *Psychoanalysis and Feminism: Freud, Reich, Laing and Women*. London: Allen Lane.
Mitchell, J. (1994) 'The urban "underclass", citizenship and public policy'. *Strathclyde Papers on Sociology and Social Policy*, no 3. Glasgow: University of Strathclyde.
Moerkerk, H. and Aggleton, P. (1990) 'AIDS prevention strategies in Europe: A comparison and critical analysis'. In Aggleton, P., Davies, P. and Hart, G. (eds) *AIDS: Individual, Cultural and Policy Dimensions*. London: Falmer Press.
Morgan, D. (1998) 'Sociological imaginings and imagining sociology: Bodies, auto/biographies and other mysteries', *Sociology*, vol. 32, no. 4, pp. 647–64.

Mort, F. (1980) 'Sexuality: regulation and contestation'. In Gay Left Collective (eds) *Homosexuality, Power and Politics*. London: Allison and Busby.

Mouffe, C. (1992) 'Feminism, citizenship and radical democratic politics'. In Butler, J. and Scott, J. W. (eds) *Feminists Theorise the Political*. New York: Routledge.

New Scientist, 24 July 1997.

New Statesman, May 1997, special edition.

New York Times, 17 July 1992.

Nixon, S. (1996) *Hard Looks: Masculinities, Spectatorship and Contemporary Consumption*. London: University College London Press.

Nye, R. A. (1999) *Sexuality*. Oxford: Oxford University Press.

Parekh, B. (1994) 'The cultural particularity of liberal democracy', Held, D. (ed.) *Prospects for Democracy*. Oxford: Polity.

Parry, G. (1969) *Political Elites*. London: Allen and Unwin.

Pateman, C. (1983) 'Feminism and democracy'. In G. Duncan (ed.) *Democratic Theory and Practice*. New York: Cambridge University Press.

Phillips, A. (1992) 'Must feminists give up on liberal democracy?' In *Prospects for Democracy*, special edition of *Political Studies*, vol. 40, pp. 68–82.

Phillips, A. (1993) *Democracy and Difference*. Cambridge: Polity Press.

Phillips, A. (1995) *The Politics of Presence*. Oxford: Clarendon Press.

Phillips, A. (1998) 'Inequality and difference', *New Left Review*, no. 224, pp. 143–53.

Phelan, S. (1997) 'Introduction'. In Phelan, S. (ed.) *Playing with Fire: Queer Politics, Queer Theories*. New York: Routledge.

Pitkin, H. (1967) *The Concept of Representation*. Berkeley: University of California Press.

Plummer, K. (1975) *Sexual Stigma: An Interactionist Account*. London: Routledge and Kegan Paul.

Plummer, K. (1995) *Telling Sexual Stories: Power, Change and Social Worlds*. London: Routledge.

Rahman, M. (1994) 'Sometimes it's hard to be a woman: The dilemma of difference and women's political ambition'. *Strathclyde Papers on Government and Politics*, no. 100. Glasgow: University of Strathclyde.

Rahman, M. (1998) 'Sexuality and rights: Problematising lesbian and gay politics'. In Carver, T. and Mottier, V. (eds) *Politics of Sexuality*. London: Routledge.

Rahman, M. and Jackson, S. (1997) 'Liberty, equality and sexuality: Essentialism and the discourse of rights', *The Journal of Gender Studies*, vol. 6, no. 2, pp. 117–29.

Ramazanoglu, C. (1993) 'Introduction'. In Ramazanoglu, C. (ed.) *Up Against Foucault*. London: Routledge.

Ramazanoglu, C. and Holland, J. (1993) 'Women's sexuality and men's appropriation of desire'. In Ramazanoglu, C. (ed.) *Up Against Foucault*. London: Routledge.

Ransom, J. (1993) 'Feminism, difference and discourse: the limits of discursive analysis for feminism'. In Ramazanoglu, C. (ed.) *Up Against Foucault.* London: Routledge.

Rayside, D. (1998) *On The Fringe: Gays and Lesbians in Politics.* Ithaca, NY: Cornell University Press.

Reinhold, S. (1994) 'Through the Parliamentary looking-glass: Real and "Pretend" families in contemporary British politics', *Feminist Review,* no. 48, pp. 61–80.

Rich, A. (1986) *Blood, Bread and Poetry.* London: Virago.

Richardson, D. (1990) 'AIDS Education and women: Sexual and reproductive issues', in Aggleton, P., Davies, P. and Hart, G. (eds) (1990) *AIDS: Individual, Cultural and Policy Dimensions.* London: Falmer Press.

Richardson, D. (1996) 'Heterosexuality and social theory'. In Richardson, D. (ed.) *Theorising Heterosexuality.* Milton Keynes: Open University Press.

Richardson, D. (1998) 'Sexuality and citizenship', *Sociology,* vol. 32, no. 1, pp. 83–100.

Rights of Women (1984) *Lesbian Mothers On Trial.* London: Community Press.

Rosario, V. (1997) 'Homosexual bio-histories: Genetic nostalgias and the quest for paternity'. In Rosario,V. (ed.) *Science and Homosexualities.* London: Routledge.

Rose, J. (1982) 'Introduction Two' from Rose, J. and Mitchell, J (eds) *Feminine Sexuality: Jacques Lacan and the Ecole Freudienne.* NewYork: Norton.

Rose, N. (1989) *Governing the Soul: The Shaping of the Private Self.* London: Routledge.

Rosenblum, D. (1996) 'Geographically sexual? Advancing lesbian and gay interests through proportional representation', *Harvard Civil Rights–Civil Liberties Law Review,* vol. 31, no. 1, pp. 119–54.

Sapiro,V. (1982) 'Private costs of public commitments or public costs of private commitments? Family roles versus political ambition', *American Journal of Political Science,* vol. 26, no. 2, pp. 265–79.

Sawicki, J. (1991) *Disciplining Foucault.* NewYork: Routledge.

Schehr, L. R. (1997) *Parts of an Andrology: On the Representations of Men's Bodies.* Stanford, CA: Stanford University Press.

Schramm-Evans, Z. (1990) 'Responses to AIDS 1986–87'. In Aggleton, P., Davies, P. and Hart, G. (eds) (1990) *AIDS: Individual, Cultural and Policy Dimensions.* London: Falmer Press.

Seidler, V. (1989) 'Reason, desire and male sexuality'. In Caplan, P. (ed.)*The Cultural Construction of Sexuality.* London: Routledge.

Seidman, S. (1991) *Romantic Longings.* NewYork: Routledge.

Seidman, S. (1996) 'Introduction'. In Seidman, S. (ed.) *Queer Theory/Sociology.* Oxford: Blackwell.

Shapiro, H. R. (1971) 'The federal principle'. In Cook, T. and Morgan, P. M. (eds) *Participatory Democracy.* San Francisco: Cranfield Press.

Shepherd, G. (1989) 'Rank, gender and homosexuality: Mombasa as a key to understanding sexual options'. In Caplan, P. (ed.) *The Cultural Construction of Sexuality.* London: Routledge.

Shilts, R. (1993) *Conduct Unbecoming: Gays and Lesbians in the US Military*. St. Martin's Press: New York.
Simons, J. (1995) *Foucault and the Political*. London: Routledge.
Simpson, M (1996) *It's a Queer World*. London: Vintage.
Sinfield, A (1994) *The Wilde Century*. London: Cassell.
Skidmore, P. (1998) 'Sexuality and the UK armed forces: judicial review of the ban on homosexuality'. In Carver, T. and Mottier, V. (eds) *Politics of Sexuality*. London: Routledge.
Smith, D. (1988) *The Everyday World As Problematic: A Feminist Sociology*. Milton Keynes: Open University Press.
Smith-Rosenberg, C. (1975) 'The female world of love and ritual', *Signs*, vol. 1, no. 1.
Smith-Rosenberg, C. (1990) 'Discourses of sexuality and subjectivity: The new woman 1870–1936'. In Duberman *et al.* (eds) *Hidden from History*. New York: Penguin.
Smyth, C. (1992) *Lesbians Talk Queer Notions*. London: Scarlet Press.
Solomos, J. (1991) *Black Youth, Racism and the State*. Cambridge: Polity Press.
Stanley, L. (1982) '"Male needs": the problems of working with gay men'. In Freidman, S. and Sarah, E. (eds) *On the Problem of Men: Two Feminist Conferences*. London: The Women's Press.
Stanley, L. (1992) *The Auto/Biographical I*. Manchester: Manchester University Press.
Stanley, L. and Wise, S. (1983) *Breaking Out*. London: Routledge.
Steedman, C. (1986) *Landscape for a Good Woman: A Story of Two Lives*. London: Virago.
Stein, A. and Plummer, K. (1996) 'I can't even think straight: "Queer theory" and the missing sexual revolution in sociology'. In Seidman, S. (ed.) *Queer Theory/Sociology*. Oxford: Blackwell.
Stein, E. (1992) 'Conclusion'. In Stein, E. (ed.) *Forms of Desire*. New York: Routledge.
Strong, P. and Berridge, V. (1990) 'No-one knew anything: Some issues in British AIDS policy' in Aggleton, P., Davies, P. and Hart, G. (eds) (1990) *AIDS: Individual, Cultural and Policy Dimensions*. London: Falmer Press.
Stychin, C. F. (1995) *Law's Desire: Sexuality and the Limits of Justice*. London: Routledge.
Sullivan, A. (1995) *Virtually Normal: An Argument about Homosexuality*. Basingstoke: Macmillan.
Times, 24 July 1996.
Turner, B. S. (ed.) (1990) *Theories of Modernity and Postmodernity*. London: Sage.
Turner, B. S. (1993) 'Baudrillard for sociologists'. In Rojek, C. and Turner, B. S. (eds) *Forget Baudrillard?* London: Routledge.
Vance, C. S. (1989) 'Social construction theory: problems in the history of sexuality'. In Altman *et al.* (eds) *Which Homosexuality?* London: Gay Men's Press.
Vines, G. (1993) *Raging Hormones*. London: Virago.

Waites, M. (1998) 'Sexual citizens: legislating the age of consent in Britain'. In Carver, T. and Mottier, V. (eds) *Politics of Sexuality*. London: Routledge.
Walby, S. (1990) *Theorising Patriarchy*. Oxford: Blackwell.
Walby, S. (1994) 'Is citizenship gendered?', *Sociology*, vol. 28, no. 2, 379–96.
Washington Post, national weekly edition, 1–7 February 1993.
Waters, M. (1994) *Modern Sociological Theory*. London: Sage.
Watney, S. (1980) 'The Ideology of the GLF'. In Gay Left Collective (eds) *Homosexuality, Power and Politics*. London: Allison and Busby.
Watney, S. (1989) 'Psychoanalysis, sexuality and AIDS'. In Shepherd, S. and Wallis, M. (eds) *Coming on Strong: Gay Politics and Culture*. London: Unwin Hyman.
Weber, M. (1976) *The Protestant Ethic and the Spirit of Capitalism*. London: Allen and Unwin.
Weeks, J. (1977) *Coming Out: Homosexual Politics in Britain from the Nineteenth Century to the Present*. London: Quartet.
Weeks, J. (1980) 'Capitalism and the organisation of sexuality'. In Gay Left Collective (eds) *Homosexuality, Power and Politics*. London: Allison and Busby.
Weeks, J. (1989) *Sex, Politics and Society*. Second edn. Harlow: Longman.
Weeks, J. (1996) *Invented Moralities: Sexual Values in an Age of Uncertainty*. Cambridge: Polity Press.
Wellings, K., Field, J., Johnson, A., and Wadsworth, J. (1994) *Sexual Behaviour in Britain: The National Survey of Sexual Attitudes and Lifestyles*. Harmondsworth: Penguin.
Whisman, V. (1996) *Queer By Choice: Lesbians, Gay Men and the Politics of Identity*. London: Routledge.
Wilson, A. R. (1997) 'Somewhere Over The Rainbow: Queer Translating'. In Phelan, S. (ed.) *Playing with Fire: Queer Politics, Queer Theories*. New York: Routledge.
Wilson, E. (1993) 'Is transgression transgressive?' In Bristow, J., and Wilson, A. (eds) *Activating Theory: Lesbian, Gay and Bisexual Politics*. London: Lawrence and Wishart.
Wittig, M. (1992) *The Straight Mind*. Hemel Hempstead: Harvester Wheatsheaf.
Young, I. M. (1989) 'Polity and group difference', *Ethics*, vol. 99, no. 2, pp. 250–74.
Young, I. M. (1994) 'Gender as seriality: Thinking about women as a social collective', *Signs*, vol. 19, no. 3, pp. 713–38.

INDEX

achieved gender, 80n
ACT UP (AIDS Coalition To Unleash Power), 53
activists, as queer, 127–8
affirmative action policies, 184
age of consent, 169
   debates on, 8
agency, 105–11, 135–41
   materiality and, 110
   and self, 85–8
   as strategy and intention, 87–8
   and structure, 99, 109
AIDS, 11, 34, 52–3, 117
   essentialist discourse and, 154, 155
   federal funding and, 178
Althusser, L., 81, 100, 102–3, 104, 106, 107
anatomy, Freud and, 61
Angelou, Maya, 2
anti-foundationalism, 132
articulation, legislation and, 172
'arts of existence', 107
associational autonomy, 165
associative democracy, 162, 186
autobiographies, articulating sociology and, 153
autonomous representation, 181

biographies, articulating sociology and, 153
Birch, Keith, 11
bisexuality, 192
Bodies That Matter (Butler), 141
Boswell, John, 22–3
bourgeois males, 30
brains, 'gay', 35
bureaucratisation, 92
Butler, Judith, 78, 108, 127, 129, 135–41

Campaign for Homosexual Equality, 50
capitalism, 30, 97, 106–7
   essentialism and, 157
castration complex, 59
Cawson, Alan, 180–1
Chicano men, 29
childhood, as pleasure seeking, 67
China, 106

Christianity, 20, 22–3, 93
citizenship, 166, 186–93
   gendered construction of, 151
   'inevitable' extension of, 17
   sexual equality and, 169–73
   strategies of, 150
Civil Rights, 11
class
   divisions, 29–30, 89
   and male relationships, 93
   politics, decline in, 53
Clinton, Bill, 1–3, 14n, 15n, 164, 196
coherent community, identity as, 158
Cole, G. D. H., 179
collective empowerment, group members and, 188
'coming out', 73, 119
commercialisation, 51, 95, 122
   of Pride, 156
commodification, 85, 156
   gay male sexual identity and, 51
competition, 92
confession, Christian practice of, 25
consensus reaching, 189
consociationalism, 174–6
consumption, 85, 106–7, 156
   identity and, 27
   sexual identity and, 180
cultural politics, Queer theorists and, 15n
culture, sexualisation of, 27

Darwin, Charles, 23
de Saussure, Ferdinand, 62
deconstruction, of essential identities, 146n
decriminalisation, 119
democracy, 149–52
   context of, 161–5
   liberal – plus?, 184–6
   participatory, 189–90
   systems of, 194n
democratic credentials, summary of, 162
democratisation, 28
Descartes, R., 25

214

Index

The Descent of Man (Darwin), 23
desire
    learning, 72–4
    transformation into discourse, 20
determinism, 71
deviance
    as identity, 131
    interactionist approach and, 65–6
    state regulation and, 166
difference, 147n
    dilemma of, 131, 187
    or inequalities?, 155–61
    social oppression and, 165–9
'dilemma of difference', 131, 187
discourse
    contesting, 152
    essentialism as, 96–9
    Foucauldian concept of, 88
'discursive formations', 95
'domestic ideology', 89
domesticity, 30–1
dominance, masculine, 39
dualism, 25

economic location, sexual identity and, 180
egalitarianism, 186
elitism
    consociationalism and, 175
    political participation and, 183, 191
Ellis, Havelock, 26, 57
emancipation, 136–7
    movements, 44
equal rights, strategies, 158
Equal Rights Amendment, US, 172
equality
    citizenship and, 169–73
    formal, 171
    liberty or?, 196–200
essential selves, constructing, 99–105
essentialism, 18
    challenging, 41–3
    as explanation of self, 55
    ideology and discourse and, 96–9
    interactionist approach and, 65–6
    as oppressive, 32
    as political strategy, 4–6
ethnic gay politics, 146n
'ethnic' identity, 18
ethnomethodology, 71
Evans, David, 85, 94, 199
evolution, 23
experiences
    identity and, 149–52
    politics of, 160
    representing, 173–4
'expert' knowledge, 86–7

family, as institution, 171
federalism, 176–9
    group closure and, 178
feminism, 52, 75, 108, 135–6, 161
    narratives and, 82
    political theorists and, 164

standpoint theorising, 71–2
Foucault, Michel, 5, 14, 19–22, 55, 76, 77, 90, 95, 107, 129, 133–4, 157
    discourse and, 98
    Queer theory and, 9, 124–5
Fraser, Nancy, 157
Freud, S., 26
    subjectivity and, 57–62
functional representation, 179–81

Gagnon, J. H., 14, 66, 67, 69, 70
Gay Activists Alliance, 50
gay 'ghettos', 8, 119, 125, 175
gay liberation, 4, 51, 52, 119, 120, 125, 154, 185
    resistance and, 21
Gay Liberation Front (GLF), 11, 50, 189, 190
gay male sexism, 190
Gay Pride march, London, 152, 156, 160, 193n
gender, 32, 89, 94–5, 137
    achieved, 80n
    conflation with sexuality, 61
    critique of, 154
    identity, 111
    inequalities, 18
    labelling and, 68
    legislation and, 172
Gender Trouble (Butler), 137, 141
genes, 'gay', 35–6
genital trauma, 58–9
geographical location, 175, 176
ghettos, 8, 119, 125, 175
Giddens, A., 101
government, democracy and, 162
Greek city-states, 28
group closure, federalism and, 178
group interests, limits of, 183
group members, collective empowerment and, 188
group representation, 151, 174
    methods of, 174–84
group-specific regulation, 167, 184
groups, ideas and presence and, 186–93
Guild Socialism Re-Stated (Cole), 179

Halperin, David, 159
Hay, Colin, 109
health policy, group input and, 178
Heath, Stephen, 22, 23
Held, David, 162
heteronormality, 117, 120, 126, 128, 131, 170
    reiterative practices of, 108
    rights and, 171
heterosexuality
    as 'norm', 35, 37, 38
    as socially produced script, 70
hierarchies, 90, 97
    of sexual categories, 75
    see also class; patriarchy
Hirst, Paul, 180
history, living within, 81–5
Hollway, Wendy, 98
homosexuality, 'explaining', 72
'homosexuals', coining of term, 47n

House of Lords, 15n
human reason, faculty of, 38–9
human rights, gay rights as, 193
humanism, radical plural, 191
husbands, subordination of wives, 168
hypothalamus, region of brain, 35–6
hysteria, 57

'I', as subject, 139
ideas, groups and, 186–93
identity
    coherent, sense of, 111
    and coherent community, 158
    emergence of sexuality as, 22–8
    experience and, 149–52
    odd relationship with politics, 121–4
    paradoxes of, 64
    and performativity, 141–2
    and politics, 116–45
    queer relationship with politics, 124–30
    sexuality as, 5, 17–47
    unified, 129
    universal, 135–6
ideological state apparatuses (ISAs), 104
ideology, 87
    essentialism as, 96–9
    neo-Weberian concepts, 98
immature sexualities, 63
immigration policies, 47n
'individual', democracy and, 163
industrialisation, 28
inequalities
    and differences, 155–61
    social basis of, 154
infantile sexuality, 58
integrity, political subject and, 173
intention, definition of, 109
interactionism, 7, 43, 81–2, 89, 138
    scripted sexuality and, 69
    self as process, 84
interactionist approach, deviance and, 65–6
interactive self, sexuality and, 66–9
interests, democracy and, 149–52
interpellation, 103
'intimate citizenship', 82, 172
issue-specific campaigns, 192

juridico–discursive power model, 21

Keen, Ann, 201n
Krafft-Ebbing, 57
Kramer, Larry, 119
Kuper, Richard, 181

labelling, 68
    theory, 49, 65
Labour government, 196
Lacan, J., 43, 77
    language, 62–5
    psychoanalysis, 115n, 147n
Laclau, E., 100, 101
Lacqueur, Thomas, 30
language, Lacan and, 62–5

legal liberties, 45–6
Lesbian and Gay Pride march, London, 152, 156, 160, 193n
LeVay, Simon, 35–6
liberal democracy, 161–5, 184–6
liberation movements, 50
Liberty, 45
liberty, or equality?, 196–200
lifestyle, and lust, 22–8
Lijphart, A., 174–6
linguistics, 62
living within history, 81–5
lust, and lifestyle, 22–8

marginality, 53
    celebration of, 128
marriage, 29–31, 106
Marshall, T. H., 169
Marx/Marxism, 81, 82–3, 96–7, 100, 161, 179
    social explanation and, 132
    structuralism, 102
masculine dominance, 39
masturbation, 34
materiality, 105–11
    agency and, 110
Mead, G. H., 66, 138
Members of Parliament, as gay or lesbian, 194n
'micro-level' of social life, 133–4
military, 3
mind/body split, 25
minorities, 164
    permanent, 6, 45, 182
    politics, 18
    protection, 158
'modern' identity, of gay politics, 51–5
modernity, 28–32
    sexuality as product of, 27–8
Mombasa, 28–9
morality, sexuality and, 43–7
movement centred approach, liberal democracy and, 185

narratives
    essentialist ideas, 153
    existence of gay and lesbian, 152
    structural production of, 82
nativist understanding *see* essentialism
'necessary fictions', 110, 111, 118
    sexualities as, 44
New Right, 52
    political prescriptions, 11
Normal Heart, The (Kramer), 119

Oedipus complex, 58
    dissolution of, 59
'On the Pulse of Morning' (Angelou), 2
ontological integrity, political subject and, 173
oppression
    sexual, 164
    social, 165–9
organisations, democracy and, 162
Origin of the Species, The (Darwin), 23

Index

OutRage, 147n

'paradoxes of identity', 56, 64
participatory democracy, 189–90
Pateman, Carole, 185
patriarchy, 30
    social explanation of, 132
penis-envy, 58–9, 60
performativity, 135–42
personal lives, sociological analysis and, 6–9
phallus, concept of, 63
Phelan, Shane, 129–30
Phillips, Anne, 184–5
philosophical resolution, liberal democracy and, 185
Plummer, Ken, 73, 75, 82, 83, 102
pluralism
    liberal democracy and, 166
    social, 186
political context, Queer theory and, 78
political elites, 183, 191
political identity, 116–41
    and performativity, 141–2
    and sexual subjectivity, 118–20
political participation, elitism and, 191
political parties, joining, 194n
political strategies, 142–5
    effective, 11–13
    essentialism, 4–6
    exploring, 149–93
political subjectivity
    querying, 112–14
    sexuality and, 48–50
    viable, criteria for, 55–7
politics
    of experience, 160
    gay, 'modern' identity of, 51–5
    of identity, identity politics and, 116–18
    odd relationship with identity, 121–4
    queer relationship with identity, 124–30
    sexuality and, 43–7
popular culture, 152
population management, 20
post-Marxist analyses, 126
post-modernism, self as process, 84
post-structuralism, 117, 126
    definition of, 115n
power
    Foucault and, 133–4
    in Queer theory, 131–5
    and sexuality, 20–2
    of veto, 188
presence, groups and, 186–93
Pride march, 156, 160
'private' realm, democracy and, 163
'process of signification', 65
procreative sex, 22, 31
proportional representation (PR), 181–2
Protestantism, 93
psychoanalysis, 7, 14, 26, 39, 62–5, 68, 77
    pathology and, 61
psychobiological identity, social constructionist approaches, 42

psychological–medical discourse, 25
psychology, 26–7
Psychology of Sex (Krafft-Ebbing), 57
'public' arena
    democracy and, 163
    state and, 172

'queer', as political term, 21, 143
Queer theorists/theory, 9–11, 55, 76–9, 81–2, 83, 95, 107, 114, 116–45, 191, 198
    cultural politics and, 15n
    development of, 146n–7n
    discursive identity and, 159
queerbashing, 84
quotas, in proportional representation, 182

race relations, 47n
racial inequalities, 19
racial politics, as minority politics, 18
rationality, 40
    biological, 33
    psychosexual health and, 54
reason, faculty of, 38–9
religious nativism, 22, 23, 25
representation
    autonomous, 181
    functional, 179–81
    group, 151, 174, 174–84
'repressive hypothesis', 20
reproductive technology, lesbians and, 177
resistance, power and, 21
rights, 150–1, 191
    gay rights as human rights, 193
    'inevitable' extension of, 17
    sexual equality and, 169–73

science, 33
scientific nativism, 23
scripted sexuality, 69–72
seduction theory, 57
self
    and agency, 85–8
    essential, construction of, 99–105
    as process, 84
    troubled, 38–41
    Victorian age and, 54
self-evident outcomes, challenging, 17–19
self-government groups, 167
self-organisation, group members and, 188
self-understanding, 48
semiology, 79n
sexism, gay male, 190
sexual activity, as allocating identity, 19
Sexual Conduct (Gagnon & Simon), 66, 67
sexual equality, citizenship and, 169–73
sexual essence, as fiction, 103
sexual identity, 115n
    ethnic versions of, 50
    materiality and, 105–11
    plasticity in, 153
sexual oppression, 164
sexual politics, Queer theory approach to, 116–45

Sexual Stigma (Plummer), 73
sexual subjectivity
  as basis for political identity, 118–20
  querying, 112–14
  in social context, 81–114
  understanding, 6, 48–79
  viable, criteria for, 55–7
sexuality
  conflation with gender, 61
  definition of, 22–3
  emergence of identity as, 22–8
  'essential', challenging, 41–3
  Freud and, 57–62
  as identity, 5, 17–47
  interactive self, 66–9
  modernity and, 28–32
  morality and, 43–7
  political subject and, 48–50
  and power, 20–2
  scripted, 69–72
  structural conditions and, 91–6
  trouble with, 32–8
signification, process of, 65
signs, as system, 62
Simon, W., 14, 66, 67, 69, 70
Smith, Chris, MP, 145n
Smith, Dorothy, 71, 75
social action theory, 66
social constructionism, 42, 49, 70
social context, sexual subjectivity in, 8, 81–114
social control, 28–32
  deviance and, 65
social inequalities, enshrinement of, 171
social investment, 112
social meaning, interactive self, 66–9
social oppression, difference and, 165–9
social organisations, 106
social process, 112
social-psychology, 112
social significance, 113
social structure, as not 'sexy', 88–91
sociology
  analysis, 197
  articulating, 152–5
  personal lives, 6–9
  of sexuality, 13
state bureaucratic procedures, 92
state regulation, deviance and, 166
Stonewall (lobbying group), 50, 169, 170, 193
strategy
  definition of, 109
  exploring political, 142–5, 149–93
structural conditions, sexuality and, 91–6
structural linguistics, 62
structure
  agency and, 85–9, 99, 109

determinism and, 71
  in Queer theory, 131–5
Studies in the Psychology of Sex (Ellis), 26, 57
Stychin, C. F., 147n
subjectivity
  achieving, 74–9
  Freud and, 57–62
  as immutable, 103
  in Queer theory, 131–5
  querying, 112–14
  in social context, 81–114
  understanding, 48–79
  viable, criteria for, 55–7
suffrage
  extension of, 174
  in liberal democracies, 165
Sullivan, Andrew, 200
symbolic interactionism, 7, 43, 65, 66, 80n

territorial representative politics, 175, 176
Three Essays on the Theory of Sexuality (Freud), 57
'Transformations of puberty' (Freud), 59
troubled self, 38–41

unconscious, 60
  as structured system, 62
unified identity, 129
United Kingdom, decriminalisation in, 119
United States
  decriminalisation in, 119
  military, 3
'universal citizen', 170

veto power, 188
Victorian age, 20
  inner self and, 54
  male in, 39–40
Virtually Normal (Sullivan), 200

Weber, M., 96–7
Weeks, Jeffrey, 24, 29, 56
welfare states, 163
West, sexuality in, 168
Western Europe, 122
Wilson, Angelia, 143
wives, subordination to husbands, 168
Wolfenden Report, 46
women
  lesbians subsumed under, 91
  social category of, 168
  subordination of, 60
  as unified subject, 135–6
women's movements, 11, 157, 190
working-class campaigns, 30
working-class male relationships, 93

Young, Iris, 157, 167, 188